DATE DUE		

VOLUME 505

SEPTEMBER 1989

THE ANNALS

of The American Academy *of* Political
and Social Science

RICHARD D. LAMBERT, *Editor*
ALAN W. HESTON, *Associate Editor*

THE PACIFIC REGION: CHALLENGES TO POLICY AND THEORY

Special Editor of this Volume

PETER A. GOUREVITCH

University of California, San Diego
La Jolla

Ⓢ SAGE PUBLICATIONS   *NEWBURY PARK   LONDON   NEW DELHI*

THE ANNALS

© 1989 *by* The American Academy *of* Political *and* Social Science

ERICA GINSBURG, *Assistant Editor*

Editorial Office: 3937 Chestnut Street, Philadelphia, PA 19104.

For information about membership* (individuals only) and subscriptions (institutions), address:

SAGE PUBLICATIONS, INC.
2111 West Hillcrest Drive
Newbury Park, CA 91320

From India and South Asia,
write to:
SAGE PUBLICATIONS INDIA Pvt. Ltd.
P.O. Box 4215
New Delhi 110 048
INDIA

From the UK, Europe, the Middle
East and Africa, write to:
SAGE PUBLICATIONS LTD
28 Banner Street
London EC1Y 8QE
ENGLAND

SAGE Production Editors: KITTY BEDNAR and LIANN LECH
*Please note that members of The Academy receive THE ANNALS with their membership.

Library of Congress Catalog Card Number 89-60677
International Standard Serial Number ISSN 0002-7162
International Standard Book Number ISBN 0-8039-3581-1 (Vol. 505, 1989 paper)
International Standard Book Number ISBN 0-8039-3580-3 (Vol. 505, 1989 cloth)
Manufactured in the United States of America. First printing, September 1989.

The articles appearing in THE ANNALS are indexed in *Book Review Index; Public Affairs Information Service Bulletin; Social Sciences Index; Monthly Periodical Index; Current Contents,* and *Combined Retrospective Index Sets.* They are also abstracted and indexed in *ABC Pol Sci, Historical Abstracts, Human Resources Abstracts, Social Sciences Citation Index, United States Political Science Documents, Social Work Research & Abstracts, Peace Research Reviews, Sage Urban Studies Abstracts, International Political Science Abstracts, America: History and Life, Sociological Abstracts, Managing Abstracts, Social Planning/Policy & Development Abstracts, Automatic Subject Citation Alert,* and/or *Family Resources Database.*

Information about membership rates, institutional subscriptions, and back issue prices may be found on the facing page.

Advertising. Current rates and specifications may be obtained by writing to THE ANNALS Advertising and Promotion Manager at the Newbury Park office (address above).

Claims. Claims for undelivered copies must be made no later than three months following month of publication. The publisher will supply missing copies when losses have been sustained in transit and when the reserve stock will permit.

Change of Address. Six weeks' advance notice must be given when notifying of change of address to insure proper identification. Please specify name of journal. Send change of address to: THE ANNALS, c/o Sage Publications, Inc., 2111 West Hillcrest Drive, Newbury Park, CA 91320.

The American Academy of Political and Social Science

3937 Chestnut Street   Philadelphia, Pennsylvania 19104

Origin and Purpose. The Academy was organized December 14, 1889, to promote the progress of political and social science, especially through publications and meetings. The Academy does not take sides in controverted questions, but seeks to gather and present reliable information to assist the public in forming an intelligent and accurate judgment.

Meetings. The Academy holds an annual meeting in the spring extending over two days.

Publications. THE ANNALS is the bimonthly publication of The Academy. Each issue contains articles on some prominent social or political problem, written at the invitation of the editors. Also, monographs are published from time to time, numbers of which are distributed to pertinent professional organizations. These volumes constitute important reference works on the topics with which they deal, and they are extensively cited by authorities throughout the United States and abroad. The papers presented at the meetings of The Academy are included in THE ANNALS.

Membership. Each member of The Academy receives THE ANNALS and may attend the meetings of The Academy.Membership is open only to individuals. Annual dues: $30.00 for the regular paperbound edition (clothbound, $45.00). Add $9.00 per year for membership outside the U.S.A. Members may also purchase single issues of THE ANNALS for $7.95 each (clothbound, $12.00).

Subscriptions. THE ANNALS (ISSN 0002-7162) is published six times annually — in January, March, May, July, September, and November. Institutions may subscribe to THE ANNALS at the annual rate: $66.00 (clothbound, $84.00). Add $9.00 per year for subscriptions outside the U.S.A. Institutional rates for single issues: $12.00 each (clothbound, $17.00).

Second class postage paid at Philadelphia, Pennsylvania, and at additional mailing offices.

Single issues of THE ANNALS may be obtained by individuals who are not members of The Academy for $8.95 each (clothbound, $17.00). Single issues of THE ANNALS have proven to be excellent supplementary texts for classroom use. Direct inquiries regarding adoptions to THE ANNALS c/o Sage Publications (address below).

All correspondence concerning membership in The Academy, dues renewals, inquiries about membership status, and/or purchase of single issues of THE ANNALS should be sent to THE ANNALS c/o Sage Publications, Inc., 2111 West Hillcrest Drive, Newbury Park, CA 91320. *Please note that orders under $25 must be prepaid.* Sage affiliates in London and India will assist institutional subscribers abroad with regard to orders, claims, and inquiries for both subscriptions and single issues.

THE ANNALS

of The American Academy *of* Political *and* Social Science

RICHARD D. LAMBERT, *Editor*
ALAN W. HESTON, *Associate Editor*

—————————— **FORTHCOMING** ——————————

HUMAN RIGHTS AROUND THE WORLD
Special Editor: Marvin E. Wolfgang

Volume 506   November 1989

PRIVATIZING AND MARKETIZING SOCIALISM
Special Editor: Jan Prybyla

Volume 507   January 1990

ENGLISH PLUS: ISSUES IN BILINGUAL EDUCATION
Special Editors: Courtney B. Cazden
Catherine Snow

Volume 508   March 1990

See page 3 for information on Academy membership and
purchase of single volumes of **The Annals.**

CONTENTS

BOOK DEPARTMENT CONTENTS

SOCIOLOGY

ECONOMICS

ANNALS, *AAPSS*, **505**, September 1989

The Pacific Rim:
Current Debates

By PETER A. GOUREVITCH

ABSTRACT: The dramatic emergence of the Pacific region poses a double challenge for policymakers and social scientists. Both need to understand change in the region as well as to adapt tools of analysis and guides to policy. Two large issues dominate debate, though there are many other important ones as well. These two are prosperity and peace: why have parts of the Asian Pacific side grown so quickly while other parts of the Pacific, much of Latin America, Africa, and other areas not; and how have these changes altered the international system of security? To answer these questions, the issue of level of analysis must be raised. Social outcomes can be interpreted by focusing on the individual, on social institutions, or on the international environment. Arguments about the role of culture, the functioning of markets, the impact of government institutions, the distribution of power in society among groups and classes, the distribution of power among countries in the state system — these are classic variables of analysis. Debates about the Pacific region give rise to new ways of integrating these variables into arguments that permit deeper analysis.

Peter A. Gourevitch is dean of the Graduate School of International Relations and Pacific Studies at the University of California, San Diego (UCSD). Before coming to UCSD in 1979, he taught at Harvard, from which he received his Ph.D. in political science, and McGill University. His publications include material on comparative politics and international relations. His most recent book is Politics in Hard Times: Comparative Responses to International Economic Crises. *He is on the editorial board of* International Organization *and the Council of the American Political Science Association.*

LARGE geopolitical shifts, by their nature, do not occur very often. The most well-known epochs lasted for centuries: the Mediterranean world of the Roman Empire, the medieval world of land-based trade through the rivers and mountains of Europe and the Silk Road through Asia, and the Atlantic world of water-based trade across that ocean to the New World. The shift from one era to another entailed massive changes in the location of wealth, power, and cultural activity. Does the emergence of the Pacific region in recent years mark another such shift? It is premature to say, but, clearly, something important is taking place. Whether it marks an epoch we must leave to another epoch to tell.

At a minimum, the Pacific Rim phenomenon is important enough to require thought. It poses a challenge to convention. It makes the world not quite as we understood it to be a few decades ago. The changes are surely large enough to pose problems for two communities who have a need to know: the community of social scientists, interested in making sense out of general social activity and the location of a particular geographical region within a theoretical context; and the community of policymakers, who, faced with the compelling need to make decisions, seek information pertinent to those decisions. Too much is made of the distinction between theory and practice, or application. These are not different types of knowledge but rather different uses of knowledge. Policy choices cannot be made without some notion, implicit or explicit, of cause and effect: what the impact will be on y of policy alternatives a, b, or c is a question inherent in any choice, and any answer contains a theory of causality. Similarly, theory building among social scientists always involves the effort to model some aspect of reality, so that changing realities alter the definitions of what needs modeling and of what constitutes satisfactory models.

The logic behind this volume lies in the reciprocal need of theory and policy application in understanding the Pacific region. Its organizing premise is that the rapid changes involving the region press against the limits of our understanding, causing an intellectual challenge to the theories used by policymakers and social scientists alike. The questions and concepts that have dominated many aspects of thought arose out of experiences and intellectual traditions shaped by other concerns. Change in the Pacific alters both analytic questions and policy issues, which in turn require change in thoughts and answers.

The interplay between changing reality, social-scientific theorizing, and policy challenges occurs in many areas. This volume has space to examine only a few. Many important areas have been left out: migration, urbanization, technology, social organization, ethnicity, family, and gender. What follows is only a partial examination of areas of interest, shaped by the availability of authors, space limits, personal familiarity with the literature, and issues of particular concern in some policy circles and intellectual debates.

In this volume on the Pacific region, Latin America is a definite realm of interest. That inclusion is not always followed. Indeed, the definition of the Pacific Rim is itself an object of controversy and struggle. Many writers see it as shorthand for Asian Pacific, the arc of countries resting on Japan and extending southward toward the newly industrializing countries (NICs). Often the term is extended to include the whole relationship of the Asian Pacific region to the United States. My usage here takes the extension another step for two reasons, one having to do with reality, the other with social-scientific inquiry. The element of reality is the growing involvement of Latin America in the dynamics of East Asian-North American relations. With the rapid intensification of the international division of labor in the manufacture of industrial products, Latin America is playing an increasing role as locus of that production: low-cost labor, proximity to the United States and Canada, plentiful natural resources, and, in some places, growing internal demand all make Latin America an increasing target of East Asian investment and production locations. At the same time, Latin American issues of contention, such as the debt, become increasingly difficult to sort out from the economic web that includes the U.S. trade deficit to East Asia and the budgetary deficits within the United States.

The social-scientific motive for including Latin America has to do with the virtues of comparison. Aristotle taught us to see the greater leverage in analytic understanding that comes from contrasting the same event or phenomenon in different places — for Aristotle, city-states; for us, countries. Latin American experiences have differed sharply from those of the Asian Pacific region in several ways, particularly as shown by recent data on economic growth. That divergence cries out for comparison. It challenges much received opinion and many theoretical approaches as well as policy indicators. Comparing the two regions allows interesting triangulation of questions: how regions relate to their economic superpower, Japan or the United States, respectively; how the regions handle debt, as illustrated by Korea and Mexico; how the regions shape public policy in relation to trade, as in export-led growth and import substitution; how the regions are differentially affected by security issues; how the regions differ in social struc-

ture, political institutions, and cultural traditions. So interesting are these comparisons that they have become the subject of several scholarly conferences, leading to publications, as well as the subject of university courses.[1] These discussions deserve wider attention.

The two major concerns of the present volume are prosperity and security, two classic issues in international affairs. How have countries assured themselves of economic growth, and why have some done better than others? How do countries obtain security, and how is the security system changing? Related to both concerns is a third — freedom, in the form of constitutional governments, procedure, rule of law, and some opportunity for democratic voice and participation.

The Pacific Rim phenomenon has forced us to think about several dimensions of these questions. First, how are we to understand what social scientists call the level-of-analysis problem — the relationship between a single unit of analysis, like the individual, and the larger system in which the individual operates, such as society? This question is intimately linked to debates over culture and structure, that is, the relationship between properties of an individual such as culture, mental outlook, and personality, on one hand, and the situation in which the individual — or unit — functions, such as the nature of incentives, rules, and institutions. While linked to the culture-structure debate, the level-of-analysis issue reappears in all the other debates as well. Thus it lies at the heart of the second dimension examined here, the factors causing stability or disorder in the international arena. What changes have

1. Gary Gereffi and Donald Wyman, eds., *Manufactured Miracles: Development Strategies in Latin America and East Asia* (Princeton, NJ: Princeton University Press, forthcoming).

taken place in the international system, in the global configuration of power among states, that promote or inhibit peace, security, prosperity, and freedom? Third, what factors cause economic growth within countries, or, put another way, what factors explain the striking differences in economic performance in recent decades? This volume is organized around the consideration of each of these dimensions.

UNIT OF ANALYSIS: CULTURE AND STRUCTURE

In dealing with subjects such as peace, security, prosperity, and freedom, we are exploring social outcomes, or the behaviors of collectivities. These goals cannot be provided by individuals acting alone but stem rather from the behavior of masses of individuals organized in some fashion or other, be it groups, nations, or groups of nations. These are collectivities. How is the behavior of collectivities to be understood? This is an old question and an old debate. We may contrast two families of answers. One, typical of Anglo-American modes of thinking, starts with the individual and moves toward larger units. Individuals have attributes — rationality, culture, emotion. Once we understand those, we can model the behavior of collections of individuals, or societies. But generalizations about larger units, or macro analysis, require a careful understanding of the properties of smaller ones, that is, micro analysis. This approach can be linked to the English theorist Thomas Hobbes.

The other mode reverses the reasoning. Systems shape the units that constitute them. Individuals have the identity that the system allows them to have and that the system shapes. Thus macro understanding precedes micro understanding. The properties of the system shape those of the unit.

This approach can be linked to the name of the French sociologist Emile Durkheim. In the social sciences, the clash between macro and micro remains very much alive in the effort to understand the Pacific region. We can see an old debate in a new location, and we can see new ways of forming older questions.[2] A striking example of this old debate in new form has to do with the treatment of culture as an explanation of social outcomes. In a region as diverse as the Pacific region, the expression of cultures is overwhelming. We find in this region one of the oldest civilizations known, China, and some of the youngest — the meso-Americans of the Western Hemisphere. With such richness, the possibility of explaining important phenomena through the causality of culture seems irresistibly tempting, and the temptation has not been resisted. Culture has been mobilized to explain many if not all of the phenomena of great interest to us.

Why is the economy of one country growing rapidly, another not at all? Why has East Asia exploded in recent years, while Latin America has not? The cultures certainly differ. East Asia is Confucian, Latin America is not. So that must be the reason. The failures of the Philippines, the one non-Confucian country of the region, are used to confirm the theory. Confucian culture, it is argued, instills values such as hard work, thrift, goal attainment, and family loyalty, among others, that prepare people for effective behavior in market economies. In Latin America, these values are lacking, hence the difference in economic outcomes. Readers will note the resonance

2. Peter Gourevitch, "The Second Image Reversed," *International Organization*, 32:881-912 (Autumn 1978); idem, *Politics in Hard Times: Comparative Responses to International Economic Crises* (Ithaca, NY: Cornell University Press, 1986).

of this interpretation with a classic of Western social science: the Protestant-ethic argument developed by Max Weber to explain why some parts of Europe launched the mercantile and industrial revolution after 1500 while other regions did not.[3]

To other social science specialists, this interpretation of growth is at best misleading and at worst simply wrong and infuriating. Just a few decades ago, the question asked of East Asia was why there was so little growth. Why was East Asia economically backward, while the economic growth of the West allowed it to dominate the world? Weber, after all, explored world religion partly to extend the discussion of culture outside the Christian West. The answer to Asian backwardness given by culture theorists pointed the finger straight at Confucianism. Confucianism meant deference to authority, resistance to change, respect for the ways of the past, aversion to risk, and other values that inhibit responsiveness to the market. If Confucianism explained the absence of growth, how can it be used as a variable to explain growth just a few years later? If culture has explanatory power, it must be relatively constant. If economic change occurs rapidly, the constant cannot account for the change.

Critics of cultural arguments note that any given culture, especially one so large as Confucianism, contains within it rather diverse and conflicting strands. Both characterizations of the Confucian tradition are correct. The decisive question for a society is which elements are allowed to dominate, and which are inhibited? The work ethic of Confucianism can emerge if it is allowed to emerge, but it can also be inhibited; deference to tradition, similarly, can be

rewarded or punished. One must turn, say the critics of the culture argument, to other factors to account for the use of culture: toward institutions, incentives, policies. Strong support for this argument can be found by looking at the Chinese. Economic change in China ground to a halt during the Cultural Revolution; later, when incentives toward production were restored in the countryside, farmers produced in abundance. Similarly, the very civilization whose productivity is low on the mainland constitutes the dynamos of Southeast Asia as the overseas Chinese. This debate occurs all over the Pacific region. Why does Japan produce so efficiently? Because of Japanese culture. Why is America experiencing economic difficulties? Because of changes in the American work ethic. And so on.

The debate over economic growth is but one example of many intellectual challenges that the emergence of the Pacific region causes for experts inside the academy and in policy circles. The Pacific region means a new agenda for country specialists, or area studies, on one side of a triangle, social sciences on the second side, and professional schools on the third. In the United States, various fields of knowledge of foreign countries traditionally were grouped in area studies programs. The focus on a specific country or region of the world consisted of specialists in language, history, literature, art and music, and, in the social sciences, that most committed to the study of culture, anthropology. Sometimes political scientists, sociologists, and economists ventured in, often not. Business, management, public policy, international relations, international competition, security, and such topics were not part of the area studies agenda. Specialists in those topics dealt with the rich and powerful

3. Max Weber, *The Protestant Ethic and the Spirit of Capitalism* (New York: Scribner's, 1958).

nations. Thus professional schools spent little time on area studies, and social sciences only some. The result was a segmentation of approach, a linking of theoretical approach to region and topic. The understanding of foreign countries was left to specialists in culture. The understanding of commerce and war was left to economics, political science, and professional schools.

The spread of economic power outside the West has altered the scene dramatically. Specialists in management security, trade, and international relations cannot possibly ignore the need to understand Japan, East Asia, Mexico, Brazil, and other active participants in the global economy. Area studies specialties are invaded by new questions and new types of experts. Some participants on each side respond by applying their traditional approach to the new agenda. Some of them feel that economies are expressions of culture. The view of others is that economies can be understood the world over with the same intellectual tool used on the United States or Europe, because behavior can be modeled as rational everywhere. In many places and increasingly, more interesting interaction occurs between these sides of the intellectual triangle. Business schools and economists talk to specialists in culture; culture specialists examine corporations and industrial relations.

The article by Eleanor Westney in this volume expresses well both the old debate and the progress of the debate toward new formulations and problems integrating different approaches. As a sociologist specializing in Japan and working at the Massachusetts Institute of Technology's Sloan School of Management, Westney charts the level-of-analysis problem. Individuals and their cultures remain important as objects of study and as explanations of events. But information about them must be integrated into a framework of institutions that specify the incentives in which individuals and their cultural propensities operate:

With a major shift in the dominant paradigms in organizational sociology, the potential role of studies of Japanese and other Asian organizations in building theory has grown immeasurably. The focus is increasingly on the institutional configuration of societies: the interactions of organizations, the flows of people, information, capital, and other resources across and within organizations, and the historical and international context in which the institutional map of the society developed. The basic premise is that organizational differences — and cultural differences — within and across societies can best be understood in terms of the relationships across organizations and how those relationships have been shaped by historical paths of change.

Westney sees in this emphasis on institutions a way of integrating the social sciences, area studies, and professional education. It is a means as well of coordinating the respective study of different regions with each other, regions whose specialists have traditionally never communicated, such as those working on Latin America and East Asia, as well as those working on the United States and Europe. Whether this integration and interaction occurs around the new institutionalism or some other approach, there is certainly a great deal of rethinking taking place around the relationship of culture to institutions and incentives, such as the work of Ronald Dore, Tom Rohlen, Christena Turner, and Mark Fruin, to name but a few. In addition, as other articles in this volume note, we see a remarkable development in cross-regional work as well as cross-disciplinary work.

The level-of-analysis issue concerning the relationship of unit to system lies at the heart of the relationship of culture to other factors. It is also at the heart of other issues of importance in the Pacific region: international relations, economic policy, and the role of the state.

THE INTERNATIONAL DIMENSION: STATES AND SYSTEMS

Students of international relations and policymakers alike have always stressed the importance of the international system in explaining events in the world arena. Countries, from this viewpoint, are actors seeking a common set of goals: security and prosperity. Their action in pursuit of these goals turns on the opportunities and constraints provided in the environment around them. Faced with weak neighbors, countries are likely to expand their influence; faced with strong neighbors, countries will be more restrained—this is but one fairly simple proposition arising from this mode of thinking. System-level thinking has an analogy to the market in economic reasoning. In economics, all actors are assumed to be alike; that is, all are rational calculators seeking to maximize welfare. The deference in behavior turns on the difference in the market that incentives provide; change the incentives and behavior will change. In the world arena, substitute countries for individuals, and the reasoning remains the same.

For policymakers, this is an important guide to action. It suggests that attention should be paid to configurations of the international environment: who has various forms of power and how it is distributed—are there many centers of power, or only one, or two? System-level thinking downplays domestic politics: country behavior turns on a country's position in the international system, not on internal considerations. Thus it matters relatively little who holds office in the country; a change of government makes little difference.

In this volume, Kurth, Gilpin, and Inoguchi explore changes in the international system by looking at just these elements in the international configuration of power that changes events. None looks only at system-level variables, and all point to aspects of domestic politics that have significant effects on policy, but in all three articles we can find interesting material pointing to the system-level issues.

The three authors note ways in which the Pacific region has altered the international order laid down in the aftermath of World War II. The international system expressed two concepts: liberal international trade and deterrence. Through the General Agreement on Tariffs and Trade and the International Monetary Fund, free trade would provide international prosperity. Through the North Atlantic Treaty Organization (NATO) and a ring of alliances around the world, deterrence would assure security from the major menace, the Soviet Union. As Kurth notes, this can be seen as an Atlantic concept. It focused on the economic rebuilding of Europe, restoring that region as a trading partner for the United States, and on Europe's political security, preventing the spread of communism either internally or through Soviet arms as in Eastern Europe.

Out of its North Atlantic perspectives, the United States developed concepts that it applied to other parts of the world, with rather more troublesome results. As Kurth writes, "The greatest disasters in U.S. security policy—toward China in the 1940s and 1950s and toward Indochina in the 1960s and 1970s—resulted from the American effort to interpret the Asian reality through the European prism, to squeeze it into the NATO model." In Europe, where Soviet troops lay minutes from the German border, finite deterrence made sense. Asian countries were not and are not likely targets of a Soviet blitzkrieg; thus for that region extended deterrence — that is, a more indirect pattern of resistance through diplomacy, negotiation, alliances, and assistance — could be more appropriate.

In economic relations, the United States promoted a regime of free trade. America held liberal views of economics within and between countries. It encouraged these in Europe through the General Agreement on Tariffs and Trade and through the Common Market. Asian countries looked at the economy rather differently. Where the United States followed liberal models, Japan, Korea, Taiwan, and other countries followed mercantilist ones. Asian capitalism embraced the market, private profit, incentives, and competition but in a rather different framework, that of cartels, subsidies, managed trade, industrial policy, and a whole host of interventions in the market mixing state and private interests.

The interaction of these two systems produces tension. American import openness combined with Japanese and other East Asian mercantilism, compounded by high American defense expenditures, produces the likely sparks of relations between the countries. It puts the international system itself under pressure, caught between two competing patterns arising out of different experiences:

The 1990s, a half century after the Pacific War, will be a period of tension between two international relations paradigms: (1) the declining one of international liberalism and extended deterrence, created by the United States in the Atlantic/European world and extended by it into the Pacific/Asian world, the paradigm of the American half century; and (2) the rising one of international mercantilism and finite deterrence, created by the Pacific/Asian powers themselves, the paradigm of the future.[4]

Kurth's exploration of the interaction between the international system and internal domestic factors resonates well with the themes of his fellow authors, Professors Gilpin and Inoguchi. Rather than repeat the points of agreement between the authors, it might be more helpful to point out separate points of emphasis made by each. Gilpin explores the relationship between economic forces of change and political-military ones. The international system has, he argues, been shaped by the distribution of power seen in military terms, the environmental setting, the economy, technology, culture, and the nature of domestic regimes. Major changes in the international system arise from changes in one or more of these. Hegemonic wars have been one massive force of change clearly visible in our era and earlier ones. Economic growth also causes big changes, through the entry of new countries into the international economic system and through the link between economic power and military potentiality. Political factors produce tremendous results; new domestic regimes alter military and economic potential and objectives.

Thus the postwar system is being altered by each of these factors. Rapid economic growth in Europe, Japan, and East Asia has ended the economic hegemony of the United States; the United States no longer produces one-half of the world's GNP but less than one-quarter. Theorists debate the implications this has for the stability of international trade: some theo-

4. James R. Kurth, "The Pacific Basin versus the Atlantic Alliance: Two Paradigms of International Relations," this issue of *The Annals* of the American Academy of Political and Social Science.

rists, Gilpin notably, have wondered whether free-trade regimes can survive in a multipolar world where no one power has the strength or the incentive to provide some of the collective goods needed to prevent protectionism in various forms. Other writers believe egoists can cooperate under anarchy, that is, that the major trading partners can learn through experience the advantages of cooperating even without a superordinate arbiter of last resort.

A second important economic transformation lies in the nature of production itself. Gilpin notes that American hegemony arose with Fordism — the efficiencies arising from mass production of standardized products for a stable mass market. With new technology, intense competition, and market instability have come alternative forms of organizing production, what some theorists have called "flexible specialization"[5] — producing specialized products tailored to specific regional markets, combining advanced technology with a wide range of economic forms, from individual highly skilled artisans to low-skilled low-wage migrants, to computerized large but programmable, hence flexible, machines. Japan and other countries have done extremely well pioneering new ways to organize manufacturing, not in the invention of new science or technology. Can other countries adjust? asks Gilpin. Do countries rise and decline because of the congruence of economic conditions with particular institutional attributes and skills, so that they rise when the fit is good and fall when it is not? Can countries alter their economic institutions when that seems appropriate, or are the rigidities rather greater than neoclassical economic theory might suggest?

Another important element of change that Gilpin notes lies in the Soviet bloc.

5. Michael Piore and Charles Sabel, *The Second Industrial Divide* (New York: Basic Books, 1984).

While the non-Soviet bloc has evolved significantly into multiple centers of economic activity and military capability, the Soviet Union has remained static for a lengthy period of time, as the Soviets have used force to control Eastern Europe. In recent years, significant debate has been taking place in the USSR itself, with uncertain prospects for change. *Perestroika* and *glasnost* have yet to alter relations within the Soviet orbit or even in East European regimes. At the same time, they are having effects on decision makers and publics in other regions, which in turn can alter intraalliance and interbloc relations. Sino-Soviet tensions have eased into a more muted mode, while in Western Europe, especially Germany, political support for militant deterrence is softening noticeably.

The complex pattern of alliance relationships is the major theme of Inoguchi's article. Countries are strongly influenced by the international system in Inoguchi's account, but they have choices. They pick from a number of options concerning their own policies and particularly concerning the alliances they make with other countries or blocs. As the world becomes increasingly multipolar, these options increase and the choices become greater and more uncertain. The postwar world no longer defines Japan's options so clearly or restrictively.

With the erosion of American hegemony comes a debate about the possible and probable prospects of the future international system. Current Japanese discussions see four scenarios: (1) Pax Americana phase 2, a revival of American power in somewhat reduced form aided by Japanese economic power; (2) bigemony, or U.S.-Japanese condominium in economic and security matters; (3) Pax Consortis, a loose, flexible association of major blocs, in overlapping issue areas with no single hegemony; and (4) Pax Nipponica, Japanese hegemony with a preeminent economic position and a nuclear arsenal.

Inoguchi sees the first two as the likely alternatives for the next quarter century, while the other two become possibilities in the longer span of a half century. Economic and technical dynamics shape the choice between Pax Americana phase 2 and Pax Nipponica, while the "nullification of nuclear arsenals is crucial in making feasible both Pax Consortis and Pax Nipponica because without it the two superpowers can remain the formidable actors."[6] What Inoguchi calls "the debt of history" may be crucial in shaping Japan's role in any of these arrangements.

In the immediate future, Inoguchi suggests, Japan's options are shaped by two primary axes of interest: relations with the United States, pro-alliance versus anti-; and relations with Europe and East Asia, or trilateralism versus Asianism. This involves a mixture of geography, economics, and security. Should Japan tilt toward East Asia on economics, or be trilateral and work with West Europe and the United States? Or can it develop an Asian pole with the other countries of the region, giving it more distance from either Europe or the United States or both? There are several possible orientations combining these dimensions.

Japan's choice between these alternatives turns on a variety of factors, some internal to Japan, some depending on decisions made elsewhere. Inside Japan there remain strong pacifist sentiment and resistance to international power politics. There are conflicting interests with respect to economic policy toward issues of import consumption, which have substantial bear-

ing on foreign economic relations. Outside Japan, there remain strong memories of World War II that inhibit regional alliances, and in the United States and Western Europe there exist sharp conflict over trade imbalances and resentments over Japanese free riding on American security expenditures.

All three authors — Kurth, Gilpin, and Inoguchi — write in an interpretive mode in which the international system plays a substantial role in shaping the behavior of states within it. In this sense the major impact of the Pacific Rim phenomenon is its effects on that system — the end of American economic hegemony and the shift to a multipolar economic world; the nuclear stalemate and its complex meaning for security issues; changes in both the United States and the Soviet Union that encourage more complex maneuvering by other countries; and shifts in ideology, technology, and institutions.[7]

Another set of issues turn our attention from the international system to nation-states and their institutions. This is a classic step in international discussions: from system-level theorizing to country-level theorizing, what Kenneth Waltz, in his famous book, called the move from "third image" to "second image" analysis.[8] In system-level theorizing, states or countries are black boxes. They behave as an integral whole, according to the pressure of exter-

6. Takashi Inoguchi, "Shaping and Sharing Pacific Dynamism," this issue of *The Annals* of the American Academy of Political and Social Science.

7. Miles Kahler, "External Ambition and Economic Performance," *World Politics*, 40(4):419-51 (July 1988); John Ruggie, "Political Structure and Change in the International Economic Order," in *The Antinomies of Interdependence: National Welfare and the International Division of Labor*, ed. John Ruggie (New York: Columbia University Press, 1983); Joann Gowa, "Political Correlates of Open International Markets: The Advantages of Bipolarity," *American Political Science Review* (forthcoming).

8. Kenneth Waltz, *Man, the State, and War* (New York: Columbia University Press, 1959).

nal incentives. But if the system-level constraints are ambiguous and states have choices, then some further analysis is needed to understand how they make those choices. What is it about a country that influences the selection of one policy alternative over others?

ECONOMIC GROWTH: POLICIES AND POLITICS

Economic growth lies at the heart of the Pacific Rim phenomenon. Without it, this issue of *The Annals* probably would not exist. Asia and Latin America have certainly been participants in the international system for decades, if not centuries. That is not new. Industrial growth in Asia is not new either: Japan has been at it for a century. The new features are the spread of that industrial dynamism to other parts of Asia; the incorporation of Asia and Latin America into the global division of labor of industrial manufacturing, not just natural-resource extraction and agriculture; and the flow of industrial products from this region into the older industrial centers of Europe and North America.

Robert Wade begins his article with an important caveat to all of these discussions of economic growth:

First, we need to define industrial success. Anyone who has experienced the pollution and congestion of East Asian cities will realize that "success" has to be used in a qualified sense, even leaving aside political aspects such as civil and political rights. I mean "success" to refer to such basics as the food in people's stomachs and the amount of income left over after caloric requirements have been met.

In that definition of success, growth has been phenomenal. Several countries have expanded at rates that break the records of a two-century-old industrial revolution. Interesting data on growth are given in the articles of this volume and need not be repeated here. The burning issue of debate is why—why has the growth occurred, how can it be explained, and, inevitably, are there lessons for elsewhere?

We may sort the controversy out into two steps, each operating at a different level of analysis. One step of the argument deals with the question, What policies promote economic growth? The second step of the argument goes one remove prior to this and asks what factors or politics cause the policies that promote economic growth.

Growth-promoting policies

The simplest explanation for economic dynamism in East Asia is neoclassical: East Asia and Japan grew because they got the prices right. Economic growth occurs in the neoclassical model when actors have the right information about real costs, which only the free market can provide, and have the incentives to achieve maximum efficiency, which, again, only the free market can provide. Create a free market, and all will take care of itself. State action can never be more informed than the information provided by the market, hence state action must by definition always be suboptimal. This sounds simple but is rather more complex.

Allowing market forces to operate is surely a central, if not the central, aspect of East Asian success. Any doubter need only look at mainland China or other regimes with extreme control over economic life. As in Europe and North America, behind economic growth in Asia lies the willingness to allow the market to provide information and incentives, to reward and to punish, to force efficiency upon many unwilling, and willing, actors. None of the participants in this debate doubts the importance of the market as a vital ingredient in any successful growth-oriented strategy. The argument turns on the sufficiency or insufficiency of basic get-the-prices-right statements for defining policy options for governments and the private sector, for explaining what effect various policies have actually had, and for recommending policy alternatives to decision makers.

In his article, Robert Wade probes the descriptive and analytic sufficiency of several studies that explain growth as the direct outcome of pure free markets. He sees three major policies that have promoted growth, each involving state action to supplement or enhance markets: capital accumulation, selective protection of industries, and selective industrial policies. First, high rates of capital accumulation produce growth, Wade argues, and high rates are not simply generated spontaneously out of trade but rather out of deliberate policies that favor them. Second, economic protection has not been all that low in Korea and Taiwan, so that its absence cannot adequately account for performance. "The point is that protection, like any powerful instrument, can be used well or it can be used badly. The predicted economic effects may not occur if the protection is arranged differently from normal." In these countries, governments acted deliberately to use tariffs to promote export. Wade cites two examples: tariffs held down domestic consumption, but exporters were exempted from duties so that they could get inputs at world prices; and exporters were given subsidies to discourage domestic consumption even further. Third, industrial policy can have, contrary to the neoclassical assumption, beneficial effects under some conditions: for Wade this can happen when industrial policy leads private actors into undertakings that they would not otherwise have been able to do.

Gereffi's article challenges the adequacy of a central distinction in much of the literature on development policies: the classification of policies into import-substituting industrialization (ISI) and export-oriented industrialization (EOI). The labels convey content: ISI sought to promote growth by shielding national economies from the gale-force winds of international competition so as to nurture infant industries to adult maturity; EOI fueled internal growth by producing directly for international markets with little or no domestic consumption of the products produced. Much current analysis thinks EOI, followed by East Asia, did better than ISI, followed by Latin America, which explains the difference between the two regions. Because EOI produces for an open world economy, many economists equate EOI with free-market policies within a country, precisely the point Wade and other contributors to this volume contest.

Gereffi questions the adequacy of the typology to understand current developments. While the distinction highlighted real differences between the two regions in the 1960s, it ignores "the subsequent interplay between inward- and outward-oriented development strategies that in fact has been essential to the economic dynamism of the NICs in each region." Latin American and East Asian NICs have converged toward mixed "strategies, which are political decisions and plans, and development patterns, which are economic outcomes that may or may not have been pursued in a strategic way by national elites." East Asian countries have invested in heavy industries leading to diversification of exports and domestic consumption, while Mexico, Brazil, and Argentina have become increasingly important participants in producing goods exported into the "global manufacturing system." Global manufacturing, the production of components in many different countries as part of an integrated network of manufacturing, exporting, and consumption, has made for considerable heterogeneity within each region of the world. The variance within East Asia and Latin America is growing rapidly, making generalizations about the regions as whole units increasingly difficult. Finding a niche in the global marketplace, Gereffi suggests, can be done in a variety of ways, so that countries can pick from a range of alternatives, rather than be restricted to a single uniform trajectory.

In comparing the international participation of Latin America with that of East Asia, Fernando Fajnzylber stresses the "capacity of countries to add intellectual value to their resource endowment." In Latin America, resource abundance has often encouraged rent-seeking behavior and, along with it, sharp income inequalities. The supposed trade-off between growth and equity may have some evidentiary support if one looks only at Latin America, but it is not supported by international comparisons. Development patterns involve an interaction of choices internal to countries and choices made by foreign actors. Countries construct the policies that produce the development sequence of "equity, austerity, growth, and competitiveness." Major powers make choices that affect developing countries greatly: the United States decides how much debt to run; Japan and Germany decide where to put their capital surplus. Other choices include how much to import and from where, and how much arms spending to sustain, high levels being inversely correlated with industrial competitiveness.

To explain the superior economic performance of the Asian Pacific region compared to other parts of the world, Krause offers five factors: societal commitment to growth; individual commitment to work as expressed through long hours; high savings rate and domestic investment rates; market-conforming policies by governments; and the "regional effect," or the bonus of being surrounded by other successful countries. Governments in this region, Krause notes, are not laissez-faire. With the exception of Hong Kong, all are quite intrusive in the economy, but their involvement seeks to guide markets, not replace or distort them. Governments used the flying-goose model of emulating leaders. Initially, it was the United States that was emulated, but already in the 1960s, Japan was a model for both the private and public sectors. Japanese imports from the region are increasing, and Japanese financial influence has grown immensely.

Fishlow focuses his analysis on financial flows. Lending surged after 1973 when oil exporters had immense payment surpluses. Banks recycled these surpluses to developing countries in the form of loans. For Latin America, the vast increase of debt has profoundly shaped economic performance and policy options. The choice between these policy options will turn on political debates currently under way.

Running through all of these discussions on best policies is a debate over the role of government. Can state action contribute to growth? The neoclassical answer is presumed to be negative: markets do better than state actors in making choices. In East Asia, though, in the very countries where growth has occurred, government involvement has been extensive. Does experience contradict theory?

Experience has at least altered the debate. Markets are vital. So are institutions. Markets cannot exist without institutions created by the state. Some institutional arrangements are better than others. So we do not have an issue of state versus markets but the complex problem of finding the right interaction between specific institutions and particular market situations. Some linkages between states and markets appear to be growth producing, while others appear to be rent seeking, or growth inhibiting.

Recent experience in East Asia and elsewhere suggests to some observers that some state interventions can promote growth in some situations — a limited claim but a real one. Growth-promoting interventions include: limits on consumption; incentives to export, to invest, to accumulate capital; investment by the state in infrastructure and education; restrictions on capital export; and other policies, which sometimes work.

The world can see a strong difference between Marcos in the Philippines and the cases of Taiwan and South Korea. Strong governments in all three cases intervened massively in the national economy. In the case of Marcos, the power was used to bilk the economy of money to benefit a few, in ways that killed growth; in Taiwan and Korea, power was used to promote growth. Along with the inequalities of the market came a tremendous expansion of wealth, pulling large numbers of people with it. What accounts for the difference? Part of the answer requires some attention to politics.[9] As Robert Wade puts it, "Rent seeking is not an inevitable accompaniment and

9. East Asian NICs provide an interesting range of alternatives in the uses of state power. For a theoretical statement that emphasizes the rent-seeking proclivities of state power, see Douglas North, *Structure and Change in Economic History* (New York: Norton, 1981). For theoretical and empirical discussion of the use of state power for developmental purposes, see Tun-jen Cheng, "Political Regimes and Development Strategies: Korea and Taiwan," in *Manufactured Miracles*, ed. Gereffi and Wyman; Stephan Haggard and Tun-jen Cheng, "State and Foreign Capital in the East Asian NICs," in *The Political Economy of New East Asian Industrialism*, ed. Frederic C. Deyo (Ithaca, NY: Cornell University Press, 1987).

distorter of government intervention; it is a function of the political regime."

Explaining the politics of policy choices

Economic growth certainly requires growth-promoting policies. But growth-promoting policies require growth-promoting politics. Policies arise from choices made by the political system. We need some understanding of the factors that inhibit or promote the choice of policies that get prices right.

Several factors are involved, among them state institutions, ideology and leadership goals, and societal interest groups and social forces. Countries differ considerably in the organization of state institutions. Haggard sees several elements of state organization that facilitate growth. Korea and Taiwan have a considerable degree of state autonomy and state capacity. Autonomy means the ability of governments to acquire some insulation from social pressures. Interest groups, lobbies, and social groups like agriculture and business all make demands on governments. Often these demands run contrary to growth-promoting policies. Certain institutional arrangements shield governments, allowing them to make tough choices. Governments also need capability: they need organizations, or bureaucracies with the skills to make and enforce policy, and they need the authority to use instruments of policy intervention. East Asian NICs have had high levels of autonomy and state capacity.

Haggard notes the importance of ideology and leadership: political leaders in East Asia placed economic growth at the top of their agenda and were influenced by international thinking about optimal policy. A variety of international institutions helped spread ideas and skills about policy choices. Whitehead notes a similar influence in his mention of policy "style."

Deyo and Haggard both explore the importance of societal pressures, interest groups, economic sectors, and classes of policymakers, as do many of the other authors in the volume at points in their articles. Deyo agrees with many of the authors in attributing considerable importance to "the insulation of development planners and corporate executives from political demands." This sort of insulation allows the choice of controversial and difficult policies, such as the limitation of consumption, the stress on export, and other growth-producing policies. Deyo's interpretation emphasizes more heavily the particular direction of the pressure for which this insulation provides the shield: the political demands of workers as expressed through the labor movement. "While political controls go some distance in explaining the political weakness of East Asian workers, the more fundamental causes are to be found, first, in the nature of employment relations in these countries and, second, in the sequencing of political and economic changes during the course of industrialization." Haggard agrees that labor weakness may have contributed to export growth, though he rejects the stronger proposition that labor controls were designed expressly for the purpose of promoting growth. The influence of other groups, Haggard notes, such as agriculture and business, was mediated through political processes of coalition building and institutional arrangements.

Whitehead concurs with several authors in noting the importance of policy style in explaining growth-generating policies: what distinguishes the growth-generating East Asian NICs from other countries in East Asia and Latin America was that all were "highly centralized and well-

disciplined societies, governed by regimes with a clear sense of direction and the ability to take a long view, if necessary, overriding temporary resistance or sectional protest." Whitehead concurs with those contributors writing on policy choices on the importance of export-promoting credit allocation and other policies made by governments.

While East Asian comparisons are interesting and useful, Whitehead cautions us about the difficulty of transferring the models. Had Latin America exported as much as the four tigers of East Asia, it would be exporting more than the United States, which would surely destabilize the international economy. The four tigers are relatively small in population. They also occupy unique and distinctive positions in geopolitics. Singapore, Hong Kong, and Taiwan are singular entities, the first two created as outward-oriented city-states, the latter overwhelmed and transformed by refugees. All four have unique places in international great-power rivalries. Certain regions of Latin America resemble these countries. The subcontinent as a whole cannot and is not likely to look the same, just as all of East Asia is not likely to follow the model of these four countries.

CONCLUSION

Whitehead's queries about the comparison of East Asia and Latin America bring us full circle to the first article of the volume. Westney notes the impact upon social science of contemporary trends in the Pacific region. The effort to make policy and the effort to comprehend converge as challenges to disciplines in the university and to policy professionals in government and business. Comparisons across region and country are both imperative and difficult. They require new ways of putting together traditional variables — culture, institutions, economics, geopolitics, micro components and macro influences, leadership, ideology. These are familiar variables. They have always been important and are likely to continue to be so as major analytic tools in understanding behavior.

But they are likely to be thought of in different ways. Culture is related to incentives and institutions. Policies and leadership may express national traditions and cultural propensities, but they also shape them. International economic patterns have substantial influence upon national choices. But countries have some role in shaping their destiny. What happens depends in part on their own choices. The micro variables of economic organization, individual motives, and the pattern of incentives, on one side, and the macro variables of the international economic system and national and international decision making — these relationships are rather more complex perhaps than either policymakers or theorists realized several decades ago. They require more interaction across area studies, disciplines, and professional schools than used to be the case — and, fortunately, some of that is taking place. This volume has sought to provide some partial sample of the issues and the debates.

Sociological Approaches to the Pacific Region

By D. ELEANOR WESTNEY

ABSTRACT: Sociology has been grounded in Western experience and philosophy, especially in the assumption that by studying the most industrialized — that is, Western — societies, sociology could produce general theories applicable to all societies. However, the growing industrial competitiveness not just of Japan but of the Asian newly industrializing countries has converged with a dissatisfaction with the current paradigms in sociology, producing a new challenge to the long-standing parochialism of American social science in general, and sociology in particular. Yet, so far, the role of sociological research on Asia in these developments has been relatively limited. This article looks closely at research on Japan in organizational and industrial sociology to address what significant sociological research has been done on Asia, what that has contributed to our understanding of Asia and to the discipline, and what the outlook is for the future as popular interest in the Pacific Rim grows. The emergence of new paradigms in sociology is increasing the prospects for using Asia as a venue for generating sociological theory as well as testing it.

Eleanor Westney is associate professor of international management at the Alfred P. Sloan School of Management at the Massachusetts Institute of Technology and holder of the Mitsubishi Career Development Chair in International Management. She received a B.A. and an M.A. in sociology from the University of Toronto and a Ph.D. in sociology from Princeton University. Her book, Imitation and Innovation: The Emulation of Western Organizational Forms in Meiji Japan, *was published in 1987.*

SOCIOLOGICAL approaches to Asia have a long and venerable history. At the turn of the century, Max Weber, one of the founding fathers of the discipline, extended his comparative inquiries on the relationship between religion and social structure to a lengthy study of China. Yet despite this promising lineage, American sociological research has been centered overwhelmingly on the United States, prompting the small number of sociologists who study East Asia to complain bitterly that someone doing research on the United States is regarded as building social theory, while someone analyzing any non-Western society is seen to be engaged in area studies.

The reason for this parochialism lies in the history of the discipline. Sociology was born out of an effort to understand the effects of industrialization on human social structure and behavior. As such it has been grounded in Western experience and philosophy, especially in the assumption that by studying the most industrialized — that is, Western — societies, sociology could produce general theories that would apply, tomorrow if not today, to all societies.

The rapid industrial growth of Japan provided less of a challenge to this assumption than one might have expected. After all, Japan's institutions were deliberately modeled on those of the West, and Japan's own leaders clearly regarded the advanced industrial societies of Europe and the United States as models for their own development. Any anomalies in Japanese social patterns could be — and usually were — regarded either as manifestations of the cultural lag, which would disappear over time, or as aspects of Japan's cultural and historical uniqueness.

But the growing industrial competitiveness not just of Japan but of the Asian newly industrializing countries has converged with a growing dissatisfaction with the current paradigms in sociology to produce a new challenge to the long-standing parochialism of American social science in general, and sociology in particular. Yet, so far, the role of sociological research on Asia in these developments has been limited. It is difficult to identify any area of sociology where the study of Asia has had an impact on paradigms and research issues comparable to that of the debate over Japanese industrial policy in political science or where significant efforts are being made to produce new theoretical paradigms comparable to Aoki's efforts to use Japanese industrial organization as a basis for a new theory of the firm in economics. The 1988 *Handbook of Sociology,* a massive tome edited by Neil Smelser, one of America's leading sociological theorists, contains in its 22 chapters and over 800 pages only four references to Japan — one fewer than to California — and two references to China.[1]

Therefore any would-be analyst of sociological approaches to Asia is confronted with several questions: What significant sociological research has been done on Asia? What has that contributed to our understanding of Asia and to the discipline? What is the outlook for the future, as popular interest in the Pacific Rim grows?

ORGANIZATIONAL SOCIOLOGY AND INDUSTRIAL SOCIOLOGY

The importance of research on Asia has been most clearly recognized in the closely related subfields of organizational sociology and industrial sociology.[2] Interest in

1. Neil J. Smelser, ed., *Handbook of Sociology* (Newbury Park, CA: Sage, 1988).

2. Organizational sociology has as its province all forms of formal organization, public and private, from corporations to schools. Industrial sociology is

Asian industrial organization has been encouraged both by popular interest in the roots of the growing competitiveness of Japan and the Asian newly industrializing countries and by recognition of the relevance of that success to theories of industrial organization. The 1988 special issue of the *American Journal of Sociology* on "organizations and institutions" included among its eight articles two that focused specifically on Asia, and a third that used a comparison of Japanese and U.S. management practices to test the explanatory power of its formal model of influence processes.

Sociological research on organizations in Asia has been concentrated overwhelmingly on Japan. As the first non-Western society to achieve very high levels of industrialization, Japan is a natural testing ground for theories about the inherent dynamics of technology and efficiency in shaping industrial organization, from Weberian theories of bureaucracy to current economics-based theories about firm internal labor markets. Japan is also the Asian country in which the lot of the social scientist is easiest: Japan itself boasts a large social science establishment, Japanese are well accustomed to filling out questionnaires, and there is a wealth of public data on virtually every aspect of social structure, from labor force statistics to public opinion polls.

*Sociological research on
Japanese industrial organization*

According to the authors of a recent review of the growing sociological literature on Japanese industrial organization,

the two fundamental sociological issues in the field are the extent to which real differences exist between Japanese and Western patterns and the extent to which any differences can be explained by existing social theories.[3] Identifying differences between societies or social groups and assessing whether those differences are real is the province of sociological methodology.

Sociological studies of Japanese industrial organizations reflect the methodological great divide in the discipline between qualitative and quantitative research methods. Either can help to identify differences across societies. Qualitative methods, which include firsthand observation, interviews, and the use of primary documents such as company rules, handbooks, and office communications, are probably most useful in this regard. They provide the rich, detailed case studies that reveal patterns not specified in existing theories, explore complex relationships between different aspects of social structure and process, and uncover informal and dynamic processes. On the other hand, quantitative methods, which employ an array of statistical techniques to assess the significance of observed patterns and to measure the association and interdependence of variables, are more useful for assessing whether the differences identified in qualitative studies or popular belief are real or whether they are the result of selective observation.

Both qualitative and quantitative methodologies are part of the sociological armory. Both have rigorous standards for establishing the credibility of the findings, and both build explicitly or implicitly on theories that identify the significant variables in organizations. Some of the best

focused on one type of organization, the factory, on related organizations, such as unions, and on the informal social processes that influence working lives.

3. James R. Lincoln and Kerry McBride, "Japanese Industrial Organization in Comparative Perspective," *Annual Review of Sociology 1987*, 13:289 (1987).

studies of Japanese organizations have used both methodologies. Ronald Dore's recent study of structural change in the Japanese economy, with a case study of the textile industry, uses both industry-level quantitative data and observation-based case studies.[4] Robert Cole's book on mobility and work organization among blue-collar workers includes both a careful quantitative study of the patterns of inter-firm and intrafirm job changes among workers in Yokohama and Detroit and a detailed qualitative description of quality-control circles in the Toyota auto body plant.[5]

Most studies, however, rely primarily on either qualitative or quantitative research methods. Ronald Dore's intensive case studies of factory organization in a British electrical equipment firm and a Japanese counterpart are an outstanding example of qualitative research.[6] He vividly portrayed the pervasive differences in the British firm between managers and workers, and the consequent antagonisms that pervaded industrial relations, both in the formal industrial relations system and the day-to-day interactions on the shop floor. This picture stood in sharp contrast to his portrayal of the elimination in the Japanese plants of many of the differences in dress, perks, and reward structure between blue-collar and white-collar workers, and the strong sense of commitment of workers to their company.

A recent example of rigorously designed quantitative research looked at a subset of the reward variables discussed in Dore's work. Kalleberg and Lincoln[7] collected data from 52 plants in seven industries in Indiana and from 46 comparable plants in Kanagawa prefecture in Japan to analyze the individual, organizational, and industry determinants of earnings inequality. Despite recent suggestions from a number of scholars and industry spokespersons that differences between Western and Japanese industrial organization are eroding, they found substantial differences between the U.S. and Japanese plants, beginning with the much greater gap between the earnings of managers and workers in the United States. The authors conclude that

American employees' earnings are heavily dependent on job/occupational characteristics, authority position, and performance reviews and job evaluations by the firm; these effects are small to nonexistent, even negative, among the Japanese. The earnings of Japanese employees, on the other hand, are more heavily conditioned by the life-cycle variables of dependents, age, and seniority.[8]

They also found that, except for women, earnings in Japanese plants are positively related to the level of automation, whereas in the U.S. plants it makes no difference to managers' salaries and gives male workers significantly lower earnings.[9] This last finding not only suggests why Japanese workers do not resist automation; it also provides a further indicator of the objective basis for Japanese workers' conviction that their welfare and that of the enterprise are inextricably linked.

4. Ronald Dore, *Flexible Rigidities: Industrial Policy and Structural Adjustment in the Japanese Economy* (Stanford, CA: Stanford University Press, 1986).

5. Robert E. Cole, *Work, Mobility, and Participation* (Berkeley: University of California Press, 1979).

6. Ronald Dore, *British Factory, Japanese Factory: The Origins of Diversity in Industrial Relations* (Berkeley: University of California Press, 1973).

7. Arne L. Kalleberg and James R. Lincoln, "The Structure of Earnings Inequality in the United States and Japan," *American Journal of Sociology*, supp., 94:S121-53 (1988).

8. Ibid., p. S149.

9. Ibid., p. S147.

In addition to methodology, studies of Japanese industrial organization differ in their comparative scope (Table 1). Some studies are explicitly designed to compare Japan and one or more other societies. Some of these studies are based on a research design that collects data in Japan and at least one other society;[10] others use data already collected and analyzed in another society and replicate the research design in Japan.[11] Still other studies focus only on Japanese organizations, making any comparisons either implicit or based on theory rather than comparative data. Rodney Clark's book, *The Japanese Company,* was a qualitative study that described the organizational structures institutionalized in the large Japanese corporation and presented a case study of how these structures were adopted by a growing Japanese manufacturing company.[12] Marsh and Mannari's quantitative analysis of Japanese factory organization analyzed the extent to which the patterns of factory organization differed across Japanese factories in different industries.[13] Part of their agenda was to see whether patterns that industrial sociology had put forward as typical of advanced industrial society characterized some industries more than others.

10. For example, Dore, *British Factory, Japanese Factory;* Kalleberg and Lincoln, "Earnings Inequality"; James R. Lincoln and Arne L. Kalleberg, "Work Organization and Workforce Commitment: A Study of Plants and Employees in the U.S. and Japan," *American Sociological Review,* 50:738-60 (1985).

11. For example, Koya Azumi and Charles J. McMillan, "Culture and Organizational Structure: A Comparison of Japanese and British Organizations," *International Studies of Management and Organization,* 35:201-18 (1981).

12. Rodney Clark, *The Japanese Company* (New Haven, CT: Yale University Press, 1979).

13. Robert M. Marsh and Hiroshi Mannari, *Modernization and the Japanese Factory* (Princeton, NJ: Princeton University Press, 1975).

Sociology's contribution to understanding Japanese industrial organization

Sociology is not alone in the effort to identify the real differences between Japanese and Western industrial organization. This is an area where sociologists rub shoulders, both literally and metaphorically, with researchers from other fields: anthropology, political science, history, economics, and management. The studies of Japanese industrial organization done by anthropologists, political scientists, and historians have been primarily qualitative, Japan-focused studies. Anthropologists have focused on case studies of the social interaction and culture of the workplace, political scientists on business-government interactions, and historians on the evolution of industrial relations at the workplace or on the system level. Economists have focused much more on comparative studies, both qualitative and quantitative, but they differ from sociologists in working primarily with public statistical data rather than data gathered in direct fieldwork. Although only a small proportion of the recent outpouring of management writing on Japan has been based on in-depth, original research, it is possible to identify at least one management study in each of the four cells of Table 1.

Sociology, therefore, possesses no monopoly on any particular methodology in studying Japanese industrial organization. In its efforts to answer the question of whether real differences exist between Japanese and Western patterns, however, it has been the prime contributor of comparative quantitative studies at the level of the organization, as opposed to the economy or the industry. Sociology as a discipline has long been dominated by quantitative research,

TABLE 1
A TYPOLOGY OF SOCIOLOGICAL STUDIES OF JAPANESE INDUSTRIAL ORGANIZATION

Comparative Scope	Methodology	
	Qualitative	Quantitative
Japan-focused	Clark, *Japanese Company*	Marsh and Mannari,
	Cole, *Japanese Blue Collar*	*Modernization and the*
		Japanese Factory
	Dore, *Flexible Rigidities*	
Comparative		
	Dore, *British Factory,*	Kalleberg and Lincoln,
	Japanese Factory	"Earnings Inequality"
	Cole, "Macropolitics of	Lincoln and Kalleberg,
	Change"	"Workforce Commitment"
		Cole, *Work, Mobility and*
		Participation
		Azumi and McMillan,
		"Culture and Structure"

and, given the bias toward U.S.-centered research, its journals and reviewers tend to prefer quantitative comparative research that has the United States as the main point of comparison. Even so, the labor and expense of data collection and analysis in more than one society means that the number of studies like Kalleberg and Lincoln's is still pitifully small.

The most widely read and frequently cited sociological studies, however, are often the qualitative, description-rich case studies. This includes both Japan-focused studies like Robert Cole's participant-observation study of workers in smaller-scale enterprises[14] and comparative studies like Dore's *British Factory, Japanese Factory* or Cole's recent comparison of the evolution and operation of quality-control circles in Sweden, Japan, and the United States.[15] Not only are they more accessible

14. Robert E. Cole, *Japanese Blue Collar: The Changing Tradition* (Berkeley: University of California Press, 1971).

15. Robert E. Cole, "The Macropolitics of Organizational Change: A Comparative Analysis of the

to a nonspecialist audience, but because they cast a wider net, they can often be used to address multiple theoretical paradigms, both within and outside sociology.

What else can be claimed for the discipline's approaches to Japanese industrial organization? One further contribution is a growing sensitivity to the importance of levels of analysis. In recent efforts to resolve some contradictory findings of earlier studies, sociologists in the field are distinguishing between industry, organization, and plant-level effects, which seem to differ in Japan and the United States. For example, comparative studies of Japanese industrial organizations in the 1970s came up with contradictory findings on whether Japanese organizational hierarchies were taller or flatter — referring to the number of levels in the hierarchy — than their Western counterparts. More recent research and some careful reexamination of the earlier findings indicate that the contradiction was

Spread of Small-group Activities," *Administrative Science Quarterly*, 30:560-85 (1985).

rooted in too loose a definition of "organization." Individual factories in a multiplant company tended to have taller organizations than their Western counterparts, whereas at the overall company level, the Japanese organizational hierarchies had flatter administrative pyramids.[16] The authors of more recent studies not only are insisting on the importance of distinguishing clearly between the levels of analysis but also are comparing the effects of each level on the variables of interest by sorting out industry effects, company effects, and plant or function effects.

This concern with the relationships between variables as well as the differences on individual variables means that when sociologists discuss the action implications of their research — for management, for policy, for social change — they often seem to focus more on the constraints on action than on setting an action agenda. Their research reveals the systemness — the complex relationships across variables — and the contextual embeddedness — the supporting web of institutions and values of the social environment — of industrial organization. Their studies therefore often emphasize the barriers to and the costs of rapid change. This can be an extremely valuable contribution to policy debates, but it is not always welcomed.

Contributions of Asia-focused research to organizational sociology

Sociological inquiry is driven by three generic questions: (1) how do we define, measure, and classify the social phenomenon of interest? (2) what causes it? and (3) what are its effects and implications for

16. For further detail, see the discussion in Lincoln and McBride, "Japanese Industrial Organization," pp. 298-99.

other social structures and processes? Not all sociological studies deal with all three questions. Many find the mapping, or empirical description and measurement, of the phenomenon a sufficiently demanding task.

Lincoln and McBride's statement of the two major research questions in the field of Japanese industrial organization — the differences between Japanese and Western patterns and the ability of existing causal theories to explain them — indicates how profoundly research in this field has been shaped by the maps of Western patterns and by the theories based on them. So far, Japan has provided a venue for testing Western-centered paradigms and identifying their shortcomings. To date, however, while this contribution to sociology has been an important one, and influential out of all proportion to the very slender volume of Japan-focused research, it has stopped short of the next step: generating theory rather than simply testing it.

In large part this has been due to the strength of the belief in the universal validity of Western-generated social theory, and of the intensity of the effort needed to challenge it, leaving little time or energy for the careful construction of alternatives. In part, however, we can attribute it to the dominant paradigms of the 1960s and 1970s. Critics of convergence theories of social organization, theories that have had a wide influence in virtually all subfields of sociology, often saw the alternative to technological or economic determinism as cultural determinism. Differences between Japanese and Western patterns proved to them the importance of national culture in shaping social patterns.

Cultural determinism, however, had serious limitations as a basis for generating alternative theories. As its critics pointed out, it tended to be tautological. Japanese industrial organization differed from Western patterns because it was Japanese, a proposition whose basic simplicity had a certain appeal, not least to Japanese. But it was impossible to falsify and difficult to use as a basis for explaining change or for explaining the variations across organizations within Japan. The debate over whether culture formed social patterns or social patterns formed culture was impossible to resolve, even as clearer definitions and measures of culture were developed.[17]

The growing importance of the institutional paradigm

With a major shift in the dominant paradigms in organizational sociology, however, the potential role of studies of Japanese and other Asian organizations in building theory has grown immeasurably. The focus is increasingly on the institutional configuration of societies: the interactions of organizations; the flows of people, information, capital, and other resources across and within organizations; and the historical and international context in which the institutional map of the society developed. The basic premise is that organizational differences — and cultural differences — within and across societies can best be understood in terms of the relationships across organizations and how those relationships have been shaped by historical paths of change.

The focus on the surrounding context of the organization is not new. In the 1960s, contingency theory explained organizational patterns in terms of the character-

17. For a much more extended definition of cultural approaches to Asian organizations, see Gary G. Hamilton and Nicole Woolsey Biggart, "Market, Culture, and Authority: A Comparative Analysis of Management and Organization in the Far East," *American Journal of Sociology*, supp., 94:S69-74 (1988).

istics of the environment, such as its stability or predictability and the speed of change. Population-ecology and resource-dependency approaches characterized the environment in terms of the level and concentration of the resources it made available to the organization.

The institutional paradigm draws on and tries to integrate the insights of earlier paradigms, but a paradigm shift in the social sciences is like the turn of a kaleidoscope: it positions familiar elements in new ways and draws attention to elements that have previously gone unnoticed. Earlier paradigms portrayed the environment as high or low on a number of continuous variables, such as complexity, turbulence, or concentration of resources. In contrast, the emerging institutional paradigm insists on the importance of what kind of institutions supply what kind of resources and what demands they place on the organization in return and on the nature as well as the number of the relationships that organizations develop with other organizations around them. This means that trying to generate theory on the basis of a single society, where there is much less variation in these factors than there is across societies, becomes an increasingly dubious enterprise.

Research on Japan and other Asian countries had little direct impact on the emergence of this paradigm, although work by Ronald Dore in particular articulated the approach before it became fashionable.[18] But the difficulty of satisfactorily accounting for the differences between Japanese and American organizational, political, and economic patterns in terms of existing paradigms was a powerful stimulus to the growing realization of their inadequacies.

18. See in particular his chapter "Late Development," in *British Factory, Japanese Factory*.

For example, the institutional paradigm pays much more attention to the role of the state in organization and management than has been the case for previous work in the subfield. Hamilton and Biggart compare features of management and organization in three Asian societies: Japan, Korea, and Taiwan. They conclude that neither economic nor cultural explanations can account for the differences these societies exhibit in the role of large-scale organizations and industrial groups, the control systems of firms, and typical market strategies. Explaining these differences demands an examination of the historical and contemporary role of the government in building the economy and in influencing the organizational structure of firms: the so-called strong state in South Korea, the reliance of the state on mediating organizations such as industrial groups and industrial associations in Japan, and the strong-society model in Taiwan.[19]

ASIA-FOCUSED RESEARCH AND SOCIOLOGY

The institutional paradigm is becoming important not only in organizational and industrial sociology but also in other subfields, including social change, the sociology of education, and social stratification. Sociologists in a growing range of subfields would echo not only Kalleberg and Lincoln's complaint about the scarcity of comparative work but also — with suitable changes in the final words — their concluding statement that "only by examining these issues in a wide range of cultural, social, and historical contexts will we ultimately be able to understand the origins and operations of the work structures

19. Ibid.

molding national patterns of economic stratification."[20]

But the growing interest in institutions and institutional contexts is by no means confined to sociology. Economics is witnessing the emergence of new paradigms and new excitement in the long-neglected area of institutional economics. A similar paradigm is having a profound effect on political economy, which is experiencing a comparable resurgence in political science. For the first time since modernization theory fell from grace in the early 1970s, the social sciences are seeing the emergence of a shared paradigm.

The study of Asian societies is particularly well positioned to benefit from this development. In the past, social scientists specializing in Asia — and sociologists in particular — have had to deal with the accusation that they have been more interested in their particular regional specialty than in cutting-edge issues in the theories of their discipline. One aspect of this was the strong pull toward eclecticism in research on Asia. The Asian studies field has long been interdisciplinary in its educational programs and its professional interactions. In contrast to the high levels of specialization that prevail in the social sciences as a whole, the Asian studies specialist in any discipline has usually shared graduate classes in language, history, and often the social sciences with fellow area concentrators from other disciplines. In the course of fieldwork in Asia, researchers from the various disciplines frequently interact informally, sharing insights and problems and building networks that are maintained and reinforced through the annual meetings of the Association for Asian Studies

20. Kalleberg and Lincoln, "Earnings Inequality," p. S150.

(AAS), which provides an interdisciplinary professional forum. Within many universities, specialists in each Asian country or region often have a primary affiliation with their disciplinary department and a secondary one with an Asian studies program or a country-focused program. With the reemergence of a shared social science paradigm, the interdisciplinary nature of the field can once again become an advantage rather than a handicap.

CONCLUSION

One immediate consequence of the emergence of the institutional paradigm is obviously the growing importance of comparative studies, especially of Asian societies, which have experienced phenomenal industrial growth but which lie outside the Western tradition. The growing receptivity of sociology journals and of academic departments to non-U.S. research lowers one of the barriers to greater contributions to sociological theory from Asia-focused research. In short, current developments in sociology raise new opportunities for research on Asia to become a venue not just for testing theories based on Western experience, but for developing new and more general — or more precisely delineated — paradigms.

A formidable barrier remains, however: the small number of sociologists trained in Asian languages and history who are able to do primary research in Asia. Sociologists make up only 3 percent of the 5000-strong membership of the national AAS. In the Japan field, for example, of the nearly 1200 Japan specialists listed in the AAS membership directory, only thirty-eight are sociologists. And in comparison with economics and management, very few Japanese researchers in sociology publish in English or do collaborative work with Western counterparts. Japanese sociology departments tend to be small, and a significant proportion of their faculty come from a more heavily Marxist intellectual tradition that makes collaboration with their North American counterparts difficult, especially in organizational or industrial sociology.

The number of sociologists who are doing comparative work within Asia is even smaller. One of the problems in most comparative work on Asia is that the base of comparison is usually the United States. We have pitifully few sociological studies that look for differences and commonalities across Asian societies, and, clearly, such studies are critically important in better understanding the roles of institutional configurations, culture, technology, and economic or market forces.

Nevertheless, the growing popular and intellectual interest in Asia that has helped fuel the demands for less parochial paradigms in sociology will undoubtedly increase the numbers of researchers doing fieldwork in Asia. The research that results will, one hopes, make important contributions to the discipline and to our understanding of Asian societies.

ANNALS, *AAPSS*, **505**, September 1989

The Pacific Basin versus the
Atlantic Alliance:
Two Paradigms of
International Relations

By JAMES R. KURTH

ABSTRACT: For many years, the study of international economy and international security, two fields of international relations, has been based respectively upon the two concepts of international liberalism and extended deterrence. Both concepts developed out of the conditions of the Atlantic/European arena after World War II; together they form the Atlantic Alliance paradigm. This paradigm poorly fits the Pacific/Asian world. In regard to the international economy, the East Asian states are adherents not of international liberalism but of international mercantilism. In regard to international security, they are cases not of extended deterrence but of finite deterrence. Together, these concepts form the Pacific Basin paradigm. The 1990s will be a period of conflict between these two international relations paradigms, the declining one of the United States and the American half century and the rising one of the East Asian powers and the future.

James R. Kurth is professor of political science at Swarthmore College, where he teaches international politics, American foreign policy, and American defense policy. During the years 1983-85, he was a visiting professor of strategy at the U.S. Naval War College. His professional publications have focused upon the political and economic sources of the foreign and defense policies of the United States and other great powers.

F OR almost half a century, the study of international relations and of two of its fields, international economy and international security, has been based upon a few central concepts. The field of international economy has been based upon the idea of international liberalism: liberal states, particularly those in North America and Western Europe, support market forces within an open international economy. This might be termed the GATT model, after the General Agreement on Tariffs and Trade, which was established in 1948. Similarly, the field of international security has been based upon the idea of extended deterrence: the United States contains Soviet military aggression, particularly in Western Europe, by the threat of nuclear escalation in response. Deterrence is said to be extended because the United States extends its commitment beyond its own territory to cover the territories of its allies. This might be termed the NATO model, after the North Atlantic Treaty Organization, which was established in 1949.

THE ATLANTIC ALLIANCE PARADIGM: INTERNATIONAL LIBERALISM AND EXTENDED DETERRENCE

The two concepts of international liberalism and extended deterrence, the two models of GATT and NATO, thus fill out the economic and security dimensions in the analysis of international relations. Together, they form a distinctive way of looking at the world, what might be called the Atlantic Alliance paradigm.

The concepts of international liberalism and extended deterrence both developed out of the conditions of what was the geographical center of world politics after World War II, namely, Europe, America, and the Atlantic Ocean that linked them, all organized by the United States within the Atlantic Alliance. But both concepts had been prefigured in the earlier economic and security policies of Great Britain, especially during the century between the Napoleonic wars and World War I. The first was also known as international liberalism; the second was known as coalition strategy.[1] After World War II, it was natural for the United States, which was replacing Britain in so many other ways and places, to replace it also as the upholder of these concepts. They are ideas that have come readily to nations that are commercial economies, liberal polities, and maritime powers.

*From the Atlantic/European
   reality to the
   Pacific/Asian reality*

It was also natural, however, for the United States, which was now both the major Atlantic power and the major Pacific power, to apply these ideas to both the Atlantic/European reality and the Pacific/Asian reality. There were, after all, many apparent similarities in the security situations of the two regions. The Soviet Union appeared to threaten both Western Europe and East Asia, it had imposed a communist revolution in Eastern Europe and supported one in China, and the two superpowers confronted each other in the two Germanies and the two Koreas. There were similarities in the economic situations as well. The shattered industries of defeated Germany and defeated Japan had

1. Karl Polanyi, *The Great Transformation: The Political and Economic Origins of Our Time* (Boston: Beacon Press, 1957), chap. 1; Paul M. Kennedy, *The Rise and Fall of British Naval Mastery* (New York: Cambridge University Press, 1976); idem, *The Rise and Fall of the Great Powers* (New York: Random House, 1988).

much in common; George Kennan included both in his famous list of the five world power centers — the others were the United States, the Soviet Union, and Britain. The U.S. response to the economic distress was the Marshall Plan in Western Europe in 1947 and the New Course in Japan in 1948. The U.S. response to the security threat was the military defense of South Korea in 1950 and the military buildup in West Germany in 1951.

The Atlantic Alliance paradigm as a Pacific Basin fantasy

This way of looking at the two realities, however, of course masked important differences, and it would lead to monumental disasters.

The way the communist revolution occurred in China was very different from the way it generally occurred in Eastern Europe. In the former, communism came to power through strong local armed forces — the People's Liberation Army — with modest support from the Soviet army in Manchuria. In the latter, communism came to power through the occupying Soviet army, with modest support from weak local communist parties.[2]

Further, the way liberal capitalism returned to power in Japan was very different from the way it returned in West Germany. In both countries, it is true, it returned with the support of the occupying U.S. army, but the local capitalist coalitions were not the same. In Germany the liberal capitalist restoration was led by German corporations and banks, with support from a now-fragmented — into the different states of the Federal Republic — bureaucracy; in the language of recent social theory, it was a case of the society leading the state. The result was that when German liberal capitalism looked to the world, it adopted a policy of international liberalism, a policy very much like that of the United States. In contrast, in Japan the liberal capitalist restoration was led by the still-centralized Japanese bureaucracy, with support from the Japanese trading companies and banks; it was a case of the state leading the society. The result was that when Japanese liberal capitalism looked to the world, it adopted international mercantilism, a policy very different from that of the United States.[3]

The greatest disasters in U.S. security policy — toward China in the 1940s and 1950s and toward Indochina in the 1960s and 1970s — resulted from the American effort to interpret the Asian reality through the European prism, to squeeze it into the NATO model. Similarly, the greatest conflicts in U.S. foreign economic policy — toward Japan and the East Asian newly industrializing countries in the 1980s — have resulted from the U.S. effort to squeeze these countries into the GATT model.

THE PACIFIC BASIN PARADIGM: INTERNATIONAL MERCANTILISM AND FINITE DETERRENCE

If we look at the Pacific/Asian world in its own terms, and not in those of the Atlantic/European world, a quite different paradigm of international relations will result, what might be called the Pacific Basin paradigm.

2. There are exceptions to this pattern, however: communism came to power in China rather as it did in Yugoslavia and Albania, and it came to power in North Korea rather as it did in the rest of Eastern Europe.

3. Clyde V. Prestowitz, Jr., *Trading Places: How We Allowed Japan to Take the Lead* (New York: Basic Books, 1988); Chalmers Johnson, *MITI and the Japanese Miracle* (Stanford, CA: Stanford University Press, 1982).

In regard to the international economy, the East Asian states are not international liberals but rather international mercantilists; that is, they believe in a strong state guiding an organic society toward effective competition in the world economy, for the purpose of increasing the power and wealth of the state and society.[4] In regard to international security, the East Asian states are not cases so much of extended deterrence as of finite deterrence. Japan, because of its insular geography, and China, because of its massive population and its own nuclear force, are much less likely targets of a Soviet blitzkrieg than Western Europe. The problem of deterring the Soviets in Asia is more soluble and the solution more stable than in Europe. The East Asian countries have acknowledged this in their own ways. Japan has recently developed its concept of "comprehensive security"; China earlier developed its concept of "people's war."[5] As we shall see, the security concept of finite deterrence also can fit neatly the economic concept of international mercantilism.

If a Pacific Basin international system based upon the concepts of international mercantilism and finite deterrence were to come into being, however, the United States would no longer be the core country in the Pacific region. If international mercantilism were adopted by all of the major states in the Pacific Basin, including the United States, the United States would close its open market. Similarly, if finite deterrence were adopted by all of the major states in the region, including the United States, the United States would withdraw its Seventh Fleet. But without the U.S. open market and the U.S. Seventh Fleet, the United States would be of little importance to Asia and the Pacific. Japan and China would become the core countries of the Pacific Basin, and the rest, including the United States, would become the periphery, rather like Latin America has been in the inter-American system.

It will be useful, therefore, to examine the historical origins of the East Asian concepts of international mercantilism and finite deterrence, in the expectation that this will better prepare us to discern their future. Although one or both of these concepts are held in some version by most East Asian states, including the so-called little tigers — South Korea, Taiwan, Hong Kong, and Singapore — what gives them their contemporary weight is the fact that they are held by Japan and China.

The modern histories of these two greatest East Asian powers have been very different, in part because they have been so intertwined, especially in the half century from the Sino-Japanese War (1895-96) to World War II. China has experienced on Chinese territory itself successively the Opium Wars, the Taiping Rebellion, a variety of foreign incursions and occupations, the Revolution of 1911, the civil wars of the warlord era, the Japanese invasion and occupation, the civil war between the Nationalists and the Communists, the Revolution of 1949, and the Cultural Revolution. The comparable events that Japan has experienced in the same period and on

4. Bruce Cumings, "The Origins and Development of the Northeast Asian Political Economy: Industrial Sectors, Product Cycles, and Political Consequences," *International Organization*, 38(1):1-40 (Winter 1984); Roy Hofheinz, Jr., and Kent E. Calder, *The Eastasia Edge* (New York: Basic Books, 1982). See also Prestowitz, *Trading Places;* Johnson, *MITI and the Japanese Miracle.*

5. Robert W. Barnett, *Beyond War: Japan's Concept of Comprehensive National Security* (McLean, VA: Pergamon-Brassey's International Defense, 1984); Ellis Joffe, "People's War under Modern Conditions: A Doctrine for Modern War," *China Quarterly,* vol. 112 (Dec. 1987); Paul H. B. Godwin, "Changing Concepts of Doctrine, Strategy and Operations in the Chinese People's Liberation Army 1978-87," ibid.

Japanese territory itself have been only the Meiji Restoration, the American bombings during World War II, and the American Occupation.

The consequence of this contrast is that throughout almost all of its modern history, China has not been a coherent state, one holding a consensus ideology and guiding a cohesive society in a concerted policy. Conversely, throughout almost all of its modern history, Japan has been very much that. It is only in recent years that the Chinese state has become coherent enough to support and sustain its own versions of international mercantilism and finite deterrence. But the Japanese state has been doing this for many decades. The Japanese story, therefore, will be the center of our discussion.

JAPAN AS AN IMPERIAL MERCANTILIST: FROM THE MEIJI RESTORATION TO THE PACIFIC WAR

The contrasting economic concepts of liberalism and mercantilism are bound up with contrasting relative positions in the timing of industrialization. The idea of liberalism came naturally to states that industrialized relatively early — particularly Britain but also the United States — and the idea of mercantilism similarly came naturally to states that industrialized relatively late, such as Germany and Japan. The reasons for this contrast have been much discussed by economic historians, and we shall not repeat them here,[6] but we can note that the late industrializers needed to protect their infant industries from the already strong early industrializers, they needed

access to foreign markets that were already dominated by the early industrializers, and they needed large amounts of capital in order to catch up with the early industrializers. For all of these reasons, they needed a strong state and a mercantilist policy to give protection and direction to the developing economy. A leading economic historian, Alexander Gerschenkron, argued that there was a general pattern that the later a country began its industrialization, the greater was the role of the state, in a sequence composed of Britain, France, Germany, Japan, and Russia.[7]

Japan as a late industrializer

Within Europe the country that exemplified mercantilism was Germany, and within Asia it was Japan. Consequently, there were numerous similarities in their histories from the 1860s — the German unification and the Meiji Restoration — to World War II. Japanese industrialization, however, began about a generation later than that of Germany. This was one factor making the Japanese state even more prominent and its policy even more mercantilist than was the case for Germany.

But while Japan was like Germany in being a late industrializer, it was like Britain in being an island country. The first condition led Japan to emphasize state guidance of the economy; the second led it to emphasize foreign markets. But because its industrialization was late, most foreign markets were already filled up by earlier industrializers. Thus Japan had to become a late imperializer as well, and because it was an island country, it had to be a sea-borne empire, one supported by naval power. In

6. James R. Kurth, "The Political Consequences of the Product Cycle: Industrial History and Political Outcomes," *International Organization*, 33(1):1-34 (Winter 1979).

7. Alexander Gerschenkron, *Economic Backwardness in Historical Perspective* (Cambridge, MA: Harvard University Press, 1962).

doing so, it began to emulate the leading maritime power of the time, Britain.

Japan between maritime power and continental power

Japan's situation in relation to its continent, Asia, was significantly different, however, from Britain's situation in relation to its continent, Europe. Because China was united under one government, which, however, was weak — while Europe was divided into several states, which, however, were strong — Japan had the opportunity to invade the Asian mainland, an opportunity that Britain had not had since it lost its territories in France in the fifteenth century. Thus Japan was a maritime power that then tried to become also a continental one. In doing so, it began to emulate the leading continental power of the time, Germany, as well as the leading maritime one, Britain.

Japan's emulation of Britain helped bring about the Anglo-Japanese alliance of 1902. This in turn enabled Japan to undertake the Russo-Japanese War of 1904-5 and to annex Korea (1905-10). In turn, the Russian defeat in that war focused British attention exclusively on Germany as the only threatening continental power and helped bring about the Anglo-Russian entente of 1907 and the British entry into World War I.

Japan's annexation of Korea was the beginning of its continental power. It was now in a position for an eventual expansion into Manchuria and even a full invasion when the opportunity or the necessity arose. The opportunity came with the Chinese Revolution and the warlord era (1911-27); the necessity would arrive with Chiang Kai-shek's efforts to reunify China after 1927 and especially with the coming of the Great Depression after 1929.

Japan between international liberalism and imperial mercantilism

By the 1920s, both Germany and Japan had developed industries that were among the most competitive in the world — principally chemicals in Germany and textiles in Japan. The prosperity of the decade meant that there was a good international market for their goods. Consequently, the ideas of international liberalism became more attractive in these two late industrializers than they had been before. But with the advent of the Great Depression, the open international market was replaced with a jungle of trade barriers. Imperial mercantilism returned, and with a vengeance. Thus Japan invaded and occupied Manchuria in 1931, becoming even more a continental power than before.

The intellectual origins of international mercantilism

By the late 1930s, Japan was the home of the most advanced mercantilist theorists in the world. Japanese economists developed sophisticated conceptions of how a state could nurture the development of its society by competing within a dynamic world economy. It would not be until the 1960s that some of these ideas, such as the product trade cycle, would appear among American economists, and then only among a few.[8] These conceptions provided the intellectual foundation for the industrial strategy of the Japanese Ministry of Commerce and Industry in the 1930s. But these beginnings of an international version of mercantilism were aborted by the fulfillment of the imperial one, the Japa-

8. Cumings, "Northeast Political Economy," pp. 2-3; Prestowitz, *Trading Places*, pp. 105-11.

nese invasion of China itself. The Ministry of Commerce and Industry would have to be converted into the Ministry of Munitions during the war before it could be born again as the Ministry of International Trade and Industry after the war.

Japan between China and America

With its invasion of China in 1937, Japan became still more a continental power. Its emulation of Germany helped bring about the Tripartite Pact with Germany and Italy in 1940. This in turn enabled Japan to expand into Indochina in 1940 and 1941 and to undertake war with the United States, beginning with a preventive strike and surprise attack at Pearl Harbor. The United States, in one of its first efforts at extended deterrence, had in 1940 moved most of its Pacific Fleet from San Diego and Long Beach to Pearl Harbor. The result was the most dramatic failure of extended deterrence in history. In turn, the Japanese war with the United State encouraged Hitler to declare war upon the United States also, uniting the European war and the Pacific war into a truly world war.[9]

The China policy was the project of the Japanese army; its purpose was to create a mercantilist empire. The Pearl Harbor strategy was the project of the Japanese navy; its purpose was to ensure military security for that empire. Together, the China policy and the Pearl Harbor strategy combined the economic and the security

9. Since Japan also attacked British possessions in East Asia at the time that it attacked Pearl Harbor, Britain was then at war with Japan as well as Germany and Italy; this technically would have linked the European and Pacific wars, even if the United States had not entered the European one. But by itself, Britain would not have been able to continue a war in the Pacific, and in practice the European and Pacific wars would have been separate ones.

goals of Japan, and they combined the army and the navy as the means to achieve them. The result was supposed to be the Greater East Asia Co-Prosperity Sphere, an ordered realm capable of international mercantilism and comprehensive security, a splendid empire of the sun. The results were actually to be the Pacific War, the largest naval battles in history, the artificial suns over Hiroshima and Nagasaki, the U.S. occupation of Japan, and the American Century.

JAPAN AS AN INTERNATIONAL MERCANTILIST: FROM THE AMERICAN OCCUPATION TO THE JAPANESE ASCENDANCY

With the end of World War II, the Japanese army was replaced by the U.S. army, which continued to perform some of the same roles as the Japanese army had before, that is, it fought and remained in Korea in large measure to ensure the military security of Japan. Similarly, the Japanese navy was replaced by the U.S. navy, which continued to perform some of the same roles as the Japanese navy had before: it provided open markets for Japanese goods in Southeast Asia and ensured the free flow of oil to Japan from Indonesia and the Persian Gulf. It had been the oil embargo of the United States, the leading oil exporter of 1941 and the Saudi Arabia of the day, that had actually driven the Japanese government to the decision to seize the oil of the Dutch East Indies, the predecessor to Indonesia, and to protect the strategic flank of that oil lifeline with a preventive strike on the U.S. Pacific Fleet at Pearl Harbor.

The supremacy of the bureaucracy

Without its own army and navy, Japan no longer had its own continental strategy or maritime strategy. What was left was a broken economy scattered about the one pillar that remained from the prewar order and that therefore became the commanding height of postwar Japan: the bureaucracy.

The American Occupation reinforced these conditions. By destroying the old military and by institutionalizing a limit on a new military within the new constitution — article 9 — the Americans removed one pillar of the prewar triple alliance of military, industry, and bureaucracy. By dismantling the industrial *zaibatsu,* if only temporarily, they also reduced a second pillar. By relying on the bureaucracy for the actual administration of Japan during the Occupation, the Americans enhanced the role of the remaining pillar and thereby confirmed its supremacy. Since it still had its own bureaucracy, Japan still had its own industrial strategy.

The synthesis of international mercantilism

Thus the MacArthur Occupation recapitulated the Meiji Restoration. The foundation was once again laid for state guidance of the economy, but this time it would be directed exclusively to an industrial strategy targeted on international markets, not imperial ones. With the conclusion of the Occupation, the Japanese state was in an even better position to lead the Japanese society than it had been before World War II and to lead it with a particular vision. That vision combined the best of the two conflicting visions of prewar Japan, the international liberalism of the 1920s and the imperial mercantilism of the 1930s. The vision was international mercantilism.

The only power that could oppose the international mercantilism of Japan was the United States, but it did not choose to

do so. Why the United States did not, when it was promoting liberalism and opposing mercantilism so vigorously in Europe, has been the subject of considerable scholarly analysis. Robert Gilpin argues that the dominant consideration in U.S. policy was international security, rather than international economy.[10] In Europe, the United States had several major allies; it could play them off against each other. In Asia, the United States had only one major ally, and that was Japan; this gave Japan much greater bargaining power than was the case with any one European ally. In any event, international mercantilism remained intact in Japan and largely has continued so down to the present day.

The international mercantilism of Japan and other East Asian states conceives of the state as guiding society toward effective competition in the world market, for the purpose of increasing the power and wealth of the state and society, but it also conceives of this competition as taking place within a context of dynamic, not static, comparative advantage, where the state helps society to move progressively higher on the ladder of technology, to shift out of low-technology and low-wage industries and into high-technology and high-wage ones. As a country moves up from a lower rung on the technological ladder, other countries — especially East Asian newly industrializing countries — will move up onto it. Thus international mercantilism conceives the world economic competition to be not a zero-sum but a positive-sum game; not only one but many countries will benefit, and these benefits will be not only short-term gains but long-term develop-

10. Robert Gilpin, *U.S. Power and the Multinational Corporation: The Political Economy of Foreign Direct Investment* (New York: Basic Books, 1975), pp. 109-11.

ment. But this mutual development requires the more advanced countries to be continually developing new technologies and new industries, so that they can devolve their old industries to less developed countries. This in turn requires the guidance of a strong and coherent state.

*The concepts of
    comprehensive security
    and finite deterrence*

Because Japan could no longer provide for its own security with its own military, it had to construct a functional equivalent with a combination of U.S. military power, its own economic power, and, in cases — for example, the Middle East — where neither of these was very useful, its own low-posture diplomacy. It is this comprehensive combination that has become the concept of comprehensive security, but the core of comprehensive security has been economic power.

Within the framework of comprehensive security, the concept of finite deterrence could become especially reasonable. Japan, because of its insular geography, is a much less likely target of a Soviet blitzkrieg than is West Germany and more generally Western Europe. The problem of deterrence of Soviet military aggression against Japan is more soluble and the solution is more stable than they are with respect to Europe.

Of course, Japanese finite deterrence, unlike that of China or France, cannot rely upon a national nuclear force. The artificial suns over Hiroshima and Nagasaki produced in Japan an enduring nuclear allergy, so there can be no Japanese nuclear deterrent. Further, Japanese finite deterrence would really be extended deterrence in the sense that it would have to be extended beyond the national territory, namely, to include South Korea. But Japanese deterrence would still be extended only into a rather small country against a rather small adversary, North Korea. South Korea is now a plausible target of only a North Korean blitzkrieg — like the one in June 1950 — not a Soviet one — unlike West Germany — and not even a Chinese one, unlike the one in November 1950.

CONTRADICTION AND
COOPERATION IN CONCEPT

At first glance it might seem that the Japanese concepts of international mercantilism and finite deterrence would be in fundamental contradiction to the American concepts of international liberalism and extended deterrence. The decade-long disputes between Japan and the United States over economic and security issues would seem to provide sufficient evidence that this is the case.

In reality, however, Japan and the other East Asian states benefit from the U.S. policies of international liberalism and extended deterrence, even though they would not adopt the policies for themselves. From their perspective, the best world is one in which the United States has policies of international liberalism and extended deterrence while they pursue policies of international mercantilism and finite deterrence. Even within the United States, however, there are important groups who find Japanese economic and security conceptions quite acceptable. This is most obviously the case with the general notion of comprehensive security, but it is also true of international mercantilism and finite deterrence, ideas that are the opposite of American ways of thinking.

Comprehensive security and complex interdependence

The Japanese concept of comprehensive security has much in common with the American concept of complex interdependence. This is the idea that economic issues have joined security issues as high politics, that economic conditions constrain military adventurism and military spending, and that international interdependence has transformed the traditional pursuit of national interests. The concept of complex interdependence is clearly consistent with, indeed is a logical extension of, the concept of international liberalism. When the advocates of complex interdependence do turn their attention to security issues, they usually support a policy of arms-control agreements with the Soviet Union, that is, the détente of the early 1970s and the new détente of the late 1980s.

Like the concept of international liberalism, the concept of complex interdependence comes naturally to a particular group within a nation, for example, to financial institutions engaged in international business. Such ideas formed the basic world- view of the City of London from the middle of the nineteenth century until World War II, and they have formed the basic worldview of the international banks of New York since the 1960s. The policy of the City of London toward Nazi Germany in the 1930s was that of appeasement; the policy of the New York banks toward the Soviet Union in the 1970s and again in the late 1980s has been that of détente.[11] This is not to say that the policy

11. James R. Kurth, "Travels between Europe and America: The Rise and Decline of the New York Foreign Policy Elite," forthcoming in a volume edited by Martin Shefter for the New York City Project of the Social Science Research Council.

of the Soviet Union has been the same as that of Nazi Germany and that the policy of détente therefore has been mistaken.

International mercantilism and international liberalism

The response of these same interests to the concept of international mercantilism, held by Japan and other Asian nations as well, is rather more complex, but it also ends in acceptance. The U.S. financial institutions can accept the combination of American international liberalism and Asian international mercantilism because the gap between the two is a void that they can fill. International mercantilism can create dynamic industries, but it is slower to develop cosmopolitan financial services; the growth of industrial exports outpaces the development of international financial connections. The dynamic industries of one country will need the sophisticated financial institutions of another country, which, however, are willing to provide these services to any rich country. Conversely, a successful mercantilism may be so successful that it can make it in the interest of almost anyone to make a deal with it. The U.S. financial community sees itself in this role vis-à-vis the mercantilist industries of Asia today, just as the City of London saw itself in this role vis-à-vis the protectionist industries of America in the nineteenth century.

The financial institutions are joined in their international liberalism by other important American interests, particularly multinational corporations that produce abroad for sale at home and professional groups — lawyers, doctors, professors — that provide services that by their nature cannot be imported and therefore do not face foreign competition. Together, they form a solid political coalition in support of international liberalism and in acceptance of the international mercantilism of other nations. On the other hand, workers engaged in the production of tradable — importable — goods are steadily displaced from their jobs. The result, or at least the cliché, is the son of a $40,000-a-year autoworker becoming a $10,000-a-year fast-food worker.

Thus the nations that adhere to international liberalism, in particular Britain and the United States, gradually divide into two parts — indeed, two nations — one that is benefited by an open economy and one that is devastated by it. Conversely, the nations that adhere to international mercantilism, especially Japan and South Korea, become even more united, indeed organic, nations than they were before.

Finite deterrence and extended deterrence

There are also groups within the United States with a similar response to the concept of finite deterrence held by Japan and other Asian nations. The U.S. military services can accept the combination of American extended deterrence and Asian finite deterrence because the gap between the two is a void that they can fill. The gap provides a role and a rationale for the U.S. Navy in the western Pacific, the U.S. Army in South Korea, the U.S. Marines in Okinawa, and the U.S. Air Force in all three.[12]

The interests of the military services, of course, are not the most important factor in deciding where they will be deployed, especially in an era when Congress will cut defense spending. But the same solid polit-

ical coalition of financial institutions, multinational corporations, and liberal professionals that prospers in the gap between American international liberalism and Asian international mercantilism also finds acceptable the gap between American extended deterrence and Asian finite deterrence. The mutual benefits that are the result of the first gap are, in their minds, protected by the extended deterrence that is part of the second.

In addition, there are emerging the elements of a grand bargain between the banks in America and the banks in Japan. The former are experienced in international lending but poor in cash — or rich in bad loans; the latter are just the reverse. The American banks hope to direct the flow of Japanese capital to their own advantage — for example, toward helping to fund the Latin American debt; the Japanese banks hope to continue to operate within the cheap security system provided for them by American military forces. The obvious bargain to be struck is for the American banks to continue to support American extended deterrence in the Pacific Basin, while the Japanese banks begin to provide capital to the grand projects of the American banks, particularly in Latin America.[13]

FROM THE PACIFIC WAR TO THE PACIFIC PACIFIC

The 1990s, a half century after the Pacific War, will be a period of tension between two international relations paradigms: (1) the declining one of international liberalism and extended deterrence, created by the United States in the Atlantic/European

12. I have discussed the maritime strategy of the U.S. Navy in my "United States and the North Pacific," in *Security and Arms Control in the North Pacific*, ed. Andrew Mack and Paul Keal (Winchester, MA: George Allen & Unwin, 1988), pp. 27-49.

13. Zbigniew Brzezinski, "America's New Geostrategy," *Foreign Affairs*, 66(4):696-99 (Spring 1988); Robert Gilpin, *The Political Economy of International Relations* (Princeton, NJ: Princeton University Press, 1987), pp. 328-39.

world and extended by it into the Pacific/Asian world, the paradigm of the American half century; and (2) the rising one of international mercantilism and finite deterrence, created by the Pacific/Asian powers themselves, the paradigm of the future. The two paradigms are in an uneasy but symbiotic relationship. The relationship between the Atlantic Alliance and the Pacific Basin paradigms is rather like the relationship between yin and yang, that famous Asian symbol that appears in many places in Asian life, including the center of the South Korean flag. The Atlantic Alliance paradigm is waning and the Pacific Basin paradigm is waxing, but each is intimately — and dialectically — connected to the other.

In its contemporary version, international mercantilism can mean economic cooperation between the states of the Pacific Basin in a reasonable but changing division of labor based upon dynamic, not static, comparative advantage in the international market. Similarly, comprehensive security can mean comprehensive cooperation between the states of the Pacific Basin, with military deterrence directed only at the most finite security objective, the protection of the national territory.

A half century ago Japan adhered to a harsher version of international mercantilism and comprehensive security: imperial mercantilism and East Asian hegemony. In pursuit of these policies, Japan warred upon the other great Asian power, China. In doing so, it came into conflict with the American paradigm of international liberalism — the open door in China — and extended deterrence — the U.S. forces in the Philippines and the U.S. fleet at Pearl Harbor. This in turn opened the way for the Pacific War, the American victory, and the American half century.

If Japan and China should again come into conflict, as they did a half century ago, the outcome of the tension between the Atlantic Alliance and the Pacific Basin paradigm is likely to be a descent into chaos and a journey into the unknown, although, of course, not necessarily in a way like the Pacific War. Conversely, if Japan and China should come into cooperation, even more than they have in the past decade, the outcome of the tension between the Atlantic Alliance and the Pacific Basin paradigms is likely to be the gradual waning of the first and waxing of the second, the dialectic of yin and yang.

The Atlantic Alliance paradigm and the American Century entered into their historic moment through the Pacific War. The Pacific Basin paradigm and the Pacific Century will enter into their historical moment only if the Pacific Basin remains pacific.

ANNALS, *AAPSS*, **505**, September 1989

Shaping and Sharing
Pacific Dynamism

By TAKASHI INOGUCHI

ABSTRACT: This article attempts to elucidate the underlying considerations and calculations of one of the major actors of the Pacific region, Japan, in shaping and sharing the much vaunted Pacific dynamism. Keeping in mind the enormous economic vigor accompanied by a measure of uncertainty in Pacific international relations, the article attempts to analyze from a Japanese perspective the current configuration of ideas and practices unfolding in the region. First, the major features of Pacific dynamism are delineated. Second, the superpowers' preoccupation with domestic difficulties are touched on as one of the major triggering mechanisms encouraging more regionalist forces throughout the world. Third, Japanese calculations surrounding Pacific dynamism are delineated, with major counteractions to Pacific dynamism by other major actors also taken into account.

Takashi Inoguchi is professor of political science at the Institute of Oriental Culture, University of Tokyo. He obtained his Ph.D. at the Massachusetts Institute of Technology in 1974. He held his previous positions at Sophia and Tokyo universities. He has also been a visiting professor or scholar at such universities as Geneva, Harvard, and Australian National. He has published 11 books and numerous articles in Japanese and in English, the latest book being The Political Economy of Japan, *vol. 2*, The Changing International Context *(1988).*

D YNAMISM — this is the best single word to characterize the evolution of the Pacific region over the past decade. Economic growth, trade expansion, and exchange-rate movements — the rise of most currencies in the Pacific region against the U.S. dollar — demonstrate the profound importance of the Pacific region in shaping global adjustments of international relations and the world economy.[1]

Dynamism contains both positive and negative aspects.[2] Positively, it means vigor and aggressiveness. Negatively, it means uncertainty and unpredictability. Because Pacific dynamism brings increasing prosperity to the Pacific region and to the entire world with its vigorous growth and expansion, it is termed positive. From this side of the looking glass, forging economic interdependence with a prosperous economic region brings economic benefits. The dramatic expansion of the Japanese market and, to a lesser degree, the markets of South Korea and Taiwan promotes the absorption of manufactured goods from the rest of the world: Japan's share of manufactured goods in total imports for the period 1979-88 has increased from 26.0 percent to slightly higher than 48.0 percent.[3]

1. Colin I. Bradford and William H. Branson, eds., *Trade and Structural Change in Pacific Asia* (Chicago: University of Chicago Press, 1987); Peter Drysdale, *International Economic Pluralism: Economic Policy in East Asia and the Pacific* (New York: Columbia University Press, 1988).
2. Takashi Inoguchi, "The International Political Economy of the Pacific Dynamism," in *Japan's Growing External Assets: A Medium for Regional Growth?* ed. Susumu Awanohara (Hong Kong: Linnan College, Centre for Asian Pacific Studies, forthcoming).
3. Peter Drysdale and Ross Garnaut, "A Pacific Free Trade Area?" (Paper delivered at "More Free Trade Areas? Outlook for World Trade Policy," Conference of the Institute for International Economics, Washington, DC, 31 Oct.-1 Nov. 1988).

At the same time, the very vigor and aggressiveness of this economic activity has been helping to create uncertainty and unpredictability in the whole arena of trade and even sometimes in security arrangements. The awesome Pacific economic growth and trade expansion in manufactured goods for the last decade and, more recently, the staggering trade surplus and financial power of Japan, Taiwan, and Korea have been causing a variety of counteractions from various countries. Thus, from the other side of the looking glass, the rapid emergence of competitive economic actors has been enormously disruptive, forcing the rest of the world to counteract with other means. One strong piece of evidence is the surge of protectionism and regionalism throughout the world in the last couple of years. Other examples range from the inability of the Uruguay Round on the General Agreement on Tariffs and Trade to come to accord for midterm review in December 1988, to the open militancy of Americans against Pacific Asians and West Europeans using their unilateral interpretations of unfair trade practices, to the ratification by the Canadians of the U.S.-Canadian bilateral free-trade agreement in December 1988, and finally to the increased self-confidence of West Europeans in devising trade and investment rules of their own toward further European integration in 1992.

In the rest of this article, I shall first describe the three major features of Pacific Asian economic relations. Then I shall analyze how the somewhat weakened leadership of the two superpowers affects the course that Pacific dynamism will take. Third, I shall focus on the considerations and calculations of the Japanese in shaping and sharing Pacific dynamism and in adapting to the counteractions of the other major actors. I shall place the Japanese conceptions of Pacific dynamism first in a historical perspective, second in relation to longer-term scenarios of Japan's place in the world, and third in the context of current policy alternatives.

THREE MAJOR FEATURES
OF PACIFIC DYNAMISM

In focusing on intra-Pacific economic interactions, three major features emerge: the flying-goose formation of economic growth, the enhancement of horizontal interactions within the Pacific Asia region, and strains between the Pacific Asia region and other parts of the world, particularly North America and Western Europe.

The flying-goose formation

The well-known phrase "flying-goose formation" was invented by Kaname Akamatsu to characterize the development pattern of East and Southeast Asia.[4] Like flying geese forming a triangular pattern headed by their leader, Pacific Asian development is spearheaded by Japan, which is followed by the Asian newly industrializing countries (NICs), including South Korea, Taiwan, Hong Kong, Singapore, Malaysia, and Thailand, and now is followed increasingly by some other countries of the Association of Southeast Asian Nations (ASEAN) and, to a far lesser degree, China, Vietnam, North Korea, and the Soviet Union. Dynamism diffuses from Japan to Korea, Taiwan, Hong Kong, and Singapore, and further to Malaysia, Thailand, Indonesia, the Philippines, and Brunei as well as to China, Vietnam, North Korea, and the Soviet Union. Uneven development in Pacific Asia has forced coun-

tries to focus energy on those industrial sectors nascently competitive with the rest and to gain from exports in a gradual fashion when its own market is not sufficiently large. The open and large market of the United States and the U.S.-led free-trade regime has been indispensable to this pattern of economic development.

There are two other mechanisms in this development pattern: (1) the success of early starters in Pacific Asia has been emulated selectively to accelerate the latecomers' catch-up process; and (2) the gradually lost competitiveness of early starters in some sectors enables latecomers to rise through the former's shift of production site from home to the latter. Thus, for instance, some Japanese electronics firms used to produce goods in Taiwan and Korea when Japanese wages and other costs soared, but as Taiwanese and Korean costs steadily rose, they began to operate more in Thailand and the Philippines. UNIDEN, an electronics company based in Japan, is now in the process of shifting all its production sites from Taiwan and Hong Kong to the Philippines and China, thus diffusing economic benefits to the Philippines and China as well.[5]

Horizontal interactions enhanced

As Pacific dynamism has unfolded to the entire region, the intraregional interactions in Pacific Asia have increased dramatically. Foremost in importance among them is the increasingly horizontal relationship between Japan and the Asian NICs, as exemplified by the dramatic increase in Japan's importation of manufactured goods from Asian NICs and ASEAN

4. Kaname Akamatsu, *Sekai keizairon* [World Economics] (Tokyo: Kunimoto shobo, 1965).

5. *Nihon keizai shimbun*, 23 May 1988.

countries, registering around 50 percent per annum since 1985.[6] There has also been a drastic decrease in exports from the Asian NICs of Korea, Taiwan, and Hong Kong to the United States as a proportion of their total exports, decreasing to one-third in 1988 from the level of one-half in 1985.[7] Among the Asian NICs as well, the complex trade pattern has emerged so as to make each country a horizontal trade partner of the others; such a relationship obtains especially between Taiwan and Korea. Although the size of such trade has not become as large as that in the European Community, the direction of the movement has become unmistakably clear. Also not to be overlooked are the vigorous moves by the Asian NICs in trade with, direct investment in, and, more recently, economic aid to some ASEAN countries, China, North Korea, and Vietnam. For instance, Taiwan is now first in terms of direct investment flows in the Philippines, surpassing both Japan and the United States. These moves are positive, as they help shape the region with regional resources rather than relying too heavily on extraregional markets. They are positive also as they make the angle of the flying-goose formation less acute and more obtuse, helping to foster a sense of equality.

Strains and stresses with other major partners

Pacific Asia must cope with the increasing salience of stresses and strains in its relationship with North America and Western Europe. In terms of saving rate, growth rate, trade surplus, and financing power, Japan and the Asian NICs are clearly one of the destabilizing forces in the world economy just as the United States and debt-ridden middle-income countries are at the other extreme. Pacific Asia has thus become party to trade frictions. As the United States increasingly resorts to what is called aggressive bilateral peacekeeping in trade,[8] frustrated as it has been with the General Agreement on Tariffs and Trade's multilateralist experiences for promoting market liberalization, these stresses and strains are most likely to continue to exist. Not only the issue of trade surplus but also all sorts of other issues characterize the rapidly intertwining economic partnership between Pacific Asia on one hand and North America and Western Europe on the other. They include intellectual property, direct investment codes, service trade, agricultural subsidies, exchange-rate regulation, nontariff barriers, industrial targeting, specific reciprocity, inward-looking regionalism, and bloc formation through bilateralism.

Three features are important when we look into the considerations and calculations of Japan concerning Pacific dynamism. First, the still-unfolding pattern of uneven development in Pacific Asia means that Pacific Asia continues to have enormous room for activating and intensifying regional economic activities within itself. In other words, much remains to be exploited in Pacific Asia to keep its dynamism moving forward. Second, the increasing intraregional transactions, when

---

6. Drysdale and Garnaut, "Pacific Free Trade Area?"

7. *Nihon keizai shimbun,* 22 Nov. 1988.

8. Robert Baldwin and J. David Richardson, "Recent U.S. Trade Policy and Its Global Implications," in *Trade and Structural Change,* ed. Bradford and Branson, pp. 121-55. See also Paula Stern and Paul A. London, "A Reaffirmation of U.S. Trade Policy," *Washington Quarterly,* 11(4):55-71 (Autumn 1988); Stephen Krasner, "Trade Conflicts and the Common Defense," *Political Science Quarterly,* 101(5):787-806 (1986).

accompanied by the relative weakening of superpower dominance and confrontation, mean the potential divergence among Pacific Asians on how to give order to a still-fluid Pacific dynamism. In other words, given the increasing prospect for the Americans to preoccupy themselves with the less than enlightened long-term globalist viewpoint, Pacific Asians might find it somewhat more difficult to organize themselves while coping with counteractions from the rest of the world to the very Pacific dynamism it has been creating.

JAPANESE CALCULATIONS:
LOOKING BACKWARD

To examine Japanese calculations, it is necessary first to point out that Japan lives in Pacific Asia with bilateral Japanese-U.S. ties in economic, technological, and security arenas kept perhaps incredibly high. A defeated nation with a developing-country status, Japan since 1945 has had to rely almost entirely on the generally favorable international environment that the victory of the Allied powers, especially the United States, brought about. The most important elements of this environment were the security umbrella and the free-trade regime. Bilateral interdependence has been further enhanced as Japan has moved up from a developing country to a country whose gross national product is more than one-half that of the United States and whose per capita income has surpassed that of the United States. Two major factors have contributed to this outcome.[9]

9. Takashi Inoguchi, "The Ideas and Structures of Foreign Policy: Looking Ahead with Caution," in *The Political Economy of Japan*, vol. 2, *The Changing International Context*, ed. Takashi Inoguchi and Daniel I. Okimoto (Stanford, CA: Stanford University Press, 1988), pp. 23-62, 490-500.

*Japanese shyness on
security matters*

The first factor is that by defeat and occupation—and by instinctive habit and cunning calculation—Japan has been accustomed to being shy about security and military matters since 1945. Japan's Self-Defense Forces (SDF) have been built primarily to satisfy the needs of the United States, first as an occupying power and later as an ally. They are not primarily for the defense of Japan but more intended to enhance the U.S. military forces confronting the Communist bloc. Even now the primary task of the Japanese SDF is to assist the U.S. armed forces in the Far East and the Pacific to meet emergencies in the Pacific and around the globe. One telling fact is that the U.S. forces in Japan are not in a position to help the Japanese land SDF on Hokkaido. Rather, they adopt a forward strategy whereby they would attack the Soviet forces deep in Soviet territories and territorial waters, with Japanese land SDF remaining vulnerable to attacking Soviet forces. Only after such an attack could the U.S. forces start their counterattack. The Japanese maritime SDF are not equipped to make amphibious operations on Hokkaido under heavy Soviet onslaught. Both the command structure and the force structure of the Japanese SDF clearly demonstrate that they exist as one component—indispensable to be sure—of the U.S. international security network.

Recent military buildup

The steady Japanese military buildup over the last decade now gives Japan number-three status after the Soviet Union and the United States in terms of military expenditure. It is clear that Japan spends enormously for defense, but much of the expenditure goes to personnel, while the bulk of nonpersonnel expenditure goes to the purchase of some of the most sophisticated and thus most expensive weapons from the United States. This pattern of Japanese military buildup has been reinforced by the more recent criticism from abroad that Japan is a free rider of the Western alliance and that Japan should contribute more to the collective defense by shouldering more of the security role. The Japanese government has to cope with three things at the same time: (1) strong pacifism at the grass roots; (2) the still intermittently expressed reminder from abroad of the Japanese psychological debt of the last war; and (3) criticism of being a free rider in the Western alliance. The result has been this peculiar pattern of Japanese defense buildup.

Evidence of Japanese determination to meet its own defense needs can be seen in at least two areas: the resolve to manufacture its next fighter support FSXs in collaboration with the United States, yet with much more local content than its counterpart likes to think, and by its vigorous emphasis on the forthcoming midterm defense estimate on the need for land-based equipment with highly sophisticated weapons allowing for the disabling of attacking forces before they reach Japanese land.[10] These developments exemplify some of the Japanese adjustments to a changed international environment. At the same time, it remains impossible to think of the Japanese SDF without the U.S. component. The

10. For FSXs, see *Asahi shimbun,* 4 June 1988; *Nihon keizai shimbun,* 26 Dec. 1988. See also Takashi Inoguchi, "Trade, Technology and Security: Implications for East Asia and the West," *Adelphi Papers,* 218:39-55 (1987). For the midterm task estimate, see *Yomiuri shimbun,* 11 May 1988; Japan Defense Agency, *White Paper on Defense 1988* (Tokyo: Government Printing Office, 1988).

Japanese constitutional prohibition, the near insanity of hollowing out the alliance with the United States, and the long-distance, fast-moving nature of military technology all inhibit any solitary view of national security in any strict sense of the word.

Unprecedented Japanese-U.S. economic interdependence

The second factor in the bilateral interdependence is that the economic interdependence with the United States is perhaps unprecedented in human history. Not only trade with and investment in each country by the other but also a huge amount of Japanese purchasing of U.S. Treasury bonds and an inestimable amount of financial trading now take place across the Pacific. The two largest and most vigorous economies of the world have every reason to increase their economic transactions with each other. Furthermore, the not-so-strange coincidence of Japanese weakness in security and American relative weakness in economic matters has reinforced Japanese economic dependence on American economic health and wealth with an astonishing speed and magnitude. To save the U.S. dollar from falling so rapidly, Japan has been intermittently spending an enormous amount of money through monetary intervention. To liberate themselves from protectionist measures, many Japanese firms have made direct investment in the United States — no other country has so vigorously invested in the United States. The more money Japan places in the form of U.S. dollars for whatever reasons, the more interdependent Japan and the United States become and the more difficult it is for them to disentangle themselves from the higher risk of losing an incredible value of their dollar assets overnight, given the somewhat shaky shape of the deficit-ridden U.S. economy.

Lax U.S. economic management

To many Japanese the problem is that the United States does not seem to manage its economy as they would like it to do. The major points of the Japanese message are the need for a drastic reduction of various expenditures including defense, the introduction of a major tax increase, the restraint of consumption through recessionary macroeconomic management, and improvement in business management and labor relations.

Some serious Japanese have begun to think about some drastic unilateral measures to discipline the somewhat lax Americans to tighten their economic management. One such move would be raising Japanese interest rates to combat quickening global inflation, which would then set off a managed decline in the dollar and U.S. bond and stock prices, forcing the United States to cut its deficit. A more moderate step would have the United States issue bonds denominated in foreign currencies. With, for instance, yen-denominated bonds, the U.S. government could not reduce its financial burden of debt simply by printing additional money.[11]

JAPANESE CALCULATIONS: LOOKING FORWARD

It is useful to recall what kind of calculation was made by Prime Minister Yasuhiro Nakasone during his tenure of 1982-87 when his policies of economic liberalization and alliance partnership were forcefully executed.[12] First, he correctly foresaw the beneficial aspects of American Japan bashing with respect to market liberalization and privatization of government-regulated sectors. Not only would economic liberalization help Japan to avert criticism from the United States and others against Japan's alleged protectionism, mercantilism, and free riding, but it also would help raise Japanese competitiveness. Second, his pro-U.S. defense efforts would help Japan to skirt criticism from the United States and others for being a free rider and also set the physical and organizational foundation on which to build stronger Japanese SDF while avoiding suspicion and criticism. As someone who had prepared 32 notebooks filled with what he would do as prime minister prior to his ascension to power, Nakasone was clear about his long-cherished nationalistic goals: more economic competitiveness and stronger SDF.

Needless to say, no fundamental reversal of power between Japan and the United States has taken place during or since Nakasone's tenure despite his success in enhancing Japan's economic and military power. But the continuing economic difficulties of the United States and the steady movement toward a U.S.-Soviet détente, along with the rise of Pacific Asia with Japan as its core driving force, have posed Japanese leaders one question: what direction should Japan take?

Japan's scenarios for the future

This is not an easy question to answer, and it has led Japanese leaders to think about Pacific dynamism much more seriously than before. To answer the question, Japanese leaders have to solve a complex set of equations involving at least three major variables: (1) economic and techno-

11. *International Herald Tribune,* 23 Dec. 1988.
12. Takashi Inoguchi, "The Legacy of a Weathercock Prime Minister," *Japan Quarterly,* 34(4):367-70 (Oct.-Dec. 1987).

logical dynamism of major countries, especially Japan and the United States; (2) prospects for the dominant military technology or the possibility of nullification of nuclear arsenals either through the U.S.-Soviet détente or through revolutionary breakthrough similar to the Strategic Defense Initiative; and (3) the debt of history as a constraining factor.[13] These are key variables in their design of future scenarios. Very briefly, they envision four major scenarios of the future in which these variables play key roles: Pax Americana phase 2, bigemony, Pax Consortis, and Pax Nipponica.

Pax Americana phase 2 is a scenario of revival of American power, if in a somewhat reduced form, helped importantly by Japan's economic power. Bigemony is the condominium of the world by the United States and Japan in both economic and security arenas. Pax Consortis envisages the loosely and flexibly aligned sets of major countries concerned in major issue areas where no one is predominant. Pax Nipponica is a world where Japan enjoys a preeminent economic position with nuclear arsenals somehow nullified. My overall scenario is that in the intermediate term of a quarter century, Pax Americana phase 2 and bigemony are feasible whereas in the longer term of half a century, Pax Consortis and Pax Nipponica may become more feasible. Economic and technological dynamism is very important in differentiating Pax Americana phase 2 and Pax Nipponica. Nullification of nuclear arsenals is crucial in making feasible both Pax Consortis and Pax Nipponica because without it the two superpowers cannot remain the formidable actors. The debt of history may be crucial in differentiating

Pax Americana phase 2 and bigemony since only without it can Japan become a full-fledged global military power along with the United States.

JAPANESE CALCULATIONS:
CURRENT POLICY
ALTERNATIVES

Along with these kinds of long-term scenario, there are short-term policy-oriented calculations. More concretely, two major dimensions that discriminate the four major foreign policy orientations are (1) favoring alliance with the United States versus opposing alliance with the United States and (2) trilateralism versus Asianism.[14] The first concerns how closely Japan should align its positions with the United States while the second concerns how much weight Japan should give to Pacific Asia. In other words, the first has to do with the distance Japan should take from the United States while the second has to do with the interest Japan should give to Western Europe, one of the three pillars of industrialized regions.

Four policy alternatives

In the space created by these two dimensions, there are four quadrants that represent major policy alternatives currently discussed in Japan: (1) the northeastern quadrant represents the thinking that emphasizes the bigemonic integration with the United States and the disinclination to institute some form of Pacific Asian community; (2) the northwestern quadrant represents the inclination to take distance from the United States in security affairs but to enhance the basic trilateral economic rela-

13. Takashi Inoguchi, "Four Japanese Scenarios for the Future," *International Affairs*, 65(1) (Winter 1988-89).

14. Takashi Inoguchi, "Japan's Images and Options: Not a Challenger, but a Supporter," *Journal of Japanese Studies*, 12(1):95-119 (Winter 1986); idem, "Ideas and Structures of Foreign Policy."

tions; (3) the southeastern quadrant represents the policy line of retaining and even enhancing the security ties with the United States while in economic matters Pacific Asia is given much more stress than Western Europe or sometimes even North America; and (4) the southwestern quadrant represents the thinking that belittles the Japanese-U.S. alliance and upgrades the economic ties with Pacific Asia. The northeastern quadrant is sometimes called the bigemonic scenario whereas the northwestern is often called the Gaullist scenario. The southeastern scenario is sometimes called the Pax Americana phase 2 scenario while the southwestern scenario is called the Pacific Asian scenario. If the Gaullist scenario is remolded in a cooperative and conciliatory spirit, it becomes more compatible with Pax Consortis, whereas if the Pacific Asian scenario becomes globalized, then it becomes more compatible with Pax Nipponica.

Two major policy agendas

These issues in Japanese thinking about Pacific dynamism can be grouped into two basic dimensions: (1) how to maintain and enhance the friendship with the United States without being wholly subjected to what Japanese see as the somewhat aggressive, irresponsible, or erratic policy lines of the United States both in security and in economics; and (2) how to foster the good, neighborly relationship with Pacific Asia in light of its continuous dynamism and the uncertainty associated with world economic health.

Japan is somewhat uneasy about the economic difficulties of the United States and what it sees as lax economic management; Japan is similarly uneasy about the prospect of the U.S.-Soviet détente and its ramifications for the Japanese-U.S. secu-

rity treaty and Japan's anti-Soviet defense buildup — and the possible emergence of a quadrangular balance-of-power situation in the north Pacific. In relation to the weakened leadership of the United States, Japan is concerned about the prospect of the possibility of Japan's further involvement in international peacekeeping operations, whether along with the United Nations peacekeeping forces or with the United States armed forces or independently. On protectionism, Japan is concerned about what it sees as the abuse of unilateralism, such as the unfair-trader charge based on clause 301 of the Trade Act, and the frequent resort to bilateralism, taking advantage of its own security hegemony over allies, as is sometimes suspected of the U.S. proposal for a bilateral free-trade agreement. Japan is concerned also about the possibilities of inward-looking regionalism and malign protectionism in Western Europe and, to a lesser extent, in North America — and Japan is increasingly convinced of the need to enhance the regional basis on which it may be able to absorb or mitigate some negative consequences of inward-looking regionalism and malign protectionism that might get momentum in other regions of the world. On Pacific Asia, Japan is concerned about the negative feeling occasionally expressed there about Japan's debt to the region and about the constraints these feelings create for Japan's attempt to enhance what it terms regional cooperation in Pacific Asia.

The basic problem confronting Japan is the paradox of dynamism. Namely, the very dynamism that Japan and Pacific Asia now demonstrate helps to create the kind of uncertainty and unpredictability of the world economy and international relations that may undermine the very foundation of the prosperity that Japan and Pacific Asia now enjoy. Pacific dynamism invites counteractions from major actors: U.S. bilateralism, Europe's regionalism, and the superpowers' détente, all intended either to enable self-restructuring and acquire competitiveness or to bring in self-closure and rest in benign protectionism — or both. To see the outcome of these complex Pacific interactions now unfolding, one needs to wait.

This article has had the modest purpose of explicating Japanese calculations concerning Pacific dynamism.

ANNALS, *AAPSS*, **505**, September 1989

International Politics in the
Pacific Rim Era

By ROBERT GILPIN

ABSTRACT: In the history of international relations, economic, technological, and demographic developments have, over the centuries, caused the center of economic and political activities to shift from one locus to another. The modern world's history can best be understood as a process of historical change that began in the Mediterranean and subsequently diffused north to Atlantic seaboard states and then spread both westward across the Atlantic and eastward across the Eurasian continent. Forces of change swept across both the North American continent and what the geographer Halford J. Mackinder called "the heartland of the Eurasian continent" in eastern Europe and European Russia. Today, historic movements of economic, political, and technological forces are converging on the Pacific. A more pluralistic world is rapidly emerging in which the Pacific Basin nations and economic forces will play an increasingly important role.

Robert Gilpin is Dwight D. Eisenhower Professor of International Affairs in the Department of Politics and the Woodrow Wilson School of Public and International Affairs at Princeton University. His primary scholarly interest is international political economy. Among his most recent publications are War and Change in World Politics *(1981) and, with the assistance of Jean M. Gilpin,* The Political Economy of International Relations *(1987).*

ON 25 September in the year 1513, the Spanish explorer Vasco Núñez de Balboa discovered what was for Western civilization a new ocean. He called this body of water, seemingly more tranquil than the turbulent waters of the Atlantic, the "Pacific Ocean." The name was appropriate with respect to more than its seemingly tranquil waters. For most of the next half millennium, the Pacific Ocean and its peripheral societies became relatively passive objects of European and North American powers. Western conquest, imperialism, and exploitation have been the fate of the Asian peoples of the immense Pacific Rim, who were economically and technologically behind the West.

During the past half century or more, however, this condition of passivity and dependence has begun to change dramatically and at an accelerating pace. In 1904-5, the Japanese delivered a devastating defeat to the Russian empire that rocked the foundations of this encroaching giant; a rising Asian power had shown that Western nations were not invincible. Then in 1931, the Japanese began their own career of imperial expansion, intended to drive the West out of Asia and to create their own empire in East Asia. The Chinese people began to stir in the middle of the nineteenth century and by the turn of the century they had revolted against the domination of both their Manchu conquerors and Western imperialists.

In the post-World War II era, the demand of Asians to be masters of their own destiny has intensified. Following a century of turmoil and weakness, Mao Zedong liberated China and established a unified, centralized state. From the ashes of colonial rebellions and international conflicts, other independent states have arisen in Indonesia, Korea, and elsewhere around the Pacific Rim. Balboa's Pacific is no longer tranquil or merely subordinate to the ambitions of external powers. As the twentieth century draws to a close, the Pacific is rapidly emerging as the world's most dynamic arena, and its peoples are driving forces of global economics and international politics.

In the history of international relations, economic, technological, and demographic developments have, over the centuries, caused the center of economic and political activities to shift from one locus to another. The modern world's history can best be understood as a process of historical change that began in the Mediterranean and subsequently diffused north to Atlantic seaboard states and then spread both westward across the Atlantic and eastward across the Eurasian continent. These forces of change swept across both the North American continent and what geographer Halford J. Mackinder called "the heartland of the Eurasian continent" in eastern Europe and European Russia.[1] Today, these historical movements of economic, political, and technological forces are converging on the Pacific.

In his massive and multivolume history of this movement of the global political economy, the French historian Fernand Braudel has told this story graphically in terms of the rise and decline of great and dominant urban centers. As one national city has replaced another, the shifts in the international distribution of power and wealth

interrupt the calm flow of history. . . . When Amsterdam replaced Antwerp, when London took over from Amsterdam, or when in about 1929, New York overtook London, it always meant a massive historical shift of forces, revealing the precariousness of the previous equi-

1. Halford J. Mackinder, *Democratic Ideals and Reality* (New York: Norton, 1962).

librium and the strengths of the one which was replacing it. The whole circle of the world-economy was affected by such changes and the repercussions were never exclusively economic, as the reader will probably already suspect.[2]

Today, the "precarious equilibrium," to use Braudel's expression, of the contemporary international system is being upset with the emergence of Tokyo, Beijing, and, in Latin America, São Paulo as global centers of accumulating material wealth and national power. The ongoing shift in the international distribution of power toward the Pacific and toward the Southern Hemisphere has placed the dominant centers in Europe and North America on the defensive. The "calm flow of history" is being disrupted, at least for most Europeans and North Americans, who have enjoyed in the postwar era both unprecedented prosperity and, with the exceptions of the Korean and Vietnam wars, what the historian John Lewis Gaddis has rightly called "the long peace."[3]

The postwar international system is changing with a rapidity unknown in human history. The spectacular rise of Japan and of other economic competitors in East Asia and elsewhere in the so-called Third World is transforming the world economy. The repercussions of this shift in the global division of labor are not exclusively economic, as Braudel suggests, but are beginning to spill over into the realm of international politics. China, which began to industrialize earlier in this century, has already become a major regional power armed with nuclear weapons and is fast becoming a global rival to the superpow-

ers. Because of its large economy, Japan's expenditure of only a little more than 1 percent of its gross national product on national defense has moved that country to third place after the United States and the Soviet Union in funding of the military. Of equal significance, the Japanese are increasingly allocating these resources in order to create a high-technology defense industry. The economic, technological, and demographic forces at work in these two major powers and throughout the Pacific Rim have unleashed a profound and far-reaching process of political change.

EXPLAINING POLITICAL
CHANGE

If we had an adequate theory of economic and political change, it would be possible to explain these historic transformations and to predict their long-term political effects. Alas, the social sciences do not and probably never will have anything like a comprehensive understanding of these matters. As the Nobel laureate and pioneer of development economics, W. Arthur Lewis, has sardonically characterized the situation, "The process of social change is much the same today as it was 2,000 years ago. . . . We can tell what change will occur if it occurs; what we cannot foresee is what change is going to occur" and, one should add, what its effects will be.[4] The best we can do is to identify what is being changed, analyze the forces producing the change, and extrapolate on the basis of past experience the likely consequences.

The explanation of international political change requires an understanding and integration of three factors that lead to major changes in international politics as they are altered and interact with one an-

2. Fernand Braudel, *The Perspective of the World-Civilization*, vol. 3, *15th-18th Century* (New York: Harper & Row, 1979), p. 32.

3. John Lewis Gaddis, *The Long Peace: Inquiries into the History of the Cold War* (New York: Oxford University Press, 1987).

4. W. Arthur Lewis, *Theory of Economic Growth* (New York: Harper & Row, 1970), pp. 17-18.

other. The first is the structure and functioning of the international system, that is, the distribution of power among the dominant states in the international system and the political relationships among the most powerful states and other states in the system. The second is what I shall call, for lack of a better term, the environmental setting of the international system, such as economic, technological, and cultural influences on economic and political behavior. The third is the nature of the domestic regimes of the actors or societies, especially those aspects that affect the ability of a country to adapt to changes in the economic and technological environment of international relations. These three factors and changes in these factors help explain the dynamics of international relations both in the past and in the present.

The primary determinant of the structure of the international system is what the French sociologist Raymond Aron called a "hegemonic war." In the words of Aron, a hegemonic war

is characterized less by its immediate causes or its explicit purposes than by the extent and the stakes involved. It affect[s] all the political units inside one system of relations between sovereign states. Let us call it, for want of a better term, a war of hegemony, hegemony being if not the conscious motive, at any rate the inevitable consequence of the victory of at least one of the states or groups.[5]

In short, what is at issue in a hegemonic war, as opposed to lesser types of wars, is the leadership and the overall structure of the existing international system. It was such a hegemonic conflict, World War II,

that created the era that is now coming to an end.

Other developments, such as the entry of new states into an international system or the decline of dominant ones, can also alter the structure of an international system. The emergence of China, Japan, and Brazil as major industrial and potentially great military powers is a contemporary example. The relative decline of the United States and the Soviet Union, both of which rose to global preeminence as a consequence of World War II, illustrates the latter type of development. In the past, such major shifts in the distribution of power among the states in an international system have led to hegemonic war. Our own age, because of the restraining force of nuclear and other weapons of mass destruction, may be the first in which a transformation of the international system occurs that is not the result of hegemonic war. As I have written in another context, the task of ensuring peaceful rather than violent change is the greatest test of statesmanship in our era.[6]

Every international system exists in an environment composed of economic, technological, and cultural factors. Although most of these components of the environment are, of course, the conscious creation of human beings, once a new idea or technology comes into existence it assumes over time a life of its own. Its influence spreads throughout the international system and affects human behavior. Thus the rise of market economies, the industrial revolution, and the enterprising spirit of capitalism transformed European society in the early modern period. Although these developments initially took place in partic-

5. Raymond Aron, "War and Industrial Society," in *War Studies from Psychology, Sociology, Anthropology*, eds. Leon Branason and George W. Goethals (New York: Basic Books, 1964), pp. 197-98.

6. Robert Gilpin, *War and Change in World Politics* (New York: Cambridge University Press, 1981).

ular European societies, they spread rapidly throughout Western Europe and enabled European civilization to advance to a dominant global position. Almost all aspects of international relations were profoundly transformed as a consequence of these developments. By the same token, significant changes in the economic and technological environment, which took place in the latter decades of the nineteenth century, brought this European-centered age to a close and ushered in by midcentury the era of the American and Soviet superpowers. Today environmental changes are once again transforming the contours of the international economic and political system.

Whether a particular society is able to take advantage of the changed environment and the opportunities that it provides to increase national wealth and power is primarily a function of the third factor causing historic change, namely, the society's economic, political, and social system as well as, one might add, good fortune. Some domestic structures are more conducive than others to adaptation to economic or technological change. For example, as Nathan Rosenberg and L. E. Birdzell, Jr., argue in their book *How the West Grew Rich* — and, one should add, "powerful" — the rise of the industrial great powers of Western Europe and North America was a consequence of their pluralistic and fluid social and political systems. In contrast to the rigid cultures of Asia and elsewhere, the flexibility of European societies facilitated institutional and technological innovation that led to economic growth and industrial supremacy. What may promote economic growth in one environmental setting, however, may fetter it in another, thereby enabling other, more suitably adapted societies to take the lead. Great Britain, which in the seventeenth century was the pioneer in the first indus-

trial revolution, which was based on the exploitation of coal, iron, and steam power, could not adapt easily to the second industrial revolution, which occurred in the late nineteenth century and was based on the exploitation of modern science.[7] As a result, it forfeited the economic and technological lead to Germany and the United States, which were better adapted to the requirements of economic success. Today these two nations as well as other industrial powers are being challenged by Japan and other Pacific Rim countries that appear more adept at exploiting contemporary scientific and technological developments.

With this simple model of political change in mind, I examine in the rest of this article the rise of the Pacific Rim and the significance of this historic development for contemporary international relations. The discussion begins with a consideration of the postwar international system and then turns to those environmental and other developments that are transforming this postwar system and elevating the Pacific Rim nations to a greatly enhanced role in the global system. These emergent Asian and Third World nations thus far appear to be better adapted than are the United States and European nations, including Eastern Europe and the Soviet Union, to take advantage of contemporary economic and technological developments. Although it is much too soon to know whether this is the case, what is certainly true is that the competition for position in the global system is intensifying.

THE POSTWAR SYSTEM

The postwar system and what we have come to call the cold war were a direct

7. W. Arthur Lewis, *Growth and Fluctuation, 1870-1913* (London: George Allen & Unwin, 1978), p. 133.

outgrowth of World War II. The conflict between the United States and the Soviet Union originated in the unwillingness of the two former allies to accept the consequences of the war and in the inability of each side to accept the other's conception of the postwar international order. Subsequently, what had originally been a geographically restricted conflict of political interest centered almost exclusively on Western Europe expanded into a global conflict between two hostile ideologies. This interest and ideological struggle quickly escalated into a power struggle and an unprecedented arms race between two military alliances and political blocs.

The American bloc

The American bloc has had two basic components: the American relationship with Western Europe and American ties with Japan. Although these two quite separate alliances have certain common features, they also have several differences that have become more significant with the increasing importance of the Pacific Rim components of the bloc.

As relations with the Soviet Union deteriorated after 1945, the United States realized that there were fundamental problems related to Western Europe that required solution. The most pressing need was to assist the revival of the West European economy while also finding a way to guarantee the military security of the West Europeans against the threat from the Soviet Union. To achieve an American commitment to the pursuit of these goals, the American people had to be linked psychologically to Western Europe. A retreat into isolationism like that which had followed World War I and contributed to the outbreak of World War II had to be prevented.

The Marshall Plan, which encouraged intra-European cooperation, and the formation of the European Economic Community (EEC), or Common Market, were regarded as the solution to the economic problem of a devastated and fragmented Europe. The creation of a huge market in Western Europe would give the West Europeans the strength to resist native Communist parties and the blandishments of the Soviet Union. Although the Common Market represented a violation of the American ideal of a multilateral world and entailed discrimination against American exports, American policymakers assumed that the Common Market with its external tariff and protective Common Agricultural Policy was a necessary stepping stone to an eventual multilateral system rather than an end in itself. It was expected that once Western Europe had regained its economic strength and confidence, it would lower its external barriers and participate in the open world economy envisioned by the United States at Bretton Woods in 1944. In the meantime, the United States required an economic quid pro quo in the form of access to the EEC for American multinational corporations. Thus the United States tolerated what it assumed would be temporary discrimination against American exports in order to rebuild Western Europe and thwart Soviet expansionist designs.

The North Atlantic Treaty Organization (NATO) was formed in 1949 to link the two sides of the Atlantic and bring Western Europe under the American nuclear umbrella. Through the strategy of extended deterrence the United States communicated to the Soviet Union that an attack on Western Europe would be tantamount to an attack on the United States itself. The stationing of American troops on European soil has been a visible sign of this commitment.

The North Atlantic Treaty identified and legitimated for Americans and West Europeans alike the linking of their security.

In Asia, the United States also found itself facing a political, economic, and strategic challenge, because World War II and its aftermath had strengthened the position of the Soviet Union in East Asia. The Red Army had gained advanced positions in the region, the Japanese economy had been even more devastated than had initially been appreciated, and North Korea and China had become Communist and part of the Soviet bloc. With the traditional markets of Japan now in hostile hands, there was an intense concern that the forces of economic gravity would pull Japan toward the Soviet Union and its Chinese ally. Today it is difficult to understand that 35 years ago American officials despaired over the problem of ensuring Japanese economic survival.

The United States wanted to integrate Japan into a larger framework of economic relationships and thereby remove the attractiveness of the Communist-dominated Asian market. There were, however, no large neighboring non-Communist economies to which the Japanese economy could be attached. In order to overcome this problem of an isolated and vulnerable Japan, the United States took several initiatives. One was to expedite the decolonization of Southeast Asia; after all, one cause of the Pacific War had been that European colonizers had closed these economies to the Japanese. The United States also sponsored Japanese membership in the so-called Western Club. Despite strong West European resistance based on intense fear of Japanese economic competition, the United States secured Japanese participation in the International Monetary Fund, the World Bank, and other international economic organizations. In addition, the

United States gave Japan relatively free access to the American market and American technology without an economic quid pro quo, although it did require strategic concessions — air and naval bases — from the Japanese.

In order to guarantee Japanese security, the United States also spread its nuclear umbrella over Japan. The American-Japanese Mutual Security Treaty (MST), however, differs fundamentally from the NATO alliance. Under the North Atlantic Treaty, an external attack on any member obliges the others to consider measures of mutual defense. In the MST, the United States agrees to defend Japan if it is attacked, but the Japanese are not obligated to defend the United States. Also, whereas the NATO agreement applies only to the territory of its members, the MST refers to the outbreak of hostilities in the entire Pacific region. Through this agreement the United States obtained the right to use air and naval bases in Japan to defend and secure its position in the western Pacific. The Japanese were given access to the American market in exchange for the right to anchor on Japan the American strategic position in East Asia.

The Soviet bloc

Naturally, much less is known about the structure and functioning of the Soviet bloc than about the American bloc. At the core of the bloc, of course, stands the Soviet Union. Its relations with its allies, however, are vastly different from those of the United States with its allies. Whereas the United States has operated largely as *primus inter pares,* the Soviet Union has behaved as a traditional imperial power. The Soviet Union has found it very difficult to treat its allies as equals. In place of consultation, it has fashioned a number of policies and institutions to maintain what the Chinese call its "hegemonic" position over the other socialist countries.

The principal instruments of Soviet domination have been the Red Army and the Warsaw Pact. In contrast to the NATO alliance and the MST, the Warsaw Pact has a twofold mission. The purpose of stationing Soviet troops in Eastern Europe, except for Bulgaria and Romania, is not only to protect the bloc against external attack but also to prevent any popular uprisings and potential defections from the Soviet system such as have occurred in every member of the Pact except Bulgaria and Romania. This military presence has been reinforced by the institutionalization of Stalinism in all of the Eastern European countries. Stalinist measures include the "leading role" of the Communist Party in political affairs, the organization of command economies based on central planning, and the linking of these economies through the state trading mechanisms of the Council for Mutual Economic Assistance.[8] The Soviet secret police (KGB) keeps Moscow well informed on the official deliberations of bloc governments. At the diplomatic level, the nations of the Warsaw Pact and the overseas socialist countries such as Cuba and Vietnam have been linked to the Soviet Union through a series of friendship treaties. Last, but not least, overarching the system is the Brezhnev Doctrine, by which the Soviet Union claims the right to intervene in socialist countries to prevent their defection from the socialist international system.

The rigidity of these instruments of Soviet domination, however, has contributed considerably to the political fragility and

economic inefficiencies of the socialist system. Soviet hegemony was a major cause of the Chinese decision in the early 1960s to break from the system, to increase economic ties with the West, and to play an independent role in the global system. Of more contemporary relevance, the traditional political instruments of Soviet policy are poorly adapted for a political world whose center of gravity is shifting toward Asia and the Pacific. The failure of the Red Army and the Brezhnev Doctrine in Afghanistan has constituted a serious setback. In Vietnam, Africa, and elsewhere, the Soviet Union finds itself with costly commitments that produce few economic or political benefits. Its traditional policies have only generated opposition and cooperation among its potential enemies. For example, the United States, China, and Japan have found common cause in resisting Soviet expansionism in East Asia.

In the economic sphere, the command economies of the Soviet bloc and the system of barter exchange connecting the socialist countries may have been well suited for the leading industries of the earlier postwar period based on heavy industry and mass production. The command economies promoted rapid reconstruction and industrialization and reduced the economic vulnerability to what Eastern-bloc leaders regarded as a threat from the West. These methods of economic organization and international trade are poorly devised, however, to take advantage of the economic revolution associated with the computer and other rapidly developing technologies.

The Soviet Union has gained relatively little in economic benefits and in fact has paid a high economic price for the security benefits provided by its system. This is not to deny the massive achievements of the Soviet Union in transforming itself from a devastated and backward country at the

8. For a discussion of these Stalinist features of Soviet societies, see Seweryn Bialer, *The Soviet Paradox: External Expansion, Internal Decline* (New York: Knopf, 1986).

end of World War II to a superpower. But these achievements are rapidly eroding. Japan has already displaced it as the world's second-largest economy. In both the political and economic realms, the Stalinist legacy and its associated institutions constitute a major impediment to the capacity of the Soviet Union and other socialist countries to adapt to the changing global economic and political system.

The transformation of the world's economic and political systems associated with the increasing importance of the Pacific Basin has begun to change the Soviet perception of its long-term interests. Secretary Mikhail Gorbachev's celebrated speech on 28 July 1986 at Vladivostok, which called for a rapprochement with China and recognized the growing economic importance of Japan and the other Pacific Rim countries, reflected this new attitude. The Soviets cannot afford to alienate a militarily significant China and a Japan flush with capital and advanced technology for export. The Soviet disengagement from Afghanistan, moves toward a settlement in Southeast Asia, and a scaling-down of its provocative naval buildup in the region are elements of a Soviet attempt to improve its position in the Pacific.

THE TRANSFORMATION OF WORLD POLITICS

The continuing transformation of world politics is due to three major changes in the environment of international relations. These technological, economic, and related changes have enhanced the role and importance of the Pacific in the international economic and political system. As in the past, the shift in the global locus of economic and military power is altering fundamental relationships.

The first environmental change is the impact of the nuclear revolution. Both the United States and the Soviet Union have realized that their political and ideological conflict cannot be resolved through military means. The contest between the superpowers has in effect resulted in a draw. The focus of this struggle in central Europe is characterized by a stalemate. The efforts of both sides to translate nuclear or conventional military power into political advantage have not succeeded. Nor have the attempts of the superpowers to break this stalemate through gaining advantage in the so-called Third World proven to be successful. This failure on the military and political planes is shifting the struggle for power in the international system to the economic realm and has dramatically increased the number of significant players. As Mackinder postulated early in this century, the increasing destructiveness of armed conflict and the decreasing utility of military force, at least between industrialized countries, appears to be causing nations to concentrate on "the struggle for relative efficiency." [9]

In the postwar era of superpower military and political rivalry, the Pacific Rim nations were at a disadvantage. Not only were they militarily inferior, but geography and recent historical experience made them dependent upon one or another of the superpowers. But in a world where the superpowers are increasingly inhibited from attempting to translate military might into political gains, the Pacific Rim nations have much greater room for maneuver and actually have certain advantages. Lacking the burden of immense military establishments, except for South Korea, and with

9. Halford J. Mackinder, "The Geographical Pivot of History," in *Democratic Ideals and Reality*, by Mackinder, p. 242 (first published in 1904).

dynamic economies, they are very well positioned to engage in the global intensification of economic competition.

The second major change in the environment of international relations is closely related. As in the latter decades of the eighteenth century and again in the late nineteenth century, the world is entering a new phase of the ongoing industrial revolution that will have equally important results. The immense scale of contemporary research and development in many countries, the decreased lead time between scientific discovery and technical application, and the pervasive influence of the computer revolution are transforming all aspects of industrial society. This technological development will be profound for the structure and functioning of the international political economy.

Since the end of the nineteenth century, the industrial economies of the world have been based on the materials and technologies of the second phase of the industrial revolution, such as steel, petroleum, and the internal-combustion engine. These technologies gave rise to the mass production and heavy industries that led to the economic, military, and political predominance of the United States and the Soviet Union. Today these industrial technologies, or what Christopher Freeman has called Fordism, are decreasingly relevant for the economic growth and competitiveness of the superpowers as well as many other advanced economies.[10] As comparative advantage in these industries shifts to the rapidly developing economies in Asia and Latin America, the developed economies must create new industrial structures based on the emergent high technologies associated with bioengineering, the com-

10. Christopher Freeman, *Technology Policy and Economic Performance: Lessons from Japan* (New York: Pinter, 1987).

puter revolution, and other science-based technologies. This situation has led to an intensified competition between the advanced countries for technological and economic leadership. As northeast Asia has become not only the most economically dynamic region on the globe but also its electronics capital, it is rapidly taking the lead in this contemporary technological revolution.

The third major environmental change is the globalization of the world economy. The liberalization of trade, the integration of financial markets, and the role of the multinational corporation in the internationalization of production have created a truly interdependent world economy. In trade, finance, and production, economic interdependence among national economies has expanded rapidly over the past several decades. The economies of such countries as Japan and the East Asian newly industrializing countries that have taken the greatest advantage of this expanding interdependence have surpassed those socialist and less developed economies that have emphasized economic autarky. As the Soviet Union under Gorbachev has acknowledged, unless an economy participates in this global interdependence, it cannot possibly develop its full potential.

This process of economic globalization and increasing interdependence, however, is not a linear one leading to the disappearance of economic and political boundaries. On the contrary, the major centers of the world economy — the United States, the Soviet Union, Western Europe, Japan, and the newly industrializing countries of East Asia, Latin America, and elsewhere — are adopting trade, industrial, and investment policies in order to strengthen their competitive position. The American Omnibus Trade Bill of 1988, Gorbachev's efforts to restructure the Soviet economy, the increased Japanese emphasis on an economic strategy based on domestic growth and overseas investment by its corporations, the decision of the EEC to create a vast internal market beginning in 1992, and the aggressive export-oriented strategies of the newly industrializing countries are all responses to what former West German Chancellor Helmut Schmidt has called "the struggle for the world product." [11] In this gathering contest, the Pacific Rim countries will play an increasingly important role and will set the pace for the rest of the world.

THE GLOBAL SIGNIFICANCE
OF THE TRANSFORMATION

A comparison of the main features of the postwar international system with those of the emergent system indicate the significance of the transformation taking place. In the former, there were sharp lines of political division between the two blocs in Western Europe; in the Pacific, the political situation is more fluid and the dividing lines are blurred. Despite the efforts of the superpowers to divide Asia into exclusive spheres of influence, the diversity and geography of the region have prevented such a development. In this region, the nations are not split by two hostile alliance systems. With the exception of the Association of Southeast Asian Nations, whose influence is very limited, the political relations are bilateral and continually in flux. Both superpowers have to adjust their cold-war policies and learn how to live with a more pluralistic international system.

The United States and the Soviet Union have also tended to subordinate the Pacific to the Atlantic. Events in the Pacific Basin

have been analyzed and interpreted from a European-centered perspective rather than as important in their own right. Americans saw Korea as the beginnings of a Soviet assault on the West, and the Soviets have been slow to appreciate the indigenous dynamism of East Asia. The strategic stalemate in central Europe and the increasing significance of the Pacific Rim are forcing both superpowers to appreciate that this region must be approached on its own special terms.

Not only the political-military system but the postwar economic system was also Atlantic centered. In every aspect of economic affairs the Pacific was subordinated to the Atlantic. For example, it is interesting to note that the subtitle of Richard Cooper's 1968 path-breaking analysis of the world economy was *Economic Policy in the Atlantic Community.* [12] The institutions of the international economy conceived at Bretton Woods in 1944 and discussed by Cooper were designed principally with Western-style economies in mind. The emphasis on the liberal economic principles of most favored nation, unconditional reciprocity, and national treatment as the means by which to liberalize world trade and create interdependencies between national economies were derived from Western experience and conceptions of economic behavior. The question, therefore, arises whether or not these rules governing global economic relations are suitable for a world economy composed of strong, non-Western economies with a much greater commitment to state intervention in the economy.

Another potential implication of the global transformation of international affairs is the decreasing relevance of tradi-

11. Helmut Schmidt, "Struggle for the World Product," *Foreign Affairs,* 52:437-51 (Apr. 1974).

12. Richard Cooper, *The Economics of Interdependence: Economic Policy in the Atlantic Community* (New York: McGraw-Hill, 1968).

tional ideologies. The postwar system has witnessed the competition between Western liberalism and Soviet Marxism for global supremacy. The former is identified with an emphasis on the market, individualism, and democracy. The latter is characterized by a commitment to state planning, collectivism, and authoritarianism. Whatever the merits of these doctrines, they are both Western and have little relevance for East Asia; as a result they are in retreat as guiding principles of political and economic affairs. In the Confucian-influenced cultures of China, Japan, and northeast Asia as well as elsewhere in the Pacific, the antipodes of market versus state, individual versus collectivity, or democracy versus authoritarianism are formulated differently.[13] The dynamism of these Asian economies and the demographic scale of these societies suggest that their conceptions of the way to organize economic,

social, and political affairs will weigh heavily in the emergent global system.

CONCLUSION

The increasing importance of the Pacific poses a major challenge to the rest of the world. It is a challenge that is global in extent and, for the moment, almost entirely on the plane of economic competition. If historical experience still has any relevance, however, this situation could change and military rivalries could result as China, Japan, and other Pacific Rim nations become more powerful. In this transformed global environment, the clash between the American and Soviet blocs, which largely determined the nature of the postwar bipolar international order, has decreased in significance. In its place, a more pluralistic and far more complex system of independent and interdependent states is rapidly coming into existence. How these many and differing players will interact and together shape the global economic and political order has yet to be determined.

13. Roy Hofheinz, Jr., and Kent E. Calder, *The Eastasia Edge* (New York: Basic Books, 1982).

ANNALS, *AAPSS*, 505, September 1989

What Can Economics Learn from East Asian Success?

By ROBERT WADE

ABSTRACT: Most economics literature on East Asian industrialization falls victim to the assumption that only those features of economic policy consistent with neoclassical principles could have contributed to good economic performance. Explanations of good performance accordingly ignore nonneoclassical features. This article suggests that new insights can be gained by carefully examining what these governments actually did. We find that much of what they did is consistent with the principles of old-style pre-1970 development economics. In particular, they gave central attention to ways of augmenting and directing the composition of investment, and much less attention to ways of increasing efficiency of resource use. They used protection as an instrument to enhance innovation and international competitiveness. In important industries they regulated both quantities and prices so as to achieve government-selected goals, preventing those parts of the economy from being guided by international prices. Economics has much to learn by embracing such nonneoclassical facts and seeking to build a theory to accommodate them.

Robert Wade is currently at the Office of Technology Assessment, U.S. Congress, on leave from the Institute of Development Studies at the University of Sussex. He worked previously on agricultural and trade policy issues at the World Bank. He is the author of Governing the Market: Economic Theory and the Role of Government in East Asian Industrialization *(forthcoming);* Village Republics: Economic Conditions for Collective Action in South India *(1988); and* Irrigation and Agricultural Politics in South Korea *(1982).*

NOTE: The views expressed in this article are not to be mistaken for the views of the institution with which the author is affiliated. The article is based on material in the author's *Governing the Market: Economic Theory and the Role of Government in East Asian Industrialization* (Princeton University Press, forthcoming).

I must immediately narrow the title of this article to "Three Propositions That Mainstream Economics Can Learn from the Industrial Success of Japan, South Korea, and Taiwan." They are (1) capital accumulation matters; (2) protection can help rather than hinder the emergence of internationally competitive industries; and (3) sectoral industrial policies that lead the market can improve upon the growth outcomes of self-adjusting markets. I make no claim that these are the only or even the most important lessons for economics, only that their implications reach far enough to warrant attention.

First, we need to define industrial success. Anyone who has experienced the pollution and congestion of East Asian cities will realize that "success" has to be used in a qualified sense, even leaving aside political aspects such as civil and political rights. I mean "success" to refer to such basics as the food in people's stomachs and the amount of income left over after caloric requirements have been met. Consider the following comparative statistics. Real wages in Western Europe, converted into hours of paid work required by an unskilled male laborer to buy one quintal of food grain, rarely fell so low as to exceed the 200-hour mark after 1400. Generalizing from Western European experience, Fernand Braudel says, "It is always serious when the 100-hours-for-one-quintal line is crossed; to cross the 200 is a danger signal; 300 is famine."[1] In much of India today the figure is over 200 hours. In France from the beginning of the twentieth century to 1920

the figure fell from about 65 hours to 40 hours. I have not made the calculation for Japan and Korea. For Taiwan, the figure remained in the range of 150 to 200 hours for one quintal of rice during the 1950s and early 1960s; by 1970 it was down to 70-120 hours; by 1980, to 40-70 hours, or in the same range as France between 1900 and 1920.[2] That is what I mean by "success," and since such a reduction in hours would not have come about had the economy not undergone rapid industrialization — for agricultural output per hectare was already very high by world standards in the 1950s — I call this "industrial success." The figure for the United States, using the minimum legal wage and the price of flour in the mid-1980s, is roughly 15 hours.

Other indicators tell the same story. Taiwan jumped from the twenty-eighth-biggest exporter of manufactures in 1965 to tenth-biggest in 1986, Korea from thirty-third to thirteenth, Japan from fourth to second. Manufactured exports from Taiwan and Korea account for 32 percent of manufactured exports from all developing countries, and about half of their manufactured exports go to the U.S. market alone. No wonder producers from other countries trying to sell in the U.S. market think of them as tigers. Even at tenth and thirteenth, however, Taiwan and Korea still have only a small combined share — 4.9 percent — of world manufactured exports. That share is nevertheless much bigger than their share of world population — 1.28 percent — and of world gross domestic product — 1.5 percent — which makes them look more like gnats than tigers.

How did it happen? In economics there is a well-trodden explanation to the effect

1. Fernand Braudel, *The Structures of Everyday Life: The Limits of the Possible* (London: Collins, 1981), p. 134. For more complete citations to material relevant to the present article, the reader is referred to Robert Wade, *Governing the Market: Economic Theory and the Role of Government in East Asian Industrialization* (Princeton, NJ: Princeton University Press, forthcoming).

2. Robert Wade, *Village Republics: Economic Conditions for Collective Action in South India* (New York: Cambridge University Press, 1988), p. 35; idem, *Governing the Market*.

70 THE ANNALS OF THE AMERICAN ACADEMY

that superior economic performance was the outcome of relatively free markets. These countries did better than comparator countries because they had freer markets or, conversely, less interventionist governments — and therefore more efficient allocation of resources. Some examples:

1. "Detailed and historical studies . . . have provided an impressive empirical validation of the theoretical case for the view that . . . free trade remains the best policy for developing (and developed) countries."[3]

2. "The evidence is quite conclusive: countries applying outward-oriented development strategies had a superior performance in terms of exports, economic growth, and employment whereas countries with continued inward orientation encountered increasing economic difficulties."[4] "Outward-orientation" exists where trade controls are nonexistent or very low and the variation in effective protection rates between different industries is also very low.[5]

3. "There can be few such clear cases in economic history of cause and effect [says Ian Little about Taiwan]. . . . Apart from the creation of [four neoclassical growth conditions — a virtual free-trade regime for exporters, a free labor market, high interest rates, and conservative government budgeting] . . . it is hard to find any good explanation of the sustained industrial boom of 1963-1973."[6]

4. Hugh Patrick declares himself to be "of the school which interprets Japanese economic performance as due primarily to the actions and efforts of private individuals and enterprises responding to the opportunities provided in quite free markets for commodities and labor.[7]

5. "The crux of the Korean example is that the active interventionist attitude of the State has been aimed at applying moderate incentives which are very close to the relative prices of products and factors that would prevail in a situation of free trade."[8]

6. "State intervention is largely absent [in Japan, Korea, Taiwan, Hong Kong, and Singapore]. What the state provided is simply a suitable environment for the entrepreneurs to perform their functions."[9]

Such is the economic legend. It is by no means wholly false. The labor market in Taiwan and Korea, for example, has been about as close to a free market as it is possible to get, due in part to government repression of unions. In addition, it is certainly the case that the overwhelming majority of academic economists in Japan, Korea, and Taiwan have believed in the virtues of the freely functioning market mechanism as an article of faith as well as of rhetoric. Yet the legend is not fully consistent with the way the governments have in practice behaved. The governments have adopted over a long period of time a much more aggressive, dirigistic set of industrial policies than free-trading princi-

3. Deepak Lal, *The Poverty of Development Economics*, Hobart Paper 16 (London: Institute of Economic Affairs, 1983), pp. 27-28.

4. Bela Balassa, *The Newly Industrializing Countries in the World Economy* (Elmsford, NY: Pergamon Press, 1981), pp. 16-17.

5. World Bank, *World Development Report 1987* (Washington, DC: World Bank, 1987).

6. Ian Little, "An Economic Reconnaissance," in *Economic Growth and Structural Change in Taiwan: The Postwar Experience of the Republic of China*, ed. W. Galenson (Ithaca, NY: Cornell University Press, 1979), pp. 474, 480.

7. Hugh Patrick, "The Future of the Japanese Economy: Output and Labor Productivity," *Journal of Japanese Studies*, 3(2):239 (Summer 1977).

8. Frederik Berger, "Korea's Experience with Export-Led Industrial Development," in *Export Promotion Policies*, Staff Working Paper 313, ed. B. de Vries (Washington, DC: World Bank, 1979), p. 64.

9. Edward Chen, *Hyper-Growth in Asian Economies: A Comparative Study of Hong Kong, Japan, Korea, Singapore, and Taiwan* (New York: Macmillan, 1979), p. 41.

ples would justify. The three propositions mentioned at the beginning of this article are derived from the experience of those policies.

CAPITAL FORMATION MATTERS

From the eighteenth century to World War I capital formation was at the heart of economic theory. Since then its place has been preempted by issues of efficient resource allocation. Capital formation enjoyed a short renaissance in the newly emerged discipline of development economics after World War II and through the 1950s into the 1960s; but in contrast to the pre-World War I classical treatment, the new discipline joined capital formation to an activist role of the state. Paul Rosenstein-Rodan and Alexander Gerschenkron, among others, emphasized the need for a "government spurt" or "big push," chiefly defined in terms of a sharp increase in capital formation under the prodding of government, allied sometimes with banks.[10] Simon Kuznets provided statistical credibility for the view that capital formation was the "engine" of growth.[11] Development economics agreed on two central imperatives for development: (1) to augment and marshal the economy's investment surplus and (2) to transfer the surplus into productive investment, by a mechanism involving a combination of government and entrepreneurs in competitive markets.

Increasingly over the 1960s, economists working on developing countries turned away from issues of capital forma-

10. Paul Rosenstein-Rodan, "Problems of Industrialization of Eastern and Southeastern Europe," *Economic Journal* (June-Sept. 1943); Alexander Gerschenkron, *Economic Backwardness in Historical Perspective* (Cambridge, MA: Harvard University Press, 1962).

11. Simon Kuznets, *Modern Economic Growth* (New Haven, CT: Yale University Press, 1966).

tion. The effects are seen in the dearth of journal articles analyzing the dynamics of capital formation in developing countries during the 1970s and 1980s. But beyond inattention, many economists denied—as part of a more general denial of a special development economics and reassertion of a single universal economics—that the volume of capital available from domestic sources is a significant constraint on development. Rather, they argued, the main determinant of more or less growth is more or less efficiency—sometimes with "enterprise" lurking ad hoc in the background—and the main determinant of efficiency is the institutional arrangement of competitive markets. Indirectly, then, the main determinant of more or less economic growth is more or less willingness on the part of governments to adopt policies that tap into the flourishing international trading system and that enlarge the scope for market allocation in the domestic economy. The agenda of the new, or neoclassical, development economics is therefore modest: to hunt out and remove price distortions, so as to enable the market, now freed of distortions, to maximize the efficiency of labor, land, and capital. The resulting rate and composition of investment constitute, with some small qualifications, the social optimum, upon which no government intention could improve. How can government bureaucrats do better than entrepreneurs with their own pocketbooks at stake? Of course, governments should also provide those things that Adam Smith called "the three duties of the sovereign," defense, law, and infrastructure.

How do these theories—the old and the new development economics—fare in light of the East Asian experience? It would be comforting for the new development economics—or, more accurately, neoclassical economics applied to developing countries — if the fast-growth East Asian countries had only average, or even lower than average, levels of investment. That would clearly be a strike against the importance attached to capital formation in the old development economics as the principal general force for economic growth.

In fact, all three economies have had very high levels of investment. Japan's 32 percent ratio of gross domestic investment to gross domestic product in 1980 was the highest among all 19 industrial market economies. Out of 18 middle-income countries — leaving out the countries of the Organization of Petroleum Exporting Countries and small countries under 10 million people — Taiwan's 33 percent ranked third, after Romania and Yugoslavia. Korea's 31 percent ranked fourth.

Not unrelated, Japan's 7.1 percent gave it the fastest growth in gross national product per capita in the period 1960-80 of the high-income industrial market economies. Taiwan, with 7.2 percent, had the second-fastest growth of the middle-income countries, next to Romania's 8.6 percent. Korea, with 7.0 percent, was third. Yugoslavia was fourth, with 5.4 percent.

So the fastest growers also tend to have the highest levels of investment. There is, of course, the question of causation. It could be that fast growth — due perhaps to freely functioning markets — caused the high levels of investment. But at the least we can say that the traditional wisdom of development economics is not contradicted by these findings.

It is clear from planning documents and from the histories of particular policy instruments — protection, tax credits, and so forth — that the governments were deeply committed to increasing and sustaining high levels of investment and to steering its composition. This provides contextual evidence that the direction of primary causa-

tion went from high investment to fast growth. Moreover, Shahid Yusuf and Kyle Peters econometrically test two models of investment in Korea, one a standard neoclassical investment model, based on a distributed lag relationship between the amount of investment and the level of and changes in output, the other based on government policy objectives. They find the latter better explains both aggregate investment during the years 1970-82 and investment in heavy industry, while the former does better on investment in light industry.[12] Abundant evidence from other countries supports the same causation from investment to growth. For example, Romer finds a strong statistical relation from investment rates to growth rates in a sample of 115 countries.[13]

PROTECTION AND THE EMERGENCE OF INTERNATIONALLY COMPETITIVE INDUSTRIES

Jagdish Bhagwati is correct to claim that belief in the superiority of what he terms the "export-promotion" strategy over the "import-substitution" strategy — others use the terms "outward-oriented" and "inward-oriented" — is all but universal among economists, "insofar as any kind of consensus can ever be found in our tribe."[14] An export-promotion (EP) strategy exists when, overall, US$1 of exports

12. Shahid Yusuf and Kyle Peters, "Is Capital Accumulation the Key to Economic Growth? Neoclassical Models and Development Economics on Korea's Investment Policies," mimeo (Washington, DC: World Bank, East Asia Programs Department, Nov. 1984).

13. P. Romer, "Crazy Explanations for the Productivity Slowdown," *Macroeconomics Annual*, 2:163-202 (1987).

14. Jagdish Bhagwati, "Rethinking Trade Strategy," in *Development Strategies Reconsidered*, ed. J. Lewis and V. Kallab (New Brunswick, NJ: Transaction Books, 1986), p. 93.

fetches, in local currency, the same as US$1 of imports, when all export subsidies and tax credits, and all import premiums resulting from quantitative restrictions and tariffs, are included. In other words, EP refers to trade neutrality, the absence of net incentives to sell either on the domestic market or on the export market. It goes with low average effective protection levels and low variation in effective protection levels between industries. It is not identical with free trade — absence of controls and tariffs — but the two concepts are very close. An EP regime may have some impediments to imports, provided their effect in giving a net incentive for domestic producers to sell on the protected domestic market is offset by export incentives; but in practice this offsetting means that the impediments to imports cannot be substantial if the regime is to meet the EP criterion.

Given the central importance of an EP or near-free trade regime as a causal condition in neoclassical explanations of East Asian success, it is odd how little solid evidence exists to confirm the existence of such regimes. One would have expected a voluminous literature showing that the central cause was indeed present. Instead, bits and pieces of evidence are adduced, the confidence in which rests upon a prior conviction that such regimes must have been in place because otherwise the economies could not have been so successful.

The *locus classicus* of the view that Korea and Taiwan have had near-free trade regimes is the six-country comparative study organized by Bela Balassa.[15] It examined the trade regimes of Korea, Taiwan, Singapore, Israel, Colombia, and Argentina for 1968 or 1969, using the same methodology for each case. It appears to show

that Taiwan and Korea — also Singapore, which we do not discuss in this article — had relatively low average effective protection for manufacturing in that year: 14 percent for Taiwan and 13 percent for Korea, as against 35 percent for Colombia and 112 percent for Argentina. It also shows that, for manufacturing as a whole, Taiwan and Korea had a low degree of trade bias — that is, they met Bhagwati's EP condition — while Argentina had a very strong trade bias in favor of the domestic market, though Colombia did not.

There are several problems with the study, which greatly reduce one's confidence in the numbers and the conclusions. Only a bald summary can be given here. The first problem is methodological, which can be illustrated by the Korean case.[16] Like the others, the Korean study ignores legal tariffs and quantitative restrictions in almost all cases. Instead it relies on price comparisons between foreign and domestically produced versions of the same item, on the assumption that effective protection is higher the higher the differential in favor of domestic substitutes. This is a crucial step, because legal tariffs in both Korea and Taiwan were high in comparison with other countries, as the authors of the studies concede. In the Korea price survey, for example, 49 percent of the 365 items were subject to legal tariffs of 60 percent or more. Legal tariffs are disregarded on the grounds that exemptions, rebates, and deferred payment mean that the tariffs actually paid were much lower. But this ignores a basic point: the exemptions, rebates, and deferrals were targeted on priority items — mainly on imports of machinery and trans-

15. Bela Balassa et al., *Development Strategies in Semi-Industrial Economies* (Baltimore, MD: Johns Hopkins University Press, 1982).

16. Richard Luedde-Neurath, *Import Controls and Export-Oriented Development: A Reassessment of the South Korean Case* (Boulder, CO: Westview Press, 1986).

port equipment and on imports to be used to make exports. These two categories, plus exemption on cereal imports, accounted for 89 percent of the total exemptions, rebates, or deferrals in the year of the study. So not much tariff exemption was available for imports of everything else for sale on the domestic market. Producers of domestic substitutes for these items received high levels of protection in line with the legal tariff.

Similarly, the Korean and Taiwanese cases ignore quantitative restrictions (QRs) in computing effective protection. Yet the Korean data show that 63 percent of the items in the price survey are subject to some form of QR, which by itself would suggest a fairly restrictive rather than a nearly free trade regime. Indeed, three-quarters of the items in the price survey had legal tariffs of 60 percent or more, or QRs, or both.

Another methodological difficulty concerns the treatment of negative price differentials. Negative price differentials, with the price of the domestic version lower than that of the foreign version, were found in no less than 45 percent of the items. How to treat them? Should they be included at negative rates of protection? Should they be excluded on the presumption that the two halves of the comparison are not really the same item, because of quality differences? Should they be included at the legal tariff? In the event the study includes most of them at zero rate of protection. It is not clear why inclusion at zero makes more sense than the alternatives. It is clear, though, that inclusion at zero results in a much lower average than inclusion at the legal tariff rate. It also results in a much higher average than inclusion at negative rates. We should note that only the Korean and Taiwanese studies show a significant portion of negative price differentials.

In addition to the methodological difficulties that make us unclear about the real value of the averages — unclear whether the average level of protection really was unusually low — there is the problem of dispersion around the averages. Neither the authors of the case studies nor subsequent commentators have paid attention to dispersions in effective protection between industries. It turns out that Korea's dispersion in effective protection rates to different industries within the manufacturing sector, with respect to their domestic market sales, was about the same as for Colombia and higher than for Argentina. Intuitively, it is plausible to conclude that the resource pulling effect, or industry bias, of a given amount of dispersion will be higher the lower the average level of protection, because from a lower average a higher percentage difference is needed to obtain the same dispersion as from a higher average. Since even with the earlier qualifications there is not much doubt that Korea's and Taiwan's average protection was much lower than Colombia's and Argentina's, Korea's similar or higher dispersion around the lower average may be presumed to have had a greater resource pulling effect. In other words, Korea's trade and industrial policies gave different incentives to different industries. Taiwan had somewhat lower dispersion than Korea but not significantly lower than Argentina's, and much the same argument holds. Both countries used the incentives of the trade regime to spur on some industries more than others.

A similar conclusion holds for both countries with respect to trade bias. The overall picture of trade neutrality results from putting together sectors with high incentives to export with those with higher incentives to sell domestically. The disaggregated figures support the view that both governments were trying to promote exports in some industries and import substitutes in others.

The principal study of Korea for a more recent year — remember that the foregoing discussion refers to data from one year only, 1968 for Korea, 1969 for Taiwan — finds that the effective rate of protection for manufacturing averaged 49 percent in both 1978 and 1982, in contrast to the figure of 13 percent from the 1968 study. It uses a somewhat different methodology from that of the earlier study, however, so one cannot compare straightforwardly. But since we can be reasonably sure that a big jump in protection did not occur between 1968 and 1978, the results of the later study lend credence to the view that Korea was a more heavily protected country in the 1960s than the Balassa study suggests and than most other economists assume has been true all along. Much the same argument applies to Taiwan.[17] One indicator can be given: in 1984, after waves of import liberalization over many years, over half of Taiwan's imports by value were covered by nontariff barriers.[18]

In short, the evidence that Korea and Taiwan have had low average protection and low dispersion around the average — low enough in relation to worse-performing developing countries to be plausibly assigned the core explanatory role in their superior performance — is not strong

17. M.-H. Hsing, *Taiwan: Industrialization and Trade Policies* (New York: Oxford University Press, 1971); Shoh-chieh Tsiang and Wen Lang Chen, "Developments towards Trade Liberalization in Taiwan" (Paper delivered at the Joint Conference on the Industrial Policies of the ROC and the ROK, Chung-hua Institution for Economic Research, Taipei, 1984).

18. C. H. Tu and W. T. Wang, "Trade Liberalization in the Republic of China on Taiwan" (Paper delivered at the Joint Conference on the Industrial Policies of the ROC and the ROK, Korea Development Institute, Seoul, 1988).

enough to support even a modest confidence. Such evidence as there is suggests that they did not have unusually low protection.

The use of protection

If Korea and Taiwan have had substantial levels of protection, how were they able to develop internationally competitive industries behind protective barriers — in the face of a general assumption among economists that this is very unlikely? The point is that protection, like any powerful instrument, can be used well or it can be used badly. The predicted economic effects may not occur if the protection is arranged differently from normal. First, both Korea and Taiwan exempted from tariffs and most QRs imports of raw materials and intermediate goods to be used for export production. This allowed exporters to get these kinds of inputs at the same terms as their foreign competitors.

Second, they both offered export subsidies to offset further any incentive to sell on the domestic market. These subsidies came in the form of concessional credit and a variety of ways by which import licenses were tied to export performance. In Korea, but not Taiwan, pressure to export went well beyond incentives, to near coercion.

Third, they tied permission to import — in the case of items whose domestic production they wished to encourage — to evidence that the makers of domestic substitutes could not meet the foreign supplier's terms on price, quality, delivery, and so forth. Of course, the domestic maker did not have to be able to meet the foreign supplier's terms exactly for the import to be refused; this was a matter for negotiation between the would-be purchaser of an imported machine tool, for example, and the domestic machine-tool makers' association, with the government in the middle. The requirement for permission was a mechanism to force producers to inform themselves about domestic supply possibilities before turning to imports. It also gave the government a way both to reduce the risks of investment in new products — by providing some protection — and to bring international competitive pressure to bear on domestic producers in a modulated way. Of course, with such discretionary power in the hands of government officials, one would expect frantic rent-seeking behavior and all the ills that the term "rent seeking" has come automatically to convey. The fact that such behavior seems to have been kept in check in Korea and Taiwan makes the more general point that rent seeking is not an inevitable accompaniment and distorter of government intervention; it is a function of the political regime.

A fourth element is that both countries made much use of QRs in addition to tariffs. QRs have merit when the acquisition of technological capacity and subsequent adaptive innovation depend on extensive interaction between users and suppliers. In addition, they allow the government to cushion domestic producers against sudden surges of imports and resulting underutilization of domestic capacity more effectively than tariffs. QRs are normally condemned on the grounds, among others, that in conditions of macroeconomic instability they generate constantly changing price signals, because with changing domestic prices the tariff equivalent of any QR changes also; so QRs amplify price instability. Since Korea and especially Taiwan had fairly stable macroeconomic conditions, this familiar cost of QRs has been much less significant there.

Let us accept that Korea, Taiwan, and Japan used protection well. What about the standard economics argument that, however well used, protection is always second best or worse? If unrestrained demand for imports leads to balance-of-payments difficulties, the standard argument runs, devalue the exchange rate and curb aggregate demand by fiscal and monetary policy. Devaluation has the merit of spurring both exports and import substitution at the same time. If for some reason it is deemed necessary to promote specific industries, use credit subsidies.[19]

What is wrong with this argument? First, experts often disagree by large margins as to what the desirable exchange rate should be, not only in developing but also in industrialized countries. Second, while there are cases where everyone agrees that the exchange rate is substantially overvalued, markets often seem to be poor at correcting the imbalances. Third, the policy instrument is the nominal exchange rate, but there may be no close connection between changes in the nominal rate and changes in the real rate except in the very short run, and it is the real rate that counts for resource allocation. Fourth, the neoclassical argument recognizes no limits on how far the exchange rate can be made to fall. A fall in the real exchange rate means a fall in the price of noninternationally traded goods and services in relation to the price of tradables. The most important nontradable is labor, so a fall in the real exchange rate means a fall in the real wage. This may be resisted politically. More generally, inflexibilities of import-dependent production processes and consumption patterns may mean that the needed fall in the exchange rate is not possible without disruption of production, inflation, social unrest, and political conflict, in the face of which a well-meaning government may look to other methods of maintaining external balance.

19. Max Corden, *Trade Policy and Economic Welfare* (New York: Oxford University Press, 1974).

The argument to replace protection with credit subsidies as a means of assisting particular industries is also open to question. First, subsidies could not buffer the impact of short-term fluctuations on the domestic economy as well as protection could. Second, there can be no presumption that the subsidies needed for infant industries to compete equally against foreign suppliers would match the finance available. Unless a close connection is assumed between the revenue-raising capacity of government and the amount of subsidies needed, the subsidies may well exceed that capacity. Third, the advantages of subsidies cannot be assumed to outweigh the distortional effects of raising revenue through the existing tax system. Fourth, subsidies are a relatively visible means of transferring resources and may therefore generate more political conflict than protection, which allows resources to be transferred more invisibly. Whether this quiet transfer is desirable depends on whether the pattern of protection makes sense in terms of a national interest. Finally, protection through tariffs raises revenue in an administratively simple way, compared to the difficulties of raising revenue through direct taxes, and it is likely to be no more difficult to administer than a direct subsidy program would be.[20]

None of this is to deny that in many countries protection has been used in a way that hinders the evolution of internationally competitive industries. It makes the point that the economic effects of protection depend critically on how it is arranged and implemented, especially on how it is integrated into a wider industrial and export strategy. This suggests directions for badly needed improvements in the economic analysis of trade regimes.

20. Luedde-Neurath, *Import Controls and Export-Oriented Development.*

SECTORAL INDUSTRIAL POLICIES THAT LEAD THE MARKET

There is surprisingly little analysis of the economic impact of industrial policy measures in East Asia, either for a particular industry or for the economy as a whole. Some of what has been said about economic impact — mainly by political scientists — is marked by the Darwinian or Malinowskian fallacy: the assumption that because something exists it must therefore be vital for the survival of the organism or society in which it exists. Translated into East Asian terms, this leads one to argue that because protection, tight financial system controls, and the like existed, they must have had a positive impact on East Asian economic performance. But the Ptolemaic fallacy — mainly from economists — is more prevalent and more inhibiting of learning: the assumption that only those features of economic policy that are consistent with neoclassical precepts could have contributed to superior economic performance, so that all nonneoclassical features can be safely ignored. In part, of course, the unsatisfactory state of the evidence reflects the fact that measuring economic impact of industrial policies is a very difficult thing to do.

The obvious way is to commensurate as many tax and subsidy programs as possible in terms of effective subsidy rates for many different industries, put them into a multisectoral model, calculate second-round effects, and then reach conclusions about the net bias of incentives in different industries. A neoclassical economist would hope to find that subsidies given to one industry are canceled out by those given to others, so that overall neutrality is the result of all those industry-specific promotion efforts. The conclusion would then be drawn that the entire array of incentives and protection could be withdrawn at a stroke, leaving relative prices and resource allocations unchanged. This is almost certainly wrong, but it is a common enough assumption in neoclassical analysis that the allocation of resources in an economy where neutrality is being contrived by policy measures is much the same as where there is no government intervention, with the prescriptive implication that the government should save all the resources going into the programs by adopting free trade.

Here I want to suggest another and more indirect way to consider the question of impact, but first I shall present some distinctions. Functional — or horizontal, or generic — industrial policies aim to strengthen a particular function without discriminating between industries in terms of who gains access to the benefits. Examples are a research and development tax break, a training subsidy, and concessional credit to small firms. Sectoral — or vertical, or industry-specific — industrial policies aim to change production and/or investment decisions in a particular industry from what they would have been without the policies.

Sectoral policies can be divided into those that lead and those that follow the market. Sectoral policies lead the market when the government (1) takes initiatives about what products or technologies should be encouraged and (2) puts public resources or influence behind these initiatives. Suppose a government proposes a project, such as a steel mill, to private firms, the private firms decline, and the government goes ahead with it as a public enterprise, which is what happened in the case of Korea's Pohang steel mill. This is a clear example of government leadership. Sectoral policies follow the market when the government adopts the proposals of private firms for new products and technologies to be encouraged. If private firms

propose to jump from 64K to 256K dynamic random-access memory chip production and ask for government help, the government help follows rather than leads the market.

Leading and following should be qualified by the degree of additionality. When the government assists firms to do what they would have done anyway without assistance, this is small followership. When the government assists firms significantly to extend the margin of their investments, this is big followership. Similarly, big leadership is a government initiative on a scale to make a substantial difference; small leadership is a government initiative that devotes too few resources or too little influence to produce a different investment outcome.

Neoclassical economics can embrace functional industrial policies in some circumstances as a means of repairing market failures. Sectoral policies — "picking winners," a term generally used in a tone of mocking derision — are much more difficult to justify. Market failures of a kind that could be repaired by sectoral policies are thought to be rare and often themselves due to government interventions. Indeed, the same causes that make for market failure produce even more likely and more socially damaging government failure, it is said. The discipline is characteristically suspicious of government's willingness to resist the temptation to misuse economic powers and of government's ability to detect business opportunities that private entrepreneurs have overlooked. More generally, it is suspicious of any arrangement in which any one agent — whether the government, a monopoly, or an oligopoly — can have a tangible impact on the aggregate outcome. A successful outcome is thought by and large to be the result of the interaction of many agents, none of whom can exercise a tangible impact on the overall result.

Neoclassical economics can recognize and accommodate functional industrial policies in East Asia without too much difficulty. But it can accommodate the fact of East Asian sectoral industrial policies only by asserting either that they hindered what would otherwise have been still better performance or that they amounted to no more than small followership or small leadership with little more causal impact than the cock's crow has on the dawn. If, however, we can demonstrate that some of the policies — some of the time and in some important industries — represented big leadership, then this line of defense is cut off, because we know that the actual production and investment outcomes differ from what would have occurred in the absence of the policies.

Space limits preclude an attempt to indicate the several kinds of evidence that suggest the existence of big leadership in East Asia.[21] Big leadership does not in itself mean that actual outcomes were better in terms of growth than otherwise; this has to be established separately. But with all due respect to the Darwinian fallacy, there is a presumption that the policies helped more than hindered the emergence of internationally competitive industries. This is more plausible than saying either that the policies had no effect — perhaps because

21. See Wade, *Governing the Market.*

promotion policies for one industry were canceled out by promotion policies for others — or that they braked what would otherwise have been still faster growth.

The challenge, then, is to find ways of making the ideas of leadership and followership more compatible with economic theory. Somehow we must become clearer about the power and influence dimension of government policies. The same type of policy instrument will have different resource effects according to the wider field of power between government and business. For example, in some kinds of polities government policies create rents but little rent-seeking behavior occurs, for reasons having to do with this wider field of power. If every official draws a gun and shoots every rent seeker, there may be much allocation of rents without rent-seeking behavior. But those parts of economics that embrace the assumption that perfect competition constitutes the optimal institutional arrangement for resource allocation are badly equipped to deal with power. There is, however, the subdiscipline of industrial organization theory, which deals with the inner workings of markets, firms, and industries, though not much with governments. This subdiscipline has little to do with the neoclassical conception of perfect competition. Future work on the role of government in industrialization should aim to integrate the political science literature on power with the economics literature on industrial organization.

ANNALS, *AAPSS*, **505**, September 1989

Growth and Equity via Austerity and Competitiveness

By FERNANDO FAJNZYLBER

ABSTRACT: In the first section of this article, a comparative analysis is undertaken of Latin America and semi-industrialized countries in other areas of the world. Attention is drawn to the specific features of Latin America as regards its lack of a strong predisposition toward the incorporation of technological progress and its dubious achievements in relation to growth, equity, and competitiveness. In the second section, a similar type of comparative analysis is applied to the leading countries. Finally, some reflections are presented with regard to directions and actions in Latin America and in the north that could contribute to confronting what in the first section is defined as the challenge of Latin America, that is, to approaching the until now empty box wherein growth converges with equity.

Fernando Fajnzylber is a Chilean engineer-economist. He studied at the School of Engineers of the University of Chile and the Centre d'études des programmes économiques in Paris, France. At present, he is chief of the joint Industry and Technology Division of the U.N. Economic Commission for Latin America and the Caribbean and the U.N. Industrial Development Organization. He has written several books and articles on industrialization and international economy, including La industrialización trunca en América Latina *(1983) and* Industrialización en América Latina: De la "caja negra" al "casillero vacío" *(1989).*

P AST experience seems to indicate that one of the most notable features of economic development is the combination of the know-how of the more advanced societies with economic and social innovations allowing for its adaptation to the specific shortcomings and potentials of the less developed countries. This accounts for the generally accepted fact that the changes that are taking place involve a variety of different essential components, directions, and institutions, as a reflection of this combination of know-how and innovation.

In the mid-1970s, when the rate of increase in the industrialized countries' productivity started to decline, the subject of the incorporation of technical progress and its impact on productivity and growth once again began to come to the fore in both political and academic circles. The way in which the classical and neoclassical schools of thought were dealing with this subject began to be viewed with dissatisfaction in various quarters. These criticisms, which were chiefly based on the ideas of Schumpeter, underscored the complexity of this phenomenon, its dynamic and unbalanced nature, and its connection with the social-institutional environment.[1]

Emphasis was placed on the fact that the stepped-up efforts and increased investments that were devoted to promoting the incorporation of technological progress — a higher ratio of research and development expenditure to gross national product and investment in the 1980s in the countries of the Organization for Economic Cooperation and Development (OECD) — had had little impact on productivity. This is the "productivity paradox" that Professor R. Solow summed up in the following terms: "We see computers everywhere except in the economic statistics."[2]

Finally, a systematic analysis was undertaken of the new types of relationships and institutional modalities linking science and technology in the 1980s, and government and business made a greater effort both to support and to base their actions on the trends that had been identified.[3] In short, the importance of this subject was recognized, but some degree of uncertainty was still felt as to how to bring about technological changes in a way that would be in keeping with economic policy objectives.

In the 1980s, the achievement of a competitive position at the international level became a prime objective, chiefly in response to the growing presence in international markets of Japan and its Southeast Asian disciples. The reorganization of production and the incorporation of technological progress came to be regarded as a more and more pressing issue in both the developed and developing countries, re-

1. Nathan Rosenberg, "The Impact of Technological Innovation: A Historical View," in *The Positive Sum Strategy*, ed. Ralph Landau and Nathan Rosenberg (Washington, DC: National Academy Press, 1986), p. 20; idem, *Perspectives on Technology* (New York: Cambridge University Press, 1976); idem, *Inside the Black Box: Technology and Economics* (New York: Cambridge University Press, 1982); C. Freeman, J. Clark, and L. Soete, *Unemployment and Technical Innovation: A Study of Long Waves and Economic Development* (London: Frances Pinter, 1982).

2. See "Aims and Organization of an International Seminar on Sciences Technology and Economic Growth" (Seminar to be held in Paris, June 1989) (Programme of Work of the Committee for Scientific and Technological Policy, Organization for Economic Cooperation and Development [OECD], 1988).

3. C. Freeman, *The Future of Information and Communication Technologies: Implications for Decision-Makers*, LGCFAM (Brighton: University of Sussex, Science Policy Research Unit, Feb. 1987); F. Chesney, "Technical Co-operation Agreements between Independent Firms: Novel Issues for Economic Analysis and the Formulation of National Technological Policies," *DSTI Review*, no. 4, in press. See "National Programmes to Promote Industrial Diffusion of New Technologies" (Synthesis report, OECD, 1987).

gardless of whether they had market or centrally planned economies.

The international market is not only an arena in which various business enterprises compete with one another; it is also a setting for encounters between different production systems, institutional schemes, and social organizations. In these encounters, business enterprises figure prominently but are nonetheless only one component of a network that links them with the educational system, the technological infrastructure, management-labor relations, the relationships between the public and private sectors, and the financial system.

In the first section of this article, a comparative analysis is undertaken of Latin America and semi-industrialized countries in other areas of the world. Attention is drawn to the specific features of Latin America as regards its lack of a strong predisposition toward the incorporation of technological progress and its dubious achievements in relation to growth, equity, and competitiveness. In the second section, a similar type of comparative analysis is applied to the leading countries. Finally, some reflections are presented with regard to directions and actions in Latin America and in the north that could contribute to confronting what in the first section is defined as the challenge of Latin America, that is, to approaching the until now empty box wherein growth converges with equity.

CHARACTERISTICS SPECIFIC
TO LATIN AMERICA:
FROM THE EMPTY BOX
TO THE BLACK BOX

Under an exceptionally wide range of circumstances, the governments of Latin America, like those in the rest of the world, regard growth and equity as being among their chief development objectives. To what extent have the countries of the region achieved either or both of these objectives in the course of their development?

For the purposes of this discussion, the growth rate of the advanced countries during the past two decades — 2.4 percent annually of per capita gross domestic product (GDP) between 1965 and 1985 — will be taken as a standard of growth, and equity will be defined in terms of the ratio between the incomes of the bottom 40 percent and the top 10 percent of the population on the income scale. In the advanced countries during the late 1970s and early 1980s, this ratio averaged 0.8, that is, the bottom 40 percent of the population in this respect had an income equivalent to 80 percent of that of the top 10 percent.

For our purposes here, the dividing line between the most equitable and least equitable countries in Latin America will be drawn on the basis of this ratio, but at a level of 0.4. This is tantamount to setting an equity target equivalent to half of that existing, on average, in the industrialized countries. If we cross-reference these two variables — growth and equity — the resulting matrix contains an empty box, which would correspond to countries having both a faster growth rate than that of the advanced countries and a higher level of equity, in terms of the reduced scale of one-half the average level of the developed countries. This empty box represents a key question in terms of the subjects under discussion here.

Approximately 66 percent of the regional GDP is generated by countries that could be described as having fast growth rates but that also suffer from disarticulation — Brazil, Colombia, the Dominican Republic, Ecuador, Mexico, Panama, and Paraguay; 13 percent of the regional GDP is accounted for by being integrated or articulated but is produced by countries whose economies are stagnant, namely, Argentina and Uruguay. The remaining 21 percent of this product corresponds to countries exhibiting both disarticulation and stagnation.

As regards the black box, the supposition is that it could only be filled by countries whose development process had moved forward. Another sort of interpretation, which might, perhaps, be more reassuring, would be to assume that there is a trade-off between growth and equity and that, accordingly, in order for a country to move up into this empty box, it would have to raise its level of development. Under this assumption, the problem of the empty box would eventually be resolved with the passage of time. Nevertheless, there are quite a few developing and semi-industrialized countries in other parts of the world that exhibit a combination of the levels of growth and equity that represent the empty box in the case of Latin America: China, Sri Lanka, Indonesia, Egypt, Thailand, Hungary, Portugal, Yugoslavia, South Korea, Israel, Hong Kong, and Spain. Indeed, these countries account for a total of 73 percent of the GDP and 58 percent of the population of the developing countries that were taken into consideration.[4]

4. Countries under consideration are those for which the World Bank gives information on growth and income distribution. The gross national product and the population of that group reaches 80 percent of the total developing countries, Latin American countries excluded. Taiwan accomplished both aims but is not included in the World Bank figures. China — for which the World Bank gives no information on income distribution — is included because, as indicated in other sources, distribution would be, at least, more favorable than that of India. See L. Emmerij, ed., *Development Policies and the Crisis of the 1980's* (Paris: OECD, 1987), pt. 4, "Asian Countries."

This group of non-Latin American countries ranges over the entire spectrum in terms of inward- and outward-oriented nations. The same degree of diversity is to be observed with respect to the relative significance of the public sector as well. The share of GDP accounted for by agriculture is comparable in the two groups of countries, as is the level of the per capita product. Some of these countries — Indonesia, Thailand, China, and Egypt — are similar to Latin America in that their position in international markets is based on their natural resources. The rest — South Korea, Spain, Hungary, Israel, Portugal, and Yugoslavia — because they do not have a large amount of natural resources upon which to draw, have had no alternative but to attempt to secure a place for themselves in the international market by means of industrialization.

*Latin America versus
growth-with-equity
industrializing countries*

As a first step in arriving at an understanding of the process of incorporating technological progress, which goes along with changes in agricultural activity, industrialization, and the establishment of a position in the international market, the comparative analysis that follows will not include certain countries in other parts of the world. These countries are the following growth-with-equity industrializing countries (GEICs): Egypt, Indonesia, and Sri Lanka, which have a low level of industrialization, this being defined as under 20 percent; Hong Kong, which lacks a significant agricultural sector; and Israel, whose geopolitical position is highly unusual. The remaining group of countries will be referred to as GEICs.

The unsatisfactory nature of the economic performance of Latin America and the sharp contrast between it and that of latecomers in other regions of the world provide the basis for this concept of GEICs. The idea of newly industrializing countries, on the other hand, arose in the 1970s as a reflection of the growing concern with which the OECD countries viewed the erosion of their competitive position in the international market.

Both groups of countries — Latin America and the GEICs — include a wide range of situations. It nonetheless appears to be possible to identify various types of significant contrasts in addition to those relating to growth and equity that were mentioned earlier, namely, a growth rate of 1.3 percent of per capita GDP for the period 1965-86 and a ratio of 0.3 between the bottom 40 percent and top 10 percent of the population in terms of income for Latin America versus a growth rate of 4.0 percent and an equity index of 0.62 for the GEICs.

The major differences, from both a theoretical and an empirical standpoint,[5] between the two are the following:

1. In terms of austerity, Latin America exhibits a markedly lower domestic saving effort. For the years 1984-86, gross domestic saving as a proportion of gross national product was an average of 16 percent, versus 28 percent. Latin America also had higher levels of external borrowing and direct foreign investment. As a proportion

5. The hypotheses that the two samples are similar has been rejected, for almost all variables, with a probability higher than 95 percent. Only for the difference in the export coefficient, the lower limit is 75 percent. For agricultural share in GDP and for GDP per capita, the two samples are similar, as shown by a T test. See R.G.D. Steel and J. H. Torrie, *Principles and Procedures of Statistics*, 2d ed. (New York: McGraw-Hill, 1980).

of GDP, Latin American debt was 79 percent, versus 38 percent, and its direct investment was 10.9 percent of GDP, versus the GEICs' 3.0 percent.

2. The growth rate of the population is higher in Latin America. In 1965-86, the rate was 2.5 percent, versus 1.4 percent.

3. The share of the GDP accounted for by the manufacturing sector is lower in Latin America — 19.4 percent in 1986, versus 33.1 percent — even though the share accounted for by the agricultural sector is similar in the two groups.

4. The relative significance of the industrial sectors that typically play an important role in technological progress — the chemical and the metal manufactures and machinery industries — is considerably less in Latin America than in the GEICs: 16.9 percent in 1985, versus 31.4 percent.

5. The performance of the industrial sector during the 1980s has been much poorer in Latin America. If 1980 = 100, then the gross value of industrial output yielded a coefficient of 98.6 in 1986 for Latin America and 127.0 for the GEICs. This is particularly significant in view of the fact that this was a period during which the technological modernization of industry proceeded at a very rapid pace at the international level.

6. Latin America's coefficient of exports of manufactures was lower — 10 percent in 1985, versus 18 percent — as was its overall coefficient for total goods and services: 21 percent versus 28 percent.

7. The level of international competitiveness, as measured by the quotient between exports and imports of manufactures, was lower in Latin America: 0.3 in 1986, versus 0.8.

In sum, as compared to the GEICs, Latin America's economy is organized in such a way that it is less equitable, shows less financial restraint, has a lower level of domestic savings, and, despite the greater contribution by external savings, is therefore less dynamic. This, in turn, inhibits the incorporation of technological progress — which is influenced by all the foregoing differences — and international competitiveness.

The black box of technological progress

As a first step in exploring the reasons why this empty box exists, it may be interesting to compare the relative position of Latin America in the international economy in various different spheres of economic activity. Such a comparison clearly brings out a fact that may provide an initial and basic research clue and that will be interpreted in these terms throughout the rest of this article: the region makes a greater contribution in terms of population than in terms of any other indicator of economic activity. More precisely, there appears to be a clear tendency for the region's share to decline as one moves up the list of indicators relating to activities with an increasing level of intellectual value added. The region's share is 8.0 percent in terms of population, 7.0 percent in terms of gross domestic product, and 6.0 percent with respect to manufacturing output. Its share plunges to 3.0 percent in the capital-goods subsector within industry and is only 2.4 percent as regards the regional share of engineers and scientists. If we then look at manufactured exports or at the resources available to these engineers and scientists as they go about their work, the region's share drops to 1.8 percent while, finally, in relation to the presence of scientific writers — making full allowance

for the unreliability of this type of indicator — Latin America accounts for just slightly more than 1.0 percent.

Rent-seeking societies: Black box and empty box

In those societies having an abundant natural resource base, which generally gives rise to a heavy concentration of property in either the private or public sector, the business leadership tends to rely on the use of profits from these natural resources. There may also be a tendency for class-based societies and wealth-oriented states to form.

Given the existence of a certain tendency toward mimicry within society — a tendency for the value expressed by the leaders to spread and be imitated throughout society — in societies where the aforementioned type of leadership prevails, this rent-seeking worldview may tend to penetrate into and spread through various spheres of the public sector, the private sector, and a wide range of institutions that help them to function, such as political parties, the armed forces, trade and labor unions, professional associations, and the bureaucracy. The specific manifestations of this dissemination of rent-seeking values — parochialism, emphasis on the short term, an aversion to risk and to technological innovation, and stress on the usefulness to the individual of given activities rather than institutional roles — seen at various levels and in various types of behavior fall outside the scope of this article; nonetheless, this is a subject that warrants further investigation, particularly with respect to Latin America, where this type of situation would appear to be of greater significance than had previously been thought. The process of urbanization, industrialization, and institutional modernization may have caused the significance of what might be referred to as a latent rent-seeking mentality to be underestimated.

The pathology and les trente glorieuses

It is quite clear to historians that in order to understand a region like Latin America it is absolutely essential to know about more than just Latin America. While this may seem to be a fairly obvious fact, it has sometimes been ignored by the methodological approaches taken to the subject of development in the region.

The acknowledgment of this shortcoming, which is associated with what we have called the empty box, is entirely compatible with a recognition of the sweeping changes that have taken place in the Latin American economy and society during the past thirty years. This period is what A. Hirschman has referred to as *les trente glorieuses* of Latin America.[6] During this period — 1950-81 — the product grew fivefold, the population grew from 155 million to nearly 400 million, and a very rapid urbanization process took place. As a result of this process, a number of the countries in the region that had more than half of their population in agriculture in 1950 saw this proportion drop to between one-fourth and one-third. In these countries, education and health services improved significantly, and institutions were created that helped to promote the economic, social, political, and cultural integration of the region. Furthermore, the foundations were laid for technological development in major areas linked to agriculture, public works, and

6. A. Hirschman, "The Political Economy of Latin American Development: Seven Exercises in Retrospection" (Paper delivered at the International Congress of the Latin American Studies Association, Boston, Oct. 1986).

energy, and the life expectancy rose significantly in all the countries of the region.

The world has grown and changed in economic, social, political, and cultural terms since the end of World War II at a pace without precedent in human history. Many of these changes have taken place in Latin America as well. An awareness of the positive changes that have occurred in the region should not, however, be seen as a cause for the complacency often displayed by countries that have played a leadership role at the international level for a number of decades, as will be discussed in the following section.

THE LEADING COUNTRIES: INSTITUTIONAL PLURALISM AND THE BLACK BOX

Why should we look at the situation of the industrialized countries? We must, if only for the following reasons. First, the leading countries — the United States, Japan, and the Federal Republic of Germany (FRG) — determine the economic and technological environment in which Latin America and the GEICs operate. Second, because these countries have resolved the syndrome of the black box and the empty box through various institutional and political instruments, their experience constitutes a necessary, though in itself insufficient, source of inspiration for regional analysis. Third, each one of them embodies a certain model of development that exercises a cultural influence on countries in neighboring regions: Japan on Asia, the FRG on Europe, and the United States on the rest of the world but particularly on Latin America. The GEICs are to be found in Asia and Europe. Fourth, it would be useful to verify whether the relationships identified in the preceding section exist in the industrialized countries.

Different approaches to
the black-box syndrome?

Taken together, the population of these three countries represents approximately 9 percent of the world total and is equal to that of Latin America. At the same time, however, these three countries account for almost half of the resources allocated to research and development worldwide and almost three-quarters of the resources that the OECD countries earmark for this purpose. In other words, the per capita availability of resources for research and development in these countries is approximately five times the world average.

Roughly 40 percent of the world's economic and industrial activity takes place in these countries. The main reason for comparing and contrasting the situation of these countries and evaluating them together is that, for the reasons mentioned before, the performance of these countries shapes the profile and determines the main features of the world industrial system. Current strains in their trading relations aside, to a large extent these three countries define the type of product, process, manufacturing techniques, institutional arrangements, and accessibility to which other countries could aspire as they develop their expertise in the various industrial sectors.

A number of significant differences exist between the United States, on one hand, and Japan and West Germany, on the other. It is well known, for example, that the United States has a very high density of scientific production in relation to its population and in comparison with that of the other two countries. In strong contrast with this solid base of scientific production, however, the relative strength of Japan and West Germany in the industrial sector is much greater than that of the United States. Taken together, the manufacturing output of Japan and West Germany is already almost 20 percent greater than that of the United States, even though the combined population of these two countries is 20 percent less.

While Japan and West Germany demonstrate a notable aptitude for transforming knowledge into highly competitive industrial production, the United States exhibits a relative disproportion between its available knowledge base and its relatively weak industrial performance. This is due, in some measure, to the asymmetry in defense expenditure, an issue to which further reference will be made later. This same situation illustrates a particular characteristic of Japan, namely, its high density of engineers and scientists. If we were to examine the relative density of lawyers, the United States would lead the pack, with 279 per 100,000 inhabitants as against 77 in the FRG and 11 in Japan.[7]

The possession of
natural resources —
a key factor

Some of the main differences in the participation of the various countries in international trade are as follows. First of all, there is a sharp contrast between, on one hand, Japan and West Germany, whose deficit in all sectors of natural resources is a structural characteristic indicative of a fragile base in this area, and, on the other hand, the situation of the United States, which, at least in the agricultural sector, posts a large and, up to the early 1980s, growing surplus. For Japan and West Germany there is no way to obtain the resources needed to acquire the natural resources that they lack other than achieving solid participation in the world manufac-

7. See *Economist*, 22 Aug. 1987.

turing trade. In contrast, the generous endowment of resources and the continental scale of the United States lead it to conceive of international trade as a strictly complementary and marginal element. Moreover, in the case of a continental economy such as that of the United States, the concern for establishing priorities among the sectors is largely irrelevant, and a neutral nonselective approach is adopted toward the various sectors. There is a perception in that country — accentuated by the preeminent position it has enjoyed over the past forty years — that its principal market is the domestic one and that while the performance of the various sectors may vary over time, at least up to the late 1970s its overall situation appeared to be one of almost absolute invulnerability. Various indications exist in the economic, political, and academic fields that confirm the perception of an approach that is centered mainly on the domestic situation.[8]

The emergence of different national models

It would be useful to compare the relationships that exist between, on one hand, the objectives of growth and equity and, on the other, two of the factors that have been given special attention: the degree of inter-

8. W. Branson, H. Giersch, and P. Peterson, "Trends in United States International Trade and Investment since World War II," in *The American Economy in Transition,* ed. Martin Feldstein (Chicago: University of Chicago Press, 1980), pp. 183-274; George C. Lodge, *The New American Ideology* (New York: New York University Press, 1987); John Zysman and Laura Tyson, eds., *American Industry in International Competition: Government Policies and Corporate Strategies* (Ithaca, NY: Cornell University Press, 1983); Oxford Analytica, *America in Perspective* (Boston: Houghton Mifflin, 1986); George C. Lodge and Ezra Vogel, eds., *Ideology and National Competitiveness: An Analysis of Nine Countries* (Boston: Harvard Business School, 1987).

national competitiveness of the industrial sector and the pattern of consumption.

If one accepts the idea that the shared objectives of the various countries in question are growth and equity, it will be seen that the Japanese model is superior to the models of the FRG and the United States, respectively, and that the model of the FRG is superior to that of the United States. The meaning of "superiority" corresponds to greater success in the achievement of both objectives. The variables and indicators are identical to those considered in the earlier section entitled "Characteristics Specific to Latin America."

This comparison suggests that there is no trade-off between the two objectives. The absence of a trade-off runs counter to one of the basic premises of conventional wisdom on these matters. This convergence is associated, however, with the presence of certain patterns of behavior and international competitiveness: the superiority of Japan over the other two countries as regards growth and equity is accompanied by greater austerity and international competitiveness, which suggests that — in keeping with the reasoning put forward in the previous section — austerity and competitiveness actually promote the convergence of the two objectives. With regard to competitiveness, one notes that the absence of natural resources has a positive impact on the greater competitiveness of the industrial sector, which in turn helps to promote growth and equity.

While sporadic growth may occur in a context of inequity and overconsumption, solid growth would seem to require simultaneously — this is the message of this model — competitiveness and austerity, a combination that is closely related to equity.

The case of the FRG represents a balance between, on one hand, a high degree of opening up to international trade, higher than that of Japan and the United States, and on the other, a high level of domestic social concertation, accompanied, moreover, by a role of the state in economic matters that is markedly greater than in the other two cases.

The U.S-Japanese contrast marks the basic difference not between different currents of macroeconomic thought but rather between a prosperous country that looks down on the world from its position of preeminence and a powerful challenger, with a history not exempt from trauma and with the will to realize its perceived destiny. The difference is between a continental economy whose language, currency, and life-style have since World War II become worldwide references, and a small island territory of which the principal asset is its population governed by a leadership whose domestic legitimacy is linked to the recovery of national dignity, one of whose manifestations has been the conquest of the international markets.

The precarious position of
the major powers in world
trade in manufactures

If we examine closely the relationship between defense expenditure — as a percentage of GDP — and international competitiveness in the industrial sector — surplus or deficit in the manufacturing sector in relation to manufacturing output — we would see that there is an inverse relationship with the USSR, China, the United States, and England at one extreme, and the FRG and Japan on the other, and France, Sweden, and Italy occupying the intermediate positions. Contrary to conventional wisdom, the multiplier effect of defense spending on international industrial competitiveness would be negative.

This last fact — which is part of an unresolved controversy about the impact of research and technological development in the military sector as a collateral effect for the industrial sector — would be a further argument in support of the idea that these are spheres in which, at least for given periods, low levels of international competitiveness in tradable goods may coexist with extremely high levels of competitiveness in the military sphere. The fact that these are activities whose challenges, procedures, periods, and forms of organization differ radically may have some influence on this.

In the military sphere, where it is necessary to define objectives and goals rather than to determine time frames, economic restrictions play a considerably less important role. The possibility of long-term programming, which exists in this sphere, does not exist in the area of industrial trade, in which the most important element is flexibility and the capacity to adapt rapidly to changing trends in international trade. Moreover, the intensification of competition in the field of industrial trade does not occur at the same rate and over the same periods as in the military sphere. The replacement of successive generations of products and the differentiation within each generation is, fortunately, not determined by the test of its performance. The military sphere is able to attract the most noted talents in science and technology, by offering them conditions of tranquility, resources, and the absence of demands for immediate results over short periods of time, quite apart from the fact that remuneration in this sphere is not subject to the implacable dynamic of the market.

All of these factors combine to create a situation in which a group of countries that have channeled substantial resources into the military sphere exhibit great precariousness in their international industrial competitiveness with respect to conventional products, while another group, which channels virtually no resources into military spending, constitutes the leaders in industrial competitiveness with respect to these products. In the case of some Latin American countries, high defense expenditures are accompanied by low international competitiveness in the industrial sector and no local expenditure on research and technological development in related areas. There, the hypothetical positive long-term multiplier effect that defense expenditure would generate on the industrial sector does not materialize.

FINAL REFLECTIONS

The following are the most salient lessons that would seem to emanate from this exploratory exercise.

First, the solidity of international participation is firmly linked to the capacity of the countries to add intellectual value to their resource endowment. It seems illusory to imagine a solid position in international markets without the participating countries' incorporating technological progress into those resources. The fact of having natural resources does not imply that a country must relinquish the revenue that they can produce, but it would seem to be vital that that revenue be utilized to transform and modernize the agricultural sector and strengthen the development of an industrial sector with a growing level of exposure and competitiveness in international markets.

Second, the widespread idea that there is a trade-off between growth and equity is not supported by the empirical evidence of a broad, varied range of national situations. It is true that, within Latin America, these two objectives have not converged and that

countries with greater equity have suffered stagnation and countries with greater dynamism do not manifest equity. This parochial view of the relationship between both objectives, however, is overcome when the Latin American pattern is contrasted with the patterns prevailing in distinct regions, with different socioeconomic systems and different levels of development.

Third, the opening of the black box of technological progress is a task that transcends the industrial and business world and forms part of a social attitude vis-à-vis the incorporation of technological progress. This new attitude of social appreciation of creativity, that is, the pursuit of formulas that respond to internal deficiencies and potentialities, assumes a modification of the leadership from which flow the values and orientations that are diffused through society as a whole. It is difficult to establish a compatibility between a leadership in which rent-seeking mentality has a weight aside from having a private or public character, and a diffusion throughout society of values in which the internal deficiencies and potentialities are converted into a conductor axis for socioeconomic transformation.

Fourth, the economic, social, political, and cultural transformation required in Latin America, whose center of gravity is internal effort, requires complementary economic backing.

If the countries with a surplus, that is, those that have the possibility of channeling resources beyond their borders — chiefly Japan and West Germany — ignore the challenge that the situation of the less developed countries represents and continue, as they have done in recent years, to concentrate their attention on the possibility of resolving the imbalances that surface between them, fundamentally in relation to the external and fiscal-deficit situation of the United States, it may very well be that they miss some formula for civilized coexistence between themselves. Nevertheless, they end up trying to ignore the growing drama that is spreading throughout the Southern Hemisphere, with well-known and implied exceptions, some of which have been discussed here.

Hence certain requirements fall into line. In the first place, the principal debtor nation, the United States, should, within the range of possibility, adopt necessary measures to adapt its life-style. In the second place, it is necessary that countries having a surplus, instead of channeling resources in order to facilitate the maintenance of the consumption pattern in the United States, gear resources precisely toward the countries of the south. In the third place, it would be vital that in those countries socioeconomic transformations be generated endogenously; that would permit the absorption of those resources to produce innovations in the direction of the development pattern.

The fifth lesson is that the sequence that seems to surface from the study of comparative experiences is the following: equity, austerity, growth, and competitiveness. In Latin America it has become increasingly delicate to continue to defer the subject of equity, although this would imply attending to unpleasant subjects from the past that appear to have withered discreetly with the advent of modernity.

Finally, an important factor in the generation of resources in the north and the modalities of their utilization in the south is the cutback in arms spending. In the north, there is a clear inverse relationship between industrial competitiveness and the military effort, which suggests that a reduction of the latter would favor the materialization of the much-desired recovery of trade and international financial equilibriums.

ANNALS, *AAPSS,* **505,** September 1989

Development Strategies and the Global Factory

By GARY GEREFFI

ABSTRACT: It has become commonplace to contrast the newly industrializing countries (NICs) in Latin America and East Asia as having followed inward-oriented and outward-oriented development strategies, respectively. These are not mutually exclusive alternatives, however. They are more appropriately seen as historically interacting approaches, with the NICs in both regions moving toward mixed strategies in the 1970s and 1980s. In particular, the development of second-stage import-substitution industries has allowed the Latin American and East Asian NICs to meet a variety of domestic development objectives and ultimately to enhance the flexibility of their export structures. The NICs today are pivotal actors in a global manufacturing system with increasingly complex product networks and an unprecedented degree of geographical specialization. This has led to greater heterogeneity in the export profiles of the NICs within each region. The new patterns of export specialization are based on distinctive industrial structures at the national level and pose special issues for industrial policy and the future internationalization of each NIC.

Gary Gereffi, associate professor in the Sociology Department at Duke University, received his B.A. degree from the University of Notre Dame and M.A. and Ph.D. degrees from Yale University. He has served as a consultant to the United Nations Centre on Transnational Corporations and organizations concerned with essential drug programs in developing nations. He is the author of The Pharmaceutical Industry and Dependency in the Third World *(1983) and coeditor, with the late Donald Wyman, of* Manufactured Miracles: Paths of Industrialization in Latin America and East Asia *(forthcoming).*

C ONVENTIONAL economic wisdom has it that the newly industrializing countries (NICs) in the world economy have followed one of two alternative development strategies: an inward-oriented path of development pursued by relatively large, resource-rich economies in which industrial production is geared mainly to the needs of a sizable domestic market; and an outward-oriented approach adopted by smaller, resource-poor nations that depend on global markets to stimulate the rapid growth of their manufactured exports. These contrasting development strategies are said to typify the experience of the two most prominent regional clusters of NICs: the three large Latin American countries — Argentina, Brazil, and Mexico — and the four tigers in East Asia — Taiwan, South Korea, Hong Kong, and Singapore — respectively.[1]

Even though this descriptive characterization is subject to a number of refinements, a very clear evaluative judgment often accompanies recent discussions of development strategies in the NICs. The World Bank's widely cited *World Development Report* for 1987 claims that "the economic performance of the outward-oriented economies has been broadly superior to that of the inward-oriented economies in almost all respects." The obvious implication is that policy reforms aimed at a greater outward orientation would lead to substantial improvements in exports, economic growth, and employment in countries that earlier had applied inward-oriented policies.[2]

The East Asian NICs thus are put forward as a model to be emulated by the rest of the developing world. Conversely, the current woes of the Latin American NICs are treated as the legacy of ill-conceived and inappropriate economic policies in the past.

This simplified view of the development trajectories and policy choices of the Latin American and East Asian NICs is profoundly misleading. It glosses over the many unique historical and geopolitical features of East Asian development that make it hazardous at best to advocate that this model be transferred to other regions of the world.[3] In addition, it fosters two general sources of bias that hinder our understanding of contemporary development in the NICs.

First, development strategy is used as a polarizing and static concept. The stereotypes of inward and outward orientation freeze history by highlighting regional differences when they were at their sharpest — Latin America's import-substituting industrialization (ISI) in the 1950s and 1960s versus East Asia's export-oriented industrialization (EOI) in the 1960s and early 1970s — while ignoring the subsequent interplay between inward- and outward-oriented development strategies that in fact has been essential to the economic dynamism of the NICs in each region. The convergence of the Latin American and East Asian NICs toward mixed strategies of ISI and EOI in the 1970s and

1. Other countries that have pursued inward-oriented development strategies in the postwar period include some South Asian nations, in particular India, as well as the European socialist countries led by the Soviet Union.

2. World Bank, *World Development Report 1987* (New York: Oxford University Press, 1987), p. 85.

Also see Bela Balassa, *The Newly Industrializing Countries in the World Economy* (Elmsford, NY: Pergamon Press, 1981), pp. 1-26; Bela Balassa et al., *Toward Renewed Economic Growth in Latin America* (Washington, DC: Institute of International Economics, 1986).

3. This topic is handled nicely in Laurence Whitehead, "Tigers in Latin America?" this issue of *The Annals* of the American Academy of Political and Social Science.

1980s is attributable to inherent limitations within each strategy, thus making an exclusive reliance on either approach unsustainable in the long run.

Second, the infatuation with regional contrasts in development strategies diverts our attention from a universal phenomenon, the globalization of production, which has reshaped the roles of the NICs in the world economy during the last two decades. The global factory has led to new patterns of export specialization that are an outgrowth of distinctive industrial structures and social forces in each of the NICs. This process is beginning to undermine the presumed internal coherence of the Latin American and East Asian development models and ultimately calls for a recasting of development theory.

The remainder of this article will look into both sets of issues.

DEVELOPMENT STRATEGIES RECONSIDERED

Development strategies are sets of government policies that define and mediate a country's relationship to the global economy. They also affect the domestic allocation of resources among industries and distinct social groups and thus embody national priorities regarding economic growth and equity. It is important to distinguish between development strategies, which are political decisions and plans, and development patterns, which are economic outcomes that may or may not have been pursued in a strategic way by national elites. The first part of this article will discuss strategies, while the latter two parts focus on new patterns of global production and export specialization.

Economic policymaking in the NICs, as in capitalist societies more generally, tends to be pragmatic and incremental, respond-

ing to immediate crises and short-term dilemmas rather than to long-range plans and comprehensive schemes for change. This was true in the Latin American and East Asian NICs, where the domestic policies associated with import substitution and export promotion frequently were short-term defensive tactics to deal with acute problems like foreign exchange shortages or inflation.[4] Over time, related incremental decisions often became established as longer-term development strategies.

Neither inward-oriented nor outward-oriented development strategies are economic panaceas, however. Both are susceptible to systemic constraints or vulnerabilities such as recurring balance-of-payments problems or the disruption of key trading relationships.[5] In order to understand how the NICs have adapted or switched development strategies in response to these problems, it is necessary to correct some common misconceptions in the literature about industrial transformation in these nations.

First, it is a mistake to think of inward-oriented and outward-oriented development strategies as mutually exclusive alternatives. Every nation, with the exception of Britain at the time of the Industrial Revolution, went through an initial stage of ISI in which protection was extended to incip-

4. See Tun-jen Cheng, "Political Regimes and Development Strategies: Korea and Taiwan," in *Manufactured Miracles: Paths of Industrialization in Latin America and East Asia,* ed. Gary Gereffi and Donald Wyman (Princeton, NJ: Princeton University Press, forthcoming); Robert R. Kaufman, "How Societies Change Development Models or Keep Them: Reflections on the Latin American Experience in the 1930s and the Post-War World," in ibid.

5. The main limitations of both import-substituting and export-oriented development strategies in the NICs are outlined in Gary Gereffi, "International Economics and Domestic Policies," in *Economy and Society: State of the Art,* ed. Alberto Martinelli and Neil Smelser (Newbury Park, CA: Sage, forthcoming).

ient manufacturing industries producing for domestic markets.[6] Furthermore, each of the NICs subsequently has pursued a combination of both advanced ISI and different types of EOI in order to avoid the inherent limitations of an exclusive reliance on domestic or external markets and also to facilitate the industrial diversification and upgrading that are required for these nations to remain competitive in the world economy. Rather than being mutually exclusive alternatives, the ISI and EOI development paths in fact have been complementary and interactive.[7]

Second, the divergence between inward-oriented and outward-oriented development strategies in the Latin American and East Asian NICs in the 1960s masks a significant convergence in their economic trajectories during the past two decades. The countries in both regions established or expanded second-stage ISI industries to meet a variety of domestic development objectives and ultimately to enhance the flexibility of their export structures.[8]

In the 1970s, South Korea and Taiwan launched major "Heavy and Chemical In-

dustrialization" programs with a focus on steel, machinery, automobiles, shipbuilding, and petrochemicals. This was justified in large part by national security concerns prompted by the United States' political rapprochement with China and the U.S. withdrawal from Vietnam, as well as import-substitution considerations.[9] Singapore used its links with multinational corporations also to push into capital-intensive sectors like oil refining, petrochemicals, telecommunications equipment, office and industrial machinery, and electronics in the 1970s.

These shifts toward heavier industries in the East Asian NICs, which paralleled similar kinds of investments in the Latin American NICs a decade or two earlier, were criticized on comparative-advantage grounds since they were energy intensive and required the massive importation of natural resources not found in the region. As we will see later in this article, however, they laid the groundwork for a far more diversified range of manufactured exports by the East Asian NICs in the 1980s.

The Latin American NICs also moved toward a strategy of export diversification in the 1980s, but from the opposite direction. Argentina, Brazil, and Mexico have strong natural-resource bases, which led them to rely heavily on commodity exports or natural-resource-based manufactured exports in the 1950s and 1960s. By the late 1970s and 1980s, however, the Latin American NICs succeeded in exporting a much broader array of manufactured products.

In Mexico, sharp currency devaluations led to a spectacular increase of labor-intensive manufactured exports from the *maquiladora* ("bonded-processing") industries located along the U.S. border. In

---

6. Even Hong Kong, the most laissez-faire of the NICs, benefited from a period of disguised ISI on the Chinese mainland. Refugees to Hong Kong from the mainland included a significant segment of the Shanghai capitalist class and a huge supply of politically unorganized labor, and they brought with them technical know-how, skills, and even machinery. See Stephan Haggard and Tun-jen Cheng, "State and Foreign Capital in the East Asian NICs," in *The Political Economy of the New Asian Industrialism*, ed. Frederic C. Deyo (Ithaca, NY: Cornell University Press, 1987), pp. 106-10.

7. This point is amply documented in Gereffi and Wyman, eds., *Manufactured Miracles*.

8. See Gary Gereffi and Donald Wyman, "Determinants of Development Strategies in Latin America and East Asia," in *Pacific Dynamics: The International Politics of Industrial Change*, ed. Stephan Haggard and Chung-in Moon (Boulder, CO: Westview Press, 1989).

9. Cheng, "Political Regimes and Development Strategies," in *Manufactured Miracles*, ed. Gereffi and Wyman.

Brazil and Argentina, the composition of industrial exports evolved toward more skill-intensive metalworking products initially developed for their domestic markets during the second stage of ISI, which focused on consumer durables, transport equipment, and capital goods.[10] The automobile industry, for example, in many ways the centerpiece of the import-substitution drive of the Latin American NICs since the mid-1950s, has emerged as one of the most dynamic export sectors for Mexico and Brazil in the 1980s. This industrial deepening along ISI lines in the Latin American and East Asian NICs contributed to a more diversified pattern of export growth in each region, illustrating the often unexpected synergy between inward-oriented and outward-oriented development strategies.

A third fallacy that distorts our perception of ISI and EOI in Latin America and East Asia is the tendency to view these development strategies as static and technologically backward. It is not uncommon to see portrayals of East Asia's export-led economies that still focus exclusively on the labor-intensive, low-tech industries that characterized the initial phase of EOI.[11] While the first significant wave of exports from the East Asian NICs in the late 1950s—from Hong Kong—and the 1960s did come from traditional, labor-intensive industries like textiles, apparel, and footwear that relied on low wages and an unskilled work force, there has been a very pronounced shift in the last decade

toward an upgraded, skill-intensive version of EOI.

These new export industries include higher-value-added items that employ sophisticated technology and require a more extensively developed, tightly integrated local industrial base. Products range from computers and semiconductors to televisions, videocassette recorders, sporting goods, and numerically controlled machine tools. This export dynamism in East Asia does not derive solely from introducing new products, however, but also from continuously upgrading traditional ones.

Thus in Hong Kong, Taiwan, and South Korea much of the export-oriented apparel industry has become modernized and fashion conscious, using expensive silk and synthetic materials, laser cutting machines for greater precision, and computer-assisted designs for positioning patterns on the cloth to minimize wastage. Exports of footwear, sporting goods, and even toys show a similar trend toward the more profitable, brand-named, and pricey end of the consumer spectrum.[12]

The portrayal of the Latin American NICs' original import-substituting industries as inefficient, low tech, and assembly oriented is similarly out of touch with today's reality. American automobile companies are setting up world-class engine plants in Mexico, partly to cope with the specter of Japanese competition. These gems of global production represent $250 million to $500 million per plant in high-tech investment, with a lean and well-trained local work force and efficiency levels comparable to those of similar plants in

---

10. Simon Teitel and Francisco E. Thoumi, "From Import Substitution to Exports: The Manufacturing Exports Experience of Argentina and Brazil," *Economic Development and Cultural Change,* 34(3):458 (Apr. 1986).

11. For example, Teitel and Thoumi refer to the East Asian NICs as still following "an export-oriented strategy largely based on unskilled labor-intensive industries." Ibid., p. 486.

12. A clothing manufacturer in Taiwan who exports most of his production to the United States told me proudly when I visited his plant, "We have moved up in quality from Filene's Basement to Bloomingdale's and Saks Fifth Avenue."

the United States.[13] Brazil also has developed state-of-the-art, technologically advanced, and increasingly export-oriented industries from an ISI base in fields like automobiles, computers, armaments, and assorted capital goods, while Argentina boasts of internationally competitive firms in the metallurgical and metalworking sectors that are generating a large share of the country's manufactured exports.

The composite picture presented thus far is one in which the NICs in Latin America and East Asia have come from quite different starting points in terms of size, natural resource endowments, and historical patterns of entry into the world system, yet they occupy a similar rank today as industrial leaders in the Third World. How did this disparate set of countries assume such a pivotal role on the world industrial stage? What are the prospects for their continued success in the future? To answer these questions, we need to look at a relatively recent phenomenon, the emergence of a global manufacturing system.

THE GLOBAL FACTORY AND
THE AMERICAN MARKETPLACE

Industrialization today is the result of an integrated system of global trade and production. International trade has allowed nations to specialize in industry as distinct from other sectors, in different manufacturing branches, and increasingly even in different stages in production. The growth in manufacturing since World War II has been fueled by an explosion of new products, new technologies, the removal of barriers to international trade, and the physical in-

tegration of world markets through improved transportation and communication networks. This process has led to the emergence of a global manufacturing system in which production capacity is dispersed to an unprecedented number of developing as well as industrialized countries.[14]

In today's global factory, production of a single good commonly spans several countries, with each nation performing tasks in which it has a cost advantage. Components for the Ford Escort, introduced in Europe, are made and assembled in 15 countries on three continents. Furthermore, the kind of production that is taking place in Third World nations is by no means limited to traditional manufacturing industries like textiles, clothes, and footwear. Machinery and transport equipment were the fastest-growing exports from developing countries between 1970 and 1984, with an average annual growth rate of 20 percent for that period.[15]

Trade and industrialization have reinforced each other. In 1980, 27 countries — of the 96 classified by the World Bank as low- and middle-income — exported goods worth $1 billion or more. By 1986, the number of developing countries exporting above the billion-dollar threshold nearly doubled to 49.[16] This expansion of Third World export capacity, particularly for manufactured goods, embraces such a di-

13. Harley Shaiken, "High Tech Goes Third World," *Technology Review,* 91(1):39-47 (Jan. 1988). One ultramodern plant, in the words of its director, brings together "U.S. managers, European technology, Japanese manufacturing systems, and Mexican workers." Ibid., p. 39.

14. See Nigel Harris, *The End of the Third World* (New York: Penguin Books, 1986), chap. 4; World Bank, *World Development Report 1987,* chap. 3.

15. World Bank, *World Development Report 1987,* p. 47. The overall average annual growth rate for labor-intensive manufactured exports from developing countries was 12.4 percent for the period 1970-84, compared to a growth rate of 15.1 percent for nontraditional manufactured exports, such as machinery and transport equipment, chemicals, and iron and steel.

16. World Bank, *World Development Report,* various issues. The high-income oil-exporting countries are excluded from these lists.

verse array of countries that it appears to be part of a general restructuring in the international economy.

The NICs are pivotal actors in the global manufacturing system. Table 1 presents data on the level and composition of exports by the Latin American and East Asian NICs in 1986. Taiwan tops the list with $40 billion in exports, followed by Hong Kong and South Korea with export totals of $35 billion each. Singapore and Brazil are in a second tier with $22 billion of exports each, followed by Mexico, with $16 billion, and then at a considerable distance by Argentina, with $7 billion. The three East Asian super exporters thus are well ahead of the other NICs in the level of their exporting activities.

The NICs vary considerably in the degree of their external orientation. The East Asian nations are export-led economies. Exports in the mid-1980s accounted for 35 percent to more than 50 percent of gross domestic product (GDP) in South Korea and Taiwan, respectively, and for well over 100 percent of GDP in the entrepôt city-states of Hong Kong and Singapore. This compares with ratios of exports to GDP of only 10 to 13 percent in the much larger Latin American NICs.[17] Thus the East Asian NICs, partly because of their smaller size, are far more dependent on external trade than their Latin American counterparts.

The NICs cluster into several strata when we look at the composition of their exports (Table 1). Manufactured products constitute over 90 percent of total exports in Taiwan, South Korea, and Hong Kong, whereas for the Latin American NICs manufactures are only about 25 to 40 percent of total exports. Singapore is an intermedi-

17. World Bank, *World Development Report 1988* (New York: Oxford University Press, 1988), tabs. 3, 11, and 12.

ate case in that one-third of its exports are primary commodities, mainly petroleum-related products, and two-thirds are manufactured goods.

This regional clustering is reinforced when one examines the types of manufactured exports produced by the NICs. The three top East Asian exporters have kept a strong base in two industries that have been economic mainstays since the start of EOI more than two decades ago, textiles and clothing, which represented one-sixth to one-third of their export totals in 1986. For the other NICs, textile and clothing exports are relatively insignificant.

More surprising is the fact that machinery and transport equipment now is the leading export sector for three of the four East Asian NICs, the exception being Hong Kong. It accounts for one-fifth to two-fifths of all their exports. Among the Latin American nations, Mexico and Brazil also were prominent exporters of machinery and transport equipment in 1986, at 18 and 15 percent, respectively, while Argentina's external sales in this sector were quite limited, at 6 percent.

The East Asian NICs thus show a considerable degree of export diversity, encompassing capital-intensive as well as traditional manufacturing industries. The Latin American NICs, on the other hand, retain a strong commitment to primary commodity exports, although manufactured exports are becoming increasingly significant.

It is important to note that despite the tremendous strides made by the NICs in expanding their export activities, the heart of the global manufacturing system remains centered in the more developed countries. Taiwan, the largest exporter of manufactured goods among the NICs, exports half what the Netherlands does and just one-third of France's total. In 1986

TABLE 1

EXPORTS BY THE LATIN AMERICAN AND EAST ASIAN NICs, 1986

Country	Exports (US$ billions)	Primary commodities	Textiles and clothing	Machinery and transport equipment	Other manufactures
		Percentage Share of Exports			
Taiwan	39.8	9	18	29	44
Hong Kong	35.4	8	35	21	36
South Korea	34.7	9	25	33	33
Singapore	22.5	33	5	38	25
Brazil	22.4	60	3	15	23
Mexico	16.2	70	2	18	10
Argentina	6.9	77	2	6	14

SOURCE: World Bank, *World Development Report 1988* (New York: Oxford University Press, 1988), tabs. 11 and 12.
NOTE: Percentages may not add up to 100 percent due to rounding error.

Hong Kong exported less than Switzerland, and South Korea's overseas sales were only half of Belgium's. The exports of the four East Asian NICs combined were just over one-half — 54 percent — of West Germany's total.[18]

The favored market for the world's top exporters of manufactured goods is, by far, the United States. This pattern is especially pronounced for the NICs. The American market has been the main destination for the NICs' overseas sales since the onset of their export-promotion efforts in the 1960s. Furthermore, the importance of the U.S. market for the NICs has been increasing over time.[19] Nonetheless, the degree of export reliance on the U.S. market varied considerably among the NICs in the mid-1980s. Mexico's dependence on the American market was the greatest, at 60 percent, followed by Taiwan, at 50 percent; South Korea, 40 percent; Hong Kong and Brazil, 30 percent; Singapore, 20 percent; and Argentina, 10 percent.[20] The second leading export market for most of the NICs today is Japan, which is under increasing pressure to have a more balanced trading relationship with the rest of the world.

The predominance of the United States and, to a lesser degree, the other industrial market economies as the main export markets for the NICs is not surprising in economic terms. But the willingness and ability of the United States to continue to fuel the NICs' export growth in the future is very questionable. The United States had a world-record trade deficit of $170 billion in 1986. With the exception of West Germany, most of the other West European nations are running trade deficits as well.

The political pressures for protectionism in the developed countries are well

18. Ibid., tab. 11.
19. The only exceptions are Argentina, whose primary export ties have been with the Soviet Union, in wheat, and with Italy, in leather; and Singapore, which relied most heavily on exports to Malaysia in the late 1960s and 1970s.

20. These rounded figures come from United Nations, *1986 International Trade Statistics Yearbook* (New York: United Nations, 1988), vol. 1.

documented and likely to grow as the advanced industrial nations seek to improve their trade balances by reducing imports and expanding their own exports. How the NICs respond to this challenge rests to a large degree on their ability to diversify their export markets, both geographically and through product specialization. It is to this latter set of issues that we now turn.

NEW PATTERNS OF EXPORT SPECIALIZATION

The global manufacturing system that has emerged in the last two decades and the related expansion in export activity by the NICs has led to increasingly complex product networks and an unprecedented degree of geographical specialization. The international division of labor has evolved beyond the old pattern by which developing nations exported primary commodities to the industrialized countries in exchange for manufactured goods. Today, as we have seen, developing countries like the East Asian NICs are among the world's most successful exporters of manufactured products. Furthermore, the NICs have diversified from traditional labor-intensive exports, such as textiles, or those based on natural resources — such as plywood, leather, paper, and basic petrochemicals — to more complex capital- and skill-intensive exports like machinery, transport equipment, and computers.

While the diversification of the NICs' exports toward nontraditional manufactured goods is now a clear trend, less well recognized is the tendency of the NICs to develop higher levels of specialization in their export profiles. This is an extremely important phenomenon because it begins to challenge several of our standard assumptions about development. The NICs within a given region, such as East Asia or Latin America, are becoming increasingly differentiated from one another as each nation is establishing specialized export niches within the world economy. In addition, countries are no longer specializing just in certain manufacturing industries but also in different stages of production within a single industry. Export networks thus are replacing the nation-state as the key unit of analysis in the contemporary global manufacturing system.

Although industry comparisons allow us to identify broad patterns of export diversification, we need more detailed information on individual products to discern new forms of export specialization in the NICs.[21] In the Latin American NICs, which have a very diverse range of exports, this specialization extends to primary products as well as manufactured goods, while in the East Asian NICs the focus is almost exclusively on the latter. A common theme, however, is that important differences in national export profiles characterize the NICs within both regions.

Primary products continued to be important foreign-exchange earners in all three Latin American NICs in 1987. In Argentina two products, leather and meat, accounted for nearly one-third of its exports to the United States. Crude oil was Mexico's leading export item throughout the 1980s, but its share of Mexico's total U.S. exports declined from one-half in 1980 to one-sixth in 1987. Brazil was more heterogeneous; petroleum products, fruits and nuts, coffee, and cocoa were four of the top five U.S. export items in 1987, constituting over one-quarter of the total. Obviously, these diverse commodities tied the

21. The product data are usually at the three-digit level of commodity classification and come from U.S. Department of Commerce, *Foreign Trade Highlights* (Washington, DC: Bureau of the Census, various years).

Latin American NICs to world markets in quite different ways.

These national contrasts are elaborated further when we turn to the manufactured exports of the Latin American NICs. Footwear was Brazil's leading export item to the United States from 1984 to 1987, surpassing $970 million – 12 percent of total exports – in the latter year. The biggest complex of manufactured exports from Brazil, however, is connected with the automotive industry – engines, auto parts, cars, and trucks – which generated over $1 billion in exports. The jump in exports of passenger motor vehicles to the United States was particularly dramatic: from $1.2 million in 1986 to over $250 million in 1987.

The automotive complex is even more significant in Mexico's exports to the United States. Passenger-motor-vehicle exports increased tenfold from $111 million in 1985 to $1.2 billion in 1987. Mexico's engine exports were valued at $880 million and its auto parts at $660 million. Television and radio receivers were another major export item, valued at over $1.2 billion in 1987. Argentina's major manufactured exports included organic chemicals, and iron, steel, and aluminum products.

Unlike the Latin American NICs, whose manufactured exports encompass a wide range of intermediate goods and industrial components, the East Asian NICs stand out as the most successful Third World exporters of finished consumer goods to the United States.[22] There are both commonalities throughout the region and quite striking patterns of specialization. Hong Kong's specialty items are clothes – outer-

wear, underwear, and sweaters – toys, watches, and clocks. Over one-fifth of Hong Kong's exports go to the People's Republic of China, so Hong Kong is an important conduit for consumer goods that make their way into China as well as the United States.

In Taiwan and South Korea, footwear has been the top export item throughout most of the 1980s. Taiwan's footwear exports to the United States totaled $2.6 billion in 1987, while South Korea's were $1.8 billion.[23] The number-two export item for most of the past decade in both countries has been baby carriages and toys.[24] This category accounted for $2 billion of Taiwan's exports and $1 billion of South Korea's exports to the United States in 1987. As with Hong Kong, apparel is also a major export item for both Taiwan and South Korea.

Taiwan has specialized in several exports that are not found in the other East Asian NICs, such as furniture and parts, with a total value of $1.4 billion in 1987; rubber and plastic articles, at $1 billion; and luggage and handbags, at $600 million. Taiwan also leads the NICs in the export of telecommunications equipment, totaling $1.3 billion, and automatic data-processing machinery, totaling $1.1 billion, and is

22. Donald B. Keesing, "Linking up to Distant Markets: South to North Exports of Manufactured Consumer Goods," *American Economic Review,* 73(2):338-42 (May 1983).

23. Hong Kong, quite surprisingly, has virtually no footwear exports to the United States despite its high profile in other traditional manufactured exports like apparel and textiles. Footwear exports to the American market are highly specialized among several of the other NICs, however. For example, South Korea's major footwear export is leather athletic shoes, Taiwan is the primary supplier of vinyl, plastic, and rubber footwear, while Brazil concentrates on leather shoes for women and on leather sandals.

24. These exports also are specialized by country. Taiwan is the leading U.S. supplier of baby carriages, strollers, and stuffed dolls. South Korea sends the largest quantity of stuffed animals, while Hong Kong is the major exporter of toys having an electric motor.

second only to Singapore in parts for office machines, at $700 million.

South Korea, like Brazil and Mexico, has dramatically expanded its exports of passenger motor vehicles to the United States in the past two years. These exports skyrocketed from only $6 million in 1985 to $850 million in 1986 and $2.2 billion in 1987, making passenger motor vehicles South Korea's largest export item and placing the country considerably above even the Latin American NICs in this category. South Korea is also a leading exporter of televisions and phonographs, including TV receivers, at $1 billion; electronic components, at $800 million; telecommunications equipment, $700 million; and automatic data-processing machinery, $600 million.

Singapore, like South Korea and Taiwan, has a well-developed machinery-export profile, but it is much weaker in clothing exports and has no automotive industry at all. Office-machine parts were the major export item to the United States in 1987, totaling $1.8 billion, followed by electronic components, $800 million; radio and TV receivers, $400 million; automatic data-processing machinery, $375 million; and telecommunications equipment, $340 million.

THE NICs IN A CHANGING WORLD ECONOMY

What conclusions are we to draw from this discussion of development strategies and the specialized export profiles that characterize the Latin American and East Asian NICs in the 1980s? First, although there are still some obvious cross-regional differences in the development strategies and patterns of export diversification of the NICs in Latin America and East Asia, a strong case can be made for increasing

heterogeneity in the export profiles of the NICs within each region. Taiwan and South Korea, for example, occupy quite distinct export niches in the world economy today, as do Brazil and Mexico, to take two of the more similar cases in each region. This should lead us to be cautious about generalizations based on the assumption that there are homogeneous Latin American or East Asian development models.

Second, this trend toward product specialization is part of the overarching process of the globalization of production, which is establishing integrated manufacturing and export networks that tie countries together in new ways using a variety of industrial agents. The semiconductor industry is an excellent example of the twin processes of specialization and integration in East Asia.[25] Although Japan is the dominant producer in the region, three of the four East Asian NICs have established special roles for themselves in the industry. South Korea has decided to focus almost exclusively on the mass production of powerful memory chips. These chips constitute the largest single segment of the semiconductor industry, whose breakneck growth has been fueled by the increasing number of consumer products to go digital. The heavy investment in chip facilities that began in 1983 is dominated by Korea's giant industrial conglomerates (*chaebols*).

Taiwan, on the other hand, is using brains instead of brawn. Rather than aiming at products like memories, Taiwan has targeted the highest-value-added segment of the market: tailor-made so-called designer chips that carry out special tasks, such as synthesizing speech or animal sounds for toys, or that are used in video

25. See "Sizzling Hot Chips: Asia Is the Source of the Semiconductor Industry's Spectacular Growth," *Far Eastern Economic Review,* 18 Aug. 1988, pp. 80-86.

games. Taiwan now has 40 chip-design houses that specialize in finding export niches and then developing products for them. This strength in design comes from the popularity of electronics engineering in Taiwan, which has allowed a number of traditional Taiwanese companies to follow the government's lead and plunge into semiconductors.

Singapore's electronics industry, which has been a mainstay of the country's economy for two decades, has moved from an emphasis on the assembly and testing of semiconductors, a labor-intensive process dominated by multinational corporations, to the higher-value-added stage of semiconductor design and fabrication. Silicon-wafer fabrication is oriented mainly toward use in Singapore's domestically produced telecommunications and data-communications devices. The microelectronics industry in Hong Kong has lagged behind that of the other East Asian NICs because the industry has not been able to count on the sort of state support that has been effective in Taiwan, Singapore, and South Korea.[26]

A third implication of these patterns in global production and trade is that the export profiles of the NICs are shaped by very different kinds of industrial structures, which in turn reflect distinctive social and political dynamics in each of these societies. There are striking national variations in the character of the leading enterprises in the Latin American and East Asian NICs.

Multinational corporations and state enterprises have been the major industrial actors in the Latin American NICs since the 1950s. Foreign firms were central to the

development of the second-stage ISI industries—motor vehicles, machinery, tires, rubber, chemicals, and so on—while state enterprises concentrated their activities in the natural-resource industries, such as oil and minerals, the transportation and communications fields, and steel production. Local private capital is quite diversified but generally tends to be a junior partner in the most dynamic industries of these countries.

In the East Asian NICs, on the other hand, local private firms are the main industrial actors. The one exception is Singapore, where multinational companies have been paramount. There are important variations in the private sector's role in each of the other three East Asian nations, however.

Taiwan and Hong Kong have based their export growth on the performance of small and medium-sized firms, which are usually family owned. Nonetheless, state enterprises also are prominent among the largest firms in Taiwan, especially in heavy industries like steel and petrochemicals.

South Korea's industrial structure, on the other hand, is dominated by giant, privately owned *chaebol* groups. The biggest Korean conglomerate, Samsung, had a sales total of $21.1 billion for 1987, which is over one-third larger than the sales of all of Taiwan's top 10 companies combined. Korea's top 10 companies—as measured by sales—are four times larger than the 10 biggest firms in Mexico and nearly two times larger than Brazil's 10 leading enterprises.[27]

These differences in national industrial structures have profound implications for industrial policy and future paths of internationalization in the Latin American and

26. For a detailed analysis of the role of the state in recent East Asian industrialization, see Robert Wade, "Industrial Policy in East Asia—Does It Lead or Follow the Market?" in *Manufactured Miracles,* ed. Gereffi and Wyman.

27. See Gary Gereffi, "Industrial Structure and Development Strategies in Latin America and East Asia," in *Manufactured Miracles,* ed. Gereffi and Wyman.

East Asian NICs. In South Korea, the *chaebols* constitute a homogeneous and very nationalistic big-business class that is available to carry out the government's objectives in terms of domestic and overseas investments, and external trade. Their large size has permitted South Korea to embark on an aggressive program of foreign investment, as in automobiles, as well as extensive local research and development in high-tech industries, such as computers and electronics, to help maintain Korea's leading international role in these industries.

In Taiwan, because of the decentralized pattern of industrialization and a low level of firm concentration, the state has been less able to implement a coordinated strategy of outward growth. Most of Taiwan's manufactured exports, like those from Hong Kong, have resulted from international subcontracting arrangements between foreign buyers and local firms. This means that these countries are more vulnerable to dislocations in their export activities if foreign buyers shift their orders to nations with lower wages or if the developed countries impose protectionist barriers to their exports. For this reason, Taiwan and Hong Kong have concentrated on creating new export niches in changing industries rather than on using South Korea's vertical integration strategy to supply distant markets.

The central role of multinational corporations in the Latin American NICs poses serious potential constraints on the formulation of national industrial policy, since foreign firms operate with a global rather than a domestic frame of reference. Mexico and Brazil have enjoyed some success, however, in getting multinational companies to use their global strategies to national advantage. This is most evident in the automotive industry, where Mexico and Brazil have become main suppliers of auto parts and motor vehicles to the United States and even Europe on the basis of American as well as Japanese investments.

This view of the NICs in the context of an interdependent, interacting, global manufacturing system raises new questions about their future development. National development strategies are oriented now to moving up the industrial ladder by capturing rapidly shifting advantages in high-value-added, skill-intensive manufacturing industries. The application of modern technologies and the creation of stable export networks is an important part of this process.

The NICs are not all cut from the same cloth, however. There are important differences within as well as between the Latin American and East Asian nations. If a key feature of successful NICs today is their ability to adapt rapidly and effectively to changing conditions in the world economy, then we should expect to find a variety of appropriate strategies as countries rely on their domestic resources and local institutions to meet this challenge.

ANNALS, *AAPSS,* **505,** September 1989

Changes in the International System: The Pacific Basin

By LAWRENCE B. KRAUSE

ABSTRACT: The economies of the Pacific Basin have been much more successful than those in other areas during the 1980s. Economic growth in the Pacific has been high and inflation has been well contained. Five factors seem to be most important in explaining this success. First, these economies have managed to form a consensus to promote growth rather than other societal goals. Second, the people work very hard. Third, they save and invest an unusually large share of their current incomes. Fourth, they implement market-conforming economic policies that are particularly outward looking. Finally, these economies benefit from a regional factor that comes from being surrounded by other successful countries. Leadership in the Pacific Basin has been supplied only by the United States; however, Japan has taken on a more prominent role in recent years and may become dominant in the future.

Lawrence B. Krause received both his bachelor's and master of arts degrees from the University of Michigan and his Ph.D. from Harvard University in 1958. He was the first professorial appointment to the new Graduate School of International Relations and Pacific Studies at the University of California at San Diego and joined the faculty on 1 January 1987. Previously he was a senior fellow of the Brookings Institution. Among his publications is The Singapore Economy Reconsidered, *coauthored with Koh Ai Tee and Lee (Tsao) Yuan (1987).*

THE variance in economic performance between different areas of the world in the 1980s is remarkable, as shown in Table 1. Observers of Latin America refer to this decade as one of crisis from beginning to end. The economic situation of most African countries deteriorated from an already minimal standard of living. While there was stirring in Europe toward the end of the 1980s, most of the decade was characterized by stagnation and high unemployment, above 10 percent. By way of contrast, some economic progress was made in North America, albeit at the cost of creating a structural economic problem in the United States. Most striking of all, however, was the rapid economic advance made by the developing countries in the Pacific Basin, defined here as the 14 economies that participate in the Pacific Economic Cooperation Conference.

The economic achievement of the Pacific Basin is shown in Table 2. The picture that emerges is one of continuing economic prosperity during the 1980s. The 1980s in fact compare very favorably to the economic progress made in the previous two decades. Inflation rates have tended to be lower than in the 1970s, and economic growth of the newly industrializing economies has been at a peak level. The Pacific Basin has not been immune to the disturbances affecting the world economy, however, so that every country in the region has suffered from some sort of slowdown or recession at some point during the 1980s. Nevertheless, these economies recovered from the second oil shock and its aftermath, and they resumed rapid growth.

What accounts for this success compared to that of countries in other regions? First should be noted a few factors that were not responsible. The decline of raw-material prices — the so-called terms of trade

shock — that inhibited natural-resource exporters in Latin America and Africa also afflicted the natural-resource exporters of the Association of Southeast Asian Nations, yet these countries performed much better. Also Korea, the Philippines, and Indonesia were major debtor countries at the start of the decade, but only in the case of the Philippines is external debt seen as a serious constraint on growth, and then only along with other, more important problems. The differences in economic performance must be found elsewhere, that is, not in the external environment, although the external environment was at least benign in the Pacific.

The answer to why the economic performance of the Pacific Basin has been better can be attributed to factors internal to each country and to the intense economic interaction between countries in the Pacific. One factor of great importance is the societal commitment to growth in each country. This means that it was possible to form a political consensus to make short-run sacrifices to promote long-term growth. This has permitted these countries to react faster to external shocks than other countries. A second factor was the willingness of people to work hard. While the number of working hours in a typical week, the number of holidays per year, and the like differ greatly from country to country, in general, the people in the Pacific work longer and possibly more intensively than people elsewhere.

High savings rates and high domestic investment rates found in Pacific Basin countries constitute a third factor helping to explain their success. Fourth, governments in the region tended to implement market-conforming economic policies. One strong characteristic of these policies has been their outward orientation, made

TABLE 1

ECONOMIC PERFORMANCE AROUND THE WORLD

	Percentage Change in Real Gross Domestic Product	
	1973-80	1980-87
Industrial countries	2.1	1.9
Developing countries	3.2	1.8
Exporters of manufactures	4.0	4.6
Highly indebted countries	2.9	−1.3
Sub-Saharan Africa	0.5	−2.9

SOURCE: World Bank, *World Development Report 1988* (Washington, DC: World Bank, 1988), p. 2.

TABLE 2

ECONOMIC PERFORMANCE IN THE PACIFIC BASIN DURING THE 1980s

	Growth Rate of Real Gross Domestic Product			
	1981-85	1986	1987	1988e*
Newly industrializing countries				
Hong Kong	5.8	11.8	13.5	7.4
Korea	7.6	11.7	11.1	11.0
Singapore	6.5	1.8	8.8	10.9
Taiwan	6.2	10.6	12.4	7.1
China	9.3	7.9	10.1	
Association of Southeast Asian Nations (minus Singapore)				
Indonesia	3.5	4.0	3.6	4.7
Malaysia	5.5	1.2	4.7	7.9
Philippines	−0.5	1.1	5.9	6.6
Thailand	5.6	3.4	10.4	11.0
Industrialized countries				
Australia	3.0	2.0	4.1	4.0
Japan	2.3	2.4	3.8	5.2
New Zealand	3.2	1.0	1.9	−2.3
United States	2.4	3.3	3.5	3.8
	Percentage Change in Consumer Prices			
	1985	1986	1987	1988e*
Newly industrializing countries				
Hong Kong	3.2	2.8	5.5	7.5
Korea	2.5	2.8	3.0	7.1
Singapore	0.5	−1.4	0.5	1.6
Taiwan	−0.2	0.7	0.6	1.4
China	6.0	8.8	6.0	7.3

(continued)

TABLE 2 continued

	Percentage Change in Consumer Prices			
	1985	1986	1987	1988e*
Association of Southeast Asian Nations (minus Singapore)				
Indonesia	4.7	5.9	9.3	8.9
Malaysia	0.3	0.7	1.1	3.5
Philippines	23.1	0.8	3.8	8.8
Thailand	2.4	1.8	2.5	3.8
Industrialized countries				
Australia	6.7	9.1	8.5	7.2
Japan	2.0	−0.2	1.1	0.5
New Zealand	13.0	18.3	9.0	13.4
United States	3.5	1.5	3.6	4.1

SOURCES: Official national income data; U.S. National Committee for Pacific Economic Cooperation, *Pacific Economic Outlook, 1989-1990* (San Francisco: U.S. National Committee for Pacific Economic Cooperation, 1989).
*The figures for 1988 are estimates.

possible by the benign external environment. Finally, there is something that could be called a regional effect, that is, an intangible bonus that comes from being surrounded by other successful countries. The remainder of this article is devoted to an elaboration of some of these factors.

SAVINGS AND INVESTMENT BEHAVIOR

Economists interested in development have long moved away from models and theories that explain growth only on the basis of rates of capital investment. Clearly, many factors are important to the complex social phenomenon that results in economic advance. Furthermore, huge amounts of capital investment can and have been wasted in countries where capital markets were distorted or where politics dictated the allocation of new investment. Indeed, in such economies large investment shares did not lead to rapid growth. Nevertheless, investment does matter, and

particularly that investment financed by domestic savings.

Some evidence of savings and investment behavior of Pacific countries is shown in Table 3. Category averages have been included to aid comparisons; categories are those used by the World Bank. An interesting difference can be noted between the share of gross savings in gross domestic product in 1965 and in 1986. In 1965, four of the nine developing countries in the region had savings rates below the average of their category, one was the same, and only four were higher. By 1986, however, seven of the nine countries were above average and generally substantially above the average of the category. The only two exceptions in 1986 were Hong Kong and the Philippines, which was subject to political disruption, but subsequently the savings rate there has risen along with economic recovery.

It is not patently obvious why high domestic savings should be so growth promoting. Of course, investment requires

TABLE 3
GROSS DOMESTIC INVESTMENT AND GROSS DOMESTIC
SAVINGS AS A PERCENTAGE OF GROSS DOMESTIC PRODUCT

Category and Country	Gross Domestic Investment		Gross Domestic Savings	
	1965	1986	1965	1986
Low-income economies	20	29	17	25
China	25	39	25	36
Lower-middle-income economies	17	19	16	17
Indonesia	8	26	8	24
Philippines	21	13	21	19
Thailand	20	21	19	25
Upper-middle-income economies	23	24	23	26
Hong Kong	36	23	29	27
Korea (ROK)	15	29	8	35
Malaysia	20	25	24	32
Singapore	22	40	10	40
Taiwan	23	17	20	38
Industrial market economies	23	21	23	21
Australia	28	22	26	21
Canada	26	21	26	22
Japan	32	28	33	32
New Zealand	28	23	26	24
United States	20	18	21	15

SOURCE: World Bank, *World Development Report 1988*, pp. 230-31.

savings, but they need not be domestic savings. Domestic investment can be financed from abroad through foreign aid, borrowing, and foreign direct investment (FDI). Indeed, since the essence of industrial growth of developing countries involves increasing technological sophistication, and since FDI usually brings technology transfers from abroad, FDI could well be more growth promoting than an equivalent amount of investment financed by domestic sources. Nevertheless, the lesson that can be drawn from the experience of the Pacific Basin is that domestic savings capacity is crucial.

The main reason why domestic savings are so important is that they permit a high level of domestic investment without incurring foreign debt. As the Latin American experience demonstrates, foreign debt can turn out to be much more difficult to service than was anticipated at the time it was undertaken. Even concessional foreign borrowing can be burdensome if, as in the case of Indonesia, it is denominated in a currency, such as the yen, that is appreciating and the country's exports are priced in a depreciating currency. The gain from financing domestic investment from domestic savings may also arise in part from the automatic containment of inflation if consumption is self-constrained. In any event, the savings rate did rise rapidly in the developing countries of the Pacific Basin and economic growth did accelerate.

If domestic savings are crucial for growth, can the domestic savings rate be a direct target of government policy? It is sometimes argued in the United States that it cannot be manipulated directly, although macroeconomic management, the structure of taxes, and the like are believed to influence it. In most countries in the Pacific Basin, the savings rate has been an explicit target of policy. For example, Singapore has devised an elaborate Central Providential Fund to force a high rate of personal savings as part of a program to raise national savings. Japanese policy in earlier periods was aimed at suppressing domestic consumption to promote higher savings. Other examples could be cited. While cause and effect are difficult to document, comprehensive government programs to raise national savings rates and the achievement of that result are positively correlated.

As also seen in Table 3, the Pacific Basin economies with few exceptions display high investment shares compared to category averages. The advantage of high investment shares needs no elaboration. It may well be, however, that high investment and high savings come out of a joint decision process by domestic entrepreneurs and that it is the action of these entrepreneurs that helps explain economic success.

OUTWARD-ORIENTED POLICY

The outward orientation of the policy of the economies of the Pacific Basin is widely recognized, and some observers attribute a major share of their success to this factor. While only a subjective determination is possible, it may well be that its importance as usually analyzed is exaggerated but that, when seen in its full dimension, it is not fully appreciated.

Outward orientation is usually characterized by a country's policy toward international trade and FDI. It is certain that almost every developing economy in the region—and that now includes China—considered itself too small to develop in a closed market, and therefore expanding industrial production and exporting industrial products went hand in hand. For example, Korea could never capture economies of scale by producing manufactures only for the domestic market. Hence export promotion was at the very heart of industrial policy in these countries. This does not mean, however, that they endorsed or practiced free trade themselves, even though they advocated it for their trading partners. Rather, they instituted mercantilist policies, that is, they limited imports while promoting exports. This was the Japanese plan for development, which was seen as a successful model to emulate.

All of the developing countries in the region, with one exception, practiced import substitution (IS). The policy was based on the usual infant-industry argument. One consequence of IS is the nurturing and training of domestic entrepreneurs and permitting them to amass some risk capital. The exception, of course, was Hong Kong, which did not restrict imports; this is the exception that proves the rule. The origin of Hong Kong's entrepreneurs was Shanghai and Canton. The training and the amassing of capital that they needed were provided by China's trade restrictions before they departed. Hence Hong Kong received the benefits of an IS policy without having to implement it.

Nevertheless, the practice of IS in the Pacific Basin has been different from that in other regions. Even at its peak, it was never as extreme as elsewhere. In some places, such as Malaysia and Singapore, it was very mild indeed. Furthermore, it seems to have ended sooner in the process of development. Nevertheless, it still persists, and rather restrictive import regimes are still found in Indonesia, the Philippines, and, until quite recently, Korea. The major point of difference, however, was the focus in the region on promoting exports rather than restricting imports per se. Thus generous exceptions from import barriers were permitted when their existence directly threatened exports.

Policies toward FDI have differed greatly between the countries in the region. During its period of rapid industrial growth, Japan made it very difficult for foreign firms to undertake equity investments. Korea emulated Japanese policy, but not so vigorously. By way of contrast, Hong Kong never made a distinction between domestic investment and FDI, and Singapore has actively encouraged investment by multinational corporations (MNCs). During the latter 1980s, FDI has been particularly important in the rapid growth of Thailand and, to a lesser extent, Malaysia. This would not have been possible if restrictive policies had been in place. Ironically, the goal of policy in countries that promoted FDI, such as Singapore, was not much different from that in Korea, which closely regulated it. In both cases, the purpose was to promote exports. Since the Singapore market was too small to be of much interest to MNCs, if they invested in Singapore, it must have only been for the purpose of exporting most of the output. Similarly, Korea regulated FDI for the purpose of ensuring that a major component of output would be exported directly or indirectly.

The same variance in policy is seen with respect to other kinds of international capital flows. For example, Hong Kong freely permits capital flows in and out of the territory, while Korea still does not permit foreigners to make portfolio investments directly into its stock market or buy real estate. In general, it can be said that current-account items — goods and services — have been treated more liberally than capital-account items throughout the region.

An important point to recognize, however, is that outward orientation goes beyond policies dealing with trade and foreign investment. The economies in this region give constant attention to more successful countries for the purpose of learning from their experience. This has been described as the "flying-goose" pattern of development, in which followers mimic the leaders and try to catch up to them. The search is for a successful pattern that then can be adapted for domestic use. Both the copying and the adapting are important in this process. It is this larger sense of outward orientation that is not frequently appreciated and that provides the regional bonus of being located in a group of successful countries.

DIRECT PARTICIPATION
OF GOVERNMENTS

The participation of governments in the process of economic development in the region is sometimes misunderstood. The difficulty occurs because a distinction is not drawn between market-distorting activities of government and the intrusiveness of government in general. It is true that there is much less market-distorting activity in this region, but this should not be interpreted as the practice of laissez-faire, except in Hong Kong. Singapore is a perfect illustration of the point. The government of Singapore does not distort markets, but it is very intrusive in running the economy. The purpose of this government activity is not to replace the market but to make the market work better and faster. An expression of this in the United States would be an active and intrusive antitrust policy.

Governments in the Pacific Basin do many things to guide the market, and if successful, without distorting it. A major area of government participation has been as an entrepreneur in state-owned enterprises (SOEs). Generally, the rationale has been that the capital requirement and/or the risk is too great for private entrepreneurs, or simply that private enterprise did not choose to undertake the activity and government has moved in to fill the vacuum. At different times SOEs have loomed very large in the economies of Korea, Malaysia, Singapore, and Taiwan. Recently, some privatization has occurred, and more is talked about. Privatization has advanced not because government activity was deemed to be illegitimate but rather because, like the POSCO steel complex in Korea, it has achieved maturity, earned considerable profits, and no longer needs government participation.

A second major activity of governments in the region has been the promotion of science and technology in industry. Governments have recognized the critical role of technology in industrial growth and have been prepared to give the market some encouragement to push the process along. Major efforts have been made in education. Indeed, once universal literacy was achieved, the mastering of technical

skills was given top priority. At first that meant sending students abroad to study. Subsequently, domestic facilities were created. Taiwan has been most active in this regard. Frequently, government laboratories were created to promote scientific work and even to do contract research for business that the firm was incapable of doing itself. Government institutes have been formed to provide a clearinghouse for technical information for business. Korea has extensively utilized such organizations. In Singapore many SOEs operate in advanced technical areas, and MNCs are encouraged to bring high technology to the country. Finally, practically all of the countries give encouragement to research and development and to technical training through special tax provisions.

Some governments in the region were even more involved in directing their economies. In the 1970s, Korea's development plans were used to direct private investment decisions. The government provided subsidized loans to firms if they would follow the government's suggestions. Furthermore, in Singapore and Korea the government became involved in wage setting for the economy. Another illustration of government involvement is in Malaysia, where the distribution of income and wealth has been a major target of policy. All of these cases depict activist governments.

How much of the economic success of these countries can be attributed to activist policies is a matter of dispute. When they were successful, they did not distort markets, but mistakes were made. In the later 1970s, Singapore restricted wage growth too intensively and created a labor shortage. To correct the shortage, wages were pushed up too rapidly, which contributed to a loss of competitiveness. In Korea in the 1970s, too much incentive was given for investment in heavy and chemical industries and as a result, overcapacity was created, losses were made by operating firms, and loans went into default. These mistakes were unusual, however. Most of the time the economies performed quite well and were assisted by policy measures.

As economies grow larger, however, it becomes increasingly harder to design policy that is intrusive, not market distorting, and helpful for growth. Larger economies are necessarily more complex. It becomes increasingly difficult for governments to have the information necessary for sound decisions. Allocative decisions are better made by private economic agents with direct interest in the outcomes and closer to markets. Hence there has been a move toward liberalization of government regulations, along with a pulling back of direct governmental economic involvement in recent years.

THE ROLE OF THE
UNITED STATES AND JAPAN

The flying-goose pattern of development in the Pacific Basin requires a leader to point the way. For most of the postwar period, that position was clearly filled by the United States. It was the United States that provided the technology that was transferred to others. It was to American universities that students went to study science, engineering, and social science as well. It was U.S.-based MNCs that made direct investments in the region, which forged organic links not only back to the United States but also to third countries in the region. It was the U.S. government that provided direct aid — at times in large amounts — to other governments, such as to Japan, Korea, the Philippines, Taiwan, and Thailand. It was U.S. foundations that supported training and research in and about the region. It was the United States, through its support of international institutions such as the World Bank and the General Agreement on Tariffs and Trade, that provided resources and an inviting external environment.

Possibly the greatest contribution that the United States made to the success of countries in the region was through having an open market that absorbed huge volumes of imported manufactures, permitting the success of an export-led growth strategy. In addition, U.S. power was critical in defining and stabilizing the political and security dimensions of the region.

The apex of American relative economic power was reached rather early in the postwar period. As European countries recovered from the war, and Japan not only recovered but entered a period of unparalleled economic acceleration, the relative position of the United States declined. The decline was speeded by U.S. involvement in Vietnam; however, in the 1970s, no other country was in position to challenge U.S. leadership. This changed in the 1980s as a result of U.S. policy choices and further acceleration of growth in the Pacific.

In the 1980s the United States no longer is the richest industrial country. When measured on a per capita basis in terms of international purchasing power — current exchange rates — the income level of Japan and several European countries has surpassed that of the United States. The United States has begun to run a huge imbalance of trade, the value of imports becoming much greater than the value of exports. In order to finance this deficit, the United States annually has to borrow large amounts abroad. The cumulation of this borrowing has quickly turned the United States into the world's largest debtor where previously it was the largest creditor.

The competitor for economic leadership in the Pacific Basin is Japan. Even in the 1960s, the Japanese model for development was being emulated in the region. Furthermore, Japan has long been the primary market for natural-resource goods produced in the region, hence the strong link between Australia and Japan. Moreover, Japanese firms rather early began to invest abroad for various purposes, relying upon the information channels of the general trading companies (*sogo shosha*). The Pacific Basin was the natural recipient of much of this investment. Recognizing its special role in the Pacific, Japan became the principal sponsor and force within the Asian Development Bank.

By the 1980s, Japanese business firms had begun to be recognized as world leaders. Where earlier they were known to be particularly competitive in heavy industries such as steel and shipbuilding, this competitiveness was explained in terms of greater capital investment. Now Japanese firms excel in high-technology industries. While the total size of the Japanese economy is smaller than that of the European Community or the United States, its industrial organization is also more concentrated. Hence the leading firms in Japan are at least the equal of those in other countries. It is Japanese management practices that are being studied intensively and being emulated everywhere. Since the appreciation of the yen, Japanese MNCs have been making large investments throughout the region and particularly in the United States. In some places, such as Thailand, Japanese firms dominate the scene. In many industries and in many countries, the goose leading the flock is Japanese.

With the shift in economic policy toward domestic-oriented growth in the late 1980s, Japanese markets are being opened to the imports of manufactured goods, and most of them are coming from Pacific Basin countries. Between 1985 and 1988, Japanese imports of manufactured goods increased by 80 percent, as measured in dollars. Korean exports have grown particularly fast in this market. Some of these goods are produced by Japanese FDI in several countries. Hence at the margin, Japan is already replacing the United States.

It is in the financial area, however, that Japanese relative power is the greatest. As a result of high domestic savings rates combined with a high level of income, the potential for Japanese investment is unmatched. Japanese institutions such as banks and insurance companies that perform the financial intermediary function have become so large as to dwarf their foreign competitors.

During the 1980s, Japan has developed almost as large a balance-of-payments surplus as the United States has developed a deficit. This surplus has been invested primarily in U.S. securities but in other foreign assets as well. Japan is clearly the largest source of foreign capital in the world.

Until recently Japan has been reluctant to take a visible leadership position in the Pacific Basin, but that is beginning to change. Japan has recently become the largest giver of foreign aid. The Japanese have become more willing to offer their own ideas for the solution of regional or even world problems. For example, the Japanese put forth a plan to deal with the debt problem of the less developed countries. Japan has also taken upon itself to become the spokesperson for the interest of Pacific countries in the annual summit meeting of industrial countries. Given Japan's relative economic power, a further evolution in the direction of assuming leadership should be expected.

Given uncertainties in all dimensions, true forecasting of major economic developments is close to worthless. Nevertheless, it is interesting to extrapolate existing trends to form a naive scenario of future prospects. Two trends will be assumed to continue: the relative economic success of the Pacific Basin and the rise of Japanese leadership.

The examination of the forces promoting relative economic success in the Pacific Basin yields systemic explanations that need not be terminated. Their applicability could spread from one country to another in the region. Indeed, if the Pacific were believed to have discovered the key to economic success, then emulation might take place in other regions. What would this mean? There would be a resurgence of the classical virtues of saving and investing for the future. There would be a new reluctance by governments to distort markets. The importance of international trade would be enhanced. Activist governments would gear their policy toward export promotion. The consequence might well be the multiplication of large private enterprises with a global focus.

The further enhancement of Japan's economic leadership might mean that the modalities by which business is conducted in Japan would determine the nature of international regimes, just as the trade system of the 1950s and 1960s reflected the United States. The international trade of Japan is managed by a handful of large firms (*keiretsu*) in a cooperative and collaborative relationship with the government, namely, with the Ministry of International Trade and Industry. Other countries have found that they need similar business firms and relationships to compete and negotiate with the Japanese. Hence a new era

of rapidly expanding but managed international trade might emerge.

The financial strength of Japan must in time be reflected in the institutions and practices of the marketplace. International commerce, especially in the Pacific, will become increasingly dependent on Japanese financing. Japanese financial institutions have a natural advantage in obtaining access to yen. Thus the competitive position of Japanese institutions will be enhanced by increasing the international role of the yen, and they can be expected to promote such usage. There is every reason to expect that they will be successful. In fact, there is a strong possibility that the world will accept the yen as its key currency, replacing the dollar. Key-currency status is not determined by the issuer of a currency but by its foreign users. If traders and investors earn most of their income in yen and must make payment in yen, then the yen will become the unit of account, the transaction currency, and the choice for reserve accumulation.

Nothing has been said in this article about Europe, and clearly the movement toward closer integration within the European Community by 1992 is a major development. What if Europe is unwilling to accept the Pacific Century under Japanese leadership? After all, the major motivation for 1992 is to strengthen European competitiveness so as not to be dominated by the United States and Japan. Europe could react to the competitive challenge of the Pacific by turning inward and erecting barriers to the outside world.

European exclusiveness, should it occur, would likely be met by some sort of regional development in the Pacific. Unlike earlier decades after World War II, when security concerns prevented an economic schism between nonsocialist countries, the relaxation of tensions between the military superpowers is likely to permit more diversity of economic relations. The fact that the world would split up into regional blocs does not mean that they would necessarily be aggressive toward one another. Indeed, there would be great economic and political incentive to avoid conflict. Nevertheless, there would be legal and practical distinctions between members and nonmembers. The Pacific bloc under Japanese leadership would be prosperous and dynamic, and very attractive to many countries.

ANNALS, *AAPSS,* **505,** September 1989

Latin American Failure against the Backdrop of Asian Success

By ALBERT FISHLOW

ABSTRACT: This article examines the principal reasons for the poor Latin American economic performance in contrast to Asian success in the last decade. These include an adverse international economy that discriminated against large debtors, a set of domestic distortions introduced by excess external debt, and a political incapacity to implement coherent and consistent adjustment policies.

Albert Fishlow is professor of economics at the University of California at Berkeley. He first joined the faculty there in 1961 upon completion of Ph.D. studies at Harvard. During the years 1978-83 he was professor of economics and director of the Center for International and Area Studies at Yale University. His research has addressed issues in economic history, Brazilian development strategy, economic relations between industrialized and developing countries, and the problem of foreign debt.

117

O NE of the salient aspects of the evolution of the world economy in the
1980s is the dismal economic performance
of Latin America and Africa. After positive
expansion during all of the postwar period,
the last decade represents a significant
break. The distinction is even more profound when compared to the development
of the Asian countries. Per capita growth
rates from 1980 to 1988 in Asia averaged
5.4 percent a year; for Africa, there was a
decrease of 1.1 percent and for Latin America a decline of 0.8 percent. The contrast to
the 1970s is especially powerful for Latin
America: a positive expansion of 3.1 percent, not much different from Asia's 3.4
percent, has given way to a decade of absolutely eroding living standards. Where
not too long ago they were far ahead, Argentina, Brazil, and Mexico now all have
lower incomes per capita than the East
Asian successes of Korea, Taiwan, Hong
Kong, and Singapore.[1]

This new reality has provoked new
thinking among economists concerned
with development issues. The dominant
thrust of this reevaluation has been to emphasize the virtues of outward orientation
and reliance on market signals. Latin
American development is seen to be
flawed by the dominance of an import substitution mentality implemented by an interventionist state. As Angus Maddison has
forcefully argued,

The economic growth performance of Latin
America since 1973 has been abysmal. . . . there
has . . . been a certain continuity in economic
policy attitudes since the 1930's, and the liberal
international order which was created by OECD
[Organization for Economic Cooperation and

Development] countries and has influenced policy in Asia has left them virtually untouched.[2]

The difficult Latin American adjustment to the external shocks of the 1970s is
thus seen as symptomatic of deeper structural defects. Asian countries, buffeted by
terms of trade deterioration, made it; Latin
America has only become mired in a continuing debt problem whose solution continues to defy the modest measures so far
taken. In this view, domestic policy is key,
and government intrusion the source of the
Latin American slowdown. Deepak Lal's
central conclusion in *The Poverty of "Development Economics"* is one that many
now find attractive: "The most serious current distortions in many developing countries are not those flowing from the inevitable imperfections of market economy but
the policy induced, and thus far from inevitable, distortions created by irrational
dirigisme."[3]

In response to the East Asian success
and Latin American failure, there has even
been a resurrection of theories of cultural
influence. Confucianism is virtuous, the
Hispanic tradition, noxious. Lawrence
Harrison has argued the latter most vigorously, concluding that "in the case of Latin
America, we see a cultural pattern, deriva-
tive of traditional Hispanic culture, that is
anti-democratic, anti-social, anti-progress,
anti-entrepreneurial, and at least among the
elite, anti-work."[4] Similar analyses,
couched in terms of inferior North Ameri-

1. Calculated from International Monetary Fund,
World Economic Outlook, 1988 (Washington, DC:
International Monetary Fund, 1988).

2. Angus Maddison, *Two Crises: Latin America
and Asia, 1929-38 and 1973-83* (Paris: OECD Development Centre, 1985), p. 53.

3. Deepak Lal, *The Poverty of "Development Economics"* (Cambridge, MA: Harvard University Press,
1985), p. 103.

4. Lawrence E. Harrison, *Underdevelopment Is a
State of Mind* (Lanham, MD: University Press of
America, 1985), p. 165.

can values, have surfaced in the context of the United States-Japan comparison.

These reactions emphasize fundamental failings in Latin American economic policies and society. They seem to me too far-reaching from the evidence in hand. There is danger in preaching secular deficiencies on the basis of a decade of results, and in sudden discovery of behavioral patterns that did nothing to brake the significant economic accomplishments of many Latin American countries during the largest part of this century. It is easy to forget that Brazilian and Mexican economic growth since 1940 stood out for their level and continuity until the 1980s.

In this article, I wish to argue an alternative view. First, I want to make clear the magnitude of the international economic deterioration faced by the countries of Latin America in the 1980s. Ironically, moreover, the reliance on market signals of low real interest rates and rising export prices induced what later was to become excess indebtedness; at the time, few Latin American countries violated a sustainability rule requiring export growth to exceed the interest rate. Second, I want to suggest that the adjustment undertaken in the 1980s has been seriously flawed by reason of the excessive priority given to achievement of balance-of-payments objectives. Latin American countries did too well in generating trade surpluses to sustain their debt service. Third, and in conclusion, I want to introduce domestic politics as a significant factor contributing to the choice of economic policies and the disappointing results deriving from them.

I justify this principal focus upon Latin America in a volume on the Pacific region for three reasons.[5] One is that it provides a

5. For a more extensive and explicitly comparative treatment of Latin America and Asia, see my "Some Reflections on Comparative Latin American

useful control experience. Explanations for Asian economic success depart from an implicit theory of Latin American failure; understanding the latter thus contributes to a better sense of which factors are special to Asia. In the second instance, it points to some of the rigidities and inflexibilities that can detract from adjustment to external shocks; for the more open Pacific economies, that question will be central in the future. Third, the impact of greater political participation upon economic performance is one of great current interest within many of the societies of the Pacific Region.

THE INTERNATIONAL
DIMENSION

The unique circumstances of developing-country debt accumulation in the 1970s are now better understood. The surge in developing-country lending after 1973 was motivated by the need to find immediate and profitable application for the sudden increase in deposits of international banks. The oil crisis had resulted in an unprecedented balance-of-payments surplus for oil-producing countries. That wealth was held in short-term form by the oil exporters. Banks somewhat unwittingly converted these deposits into long-term development finance by recycling petrodollars. Middle-income developing countries were attractive borrowers by virtue of their accelerating growth and persistent shortage of capital and foreign exchange. In the midst of successful expansion, many Latin American countries were especially eager to sustain growth in the face of adverse international conditions.[6]

Economic Performance and Policy" (Economics Working Paper 8754, University of California, Berkeley, Sept. 1987).

6. For fuller discussion of Latin American response to the oil shocks and other aspects of the debt

Private market intermediation sustained global demand in the 1970s and averted the international depression that some feared. Oil-exporter surpluses were matched by developing-country deficits used to sustain imports of oil and manufactures. The arrangements had novel, and potentially costly, features. Banks, and increasingly large numbers of them, were the ultimate holders of the loans and hence directly vulnerable to developing-country performance. Countries took on exchange and interest rate risks as they elaborated ambitious investment projects; they correspondingly reduced their margin of policy maneuver.

Neither party to the transaction fully understood the inherent temporary character of the access to credit. The new capital flows did not emerge as a result of a sustained increase in global saving that was seeking continuing productive outlet. Banks did not consciously decide to provide longer-term development finance and set aside loan loss provisions to compensate for the higher risk in sovereign exposure. Profits were initially large, particularly for lead banks and those also participating in developing-country domestic markets, and that was enough. Very little thought, and less concern, was given to the importance of a continuous stream of lending; all of the emphasis was on moving the money out in the first place.

On the side of the countries, however, the capital inflows became a regular, and increasingly necessary, input into the bal-

ance of payments. Neither productive capacity nor exports immediately increased to provide the incremental resources to service debt. Even when some projects did produce that result, it was attractive to continue to borrow to take on still more ambitious, and slowly maturing, investment opportunities. Countries were not prepared to desist from import surpluses while there was finance to permit them. Soon that finance was diverted to other purposes. Borrowing today was necessary to pay the interest on yesterday's loan. Debt dynamics meant that constant inflows transferred progressively less real resources.

Latin American countries, in particular, erred in two respects in following a strategy of reliance on debt finance. First, they opened to the international economy in an asymmetrical way: increases in debt were disproportional to their attention to exports. The asymmetry became self-fulfilling. Large capital flows permitted overvalued exchange rates that facilitated imports and discouraged exports. The unfavorable status of the current account was subordinated to the satisfactory state of the balance of payments as a whole. This was true of oil-exporting Mexico after 1976, which failed to stanch excess imports because cheap loans were readily available; of oil-importing Brazil, which undertook an ambitious program of industrial expansion; and of Argentina and Chile, implementing overvalued exchange rates as an integral part of anti-inflationary strategy. Diverse paths led a number of countries to the same defective exchange-rate policies and excess dependence on continuing capital flows.

In the second place, state enterprises in Latin America rapidly became the preferred vehicle for absorbing external resources. Chile was the principal exception, where large private banks on-lent dollars,

crisis, see my "Latin American Adjustments to the Oil Shocks of 1973 and 1979," in *Latin American Political Economy,* by Jonathan Hartlyn and Samuel A. Morley (Boulder, CO: Westview Press, 1986); idem, "Alternative Approaches and Solutions to the Debt of Developing Countries," in *International Finance and Trade in a Polycentric World,* ed. S. Borner (New York: Macmillan, 1988).

principally to associated enterprises. The public guarantee was attractive to external lenders who had limited information on the risks of lending to private creditors. Public enterprises could directly implement programs of increased investment, particularly in the intermediate-goods sectors. In addition, this channel assured direct control over the foreign-exchange proceeds to the national government; projects even became shells to conceal balance-of-payments financing. The problems of the public sector are in no small way a heritage of the style of Latin American accommodation to capital-market access in the 1970s.

Another symptom of the inadequacy of that accommodation was the emergence of large-scale capital flight. It is no accident that Venezuela, Mexico, and Argentina were by far the worst offenders. Oil exporters had less need to borrow; in Argentina, the military government was not pursuing a policy of increased growth and investment. At the same time that the public sector was borrowing foreign exchange, private citizens were acquiring it to send it back abroad. There can hardly be a better index of excess borrowing than a reverse flow of the surplus foreign exchange unneeded for imports or reserves. Capital flight goes beyond simply rectifying the capital account. Its irregularity, in response to changing expectations, helps to create and intensify foreign-exchange crises. It also saddles the public sector, and ultimately the country, with debt service on assets that yield no domestic return. Borrowing does not then create the means for its own repayment. There is thus a continuing and important shortfall in earnings that must be domestically compensated at the expense of other applications.

By contrast, historical excess borrowing had its typical counterpart in the overbuilding of infrastructure beyond current

demand, a problem soon rectified by the inevitable subsequent boom. Lack of compensating earnings was temporary, not permanent. Mistakes might be made in undertaking particular projects. But such capital loss was not of the order of the capital flight of 40 to 100 percent of the borrowing undertaken by Mexico, Argentina, and Venezuela. The physical assets eventually would prove useful.

The capital market seemed to work well enough in recycling vast amounts of petrodollars in the 1970s without official intervention. It did so because favorable capital-supply conditions and satisfactory trade performance were extrapolated by optimistic countries and banks. Banks lent enough at low real interest rates, and countries serviced their obligations. The majority of Latin American countries satisfied a debt-sustainability criterion of greater export growth than interest rates; of those that did not, only Brazil had a debt-export ratio larger than 2.[7]

A first best scenario that masked the latent dangers of the sudden increase in developing-country debt was in fact realized from 1975 to 1978. These dangers only became apparent when the international economy began to falter with the second oil-price shock and disinflation in the industrial economies from 1979 on.

Latin American countries have been especially prejudiced by the poor performance of the international economy in the 1980s. One can differentiate two phases. In the early 1980s, their relatively high level of indebtedness made them especially susceptible to changes in the terms and amount of lending. While the more open East Asian economies were buffeted by deteriorating trade conditions, both in vol-

7. For these calculations, see Anne O. Krueger, "Origins of the Developing Countries' Debt Crisis," *Journal of Development Economics*, 27:175 ff. (1987).

ume and in terms of trade, the Latin American countries were sensitive to increases in interest rates and reductions in capital inflow. These effects were more serious because they threw Latin American countries suddenly back upon the trade account to compensate. Asian countries had already in the 1970s opted for increased competitiveness in world markets and had acquired valuable experience in adjustment that was put to good use in the later crisis.

With no access to new capital, large debtors — which were on the whole Latin American — had no alternative but to adjust their balance of payments immediately by achieving surpluses on the merchandise account. Most came on the import side. Imports declined by $40 billion between 1981 and 1983, or by more than 40 percent in terms of volume. For relatively closed economies, a larger change in income is needed to produce a given decline in imports because import propensities are small. The Latin American decline in production of 4 percent is actually much below what might have been expected; it was as small as it was because domestic supply was relatively successful in substituting for imports. It was easier for the Asian economies to adjust to the second oil shock simply because smaller income adjustments could produce larger trade consequences, quite apart from their longer-standing emphasis upon an export solution made easier by continuing finance.[8]

In the years after 1983, Latin American countries suffered from a continued curtailment of capital flows but also increasingly felt the consequences of a slide in primary commodity prices that became more severe than the post-Korean War de-

8. For a detailed discussion, see Fishlow, "Some Reflections," pp. 3-10. See also Krueger, "Origins," for discussion of comparative Latin American and Korean adjustment effort.

cline. Resource richness worked against the region. From 1983 to 1986, Latin American terms of trade declined by almost 15 percent, the Asian by 6.5 percent. New commitments to increased exports were frustrated by falling prices. Countries experienced very different patterns. Argentina and Peru were especially hard hit, and even Mexico was adversely affected by falling oil prices in 1986.

In the aggregate, had 1986 terms of trade for the region remained at their 1980 level, and 1986 interest rates conformed to a real rate of 3 percent, the 1986 Latin American balance of payments would have registered a net improvement of almost $25 billion. Many independent estimates of the capital flow required by the region to resume an adequate rate of growth, say, of about 5 percent are of this order of magnitude. The region would not need capital inflows to grow had the world economy performed more satisfactorily. When it did not, external flows could not cushion the shocks because Latin American countries had borrowed earlier, and in the new environment of high real interest rates, banks could not justify further voluntary lending.

Another, and differential, measure of the impact of the adverse turn of the international economy is the following exercise. If terms of trade and real interest rates had remained at their 1980 levels, and net capital inflows had been sustained at the 1980 rate, then cumulative 1981-88 imports could have been 53 percent higher for Latin America. That would have been sufficient to support quite positive economic growth. A comparable calculation for the Asian countries yields a reduction of import capacity of only 10 percent. Prices of manufactured exports fared better, debt was relatively smaller and contracted at cheaper official rates, and net capital inflows were better sustained.

The persistent disequilibrium in the United States' balance of payments contributes to the disadvantage of Latin America. Put in its strongest form, the United States buys manufacturing imports from Asian newly industrializing countries while siphoning off potential capital flow from Latin America. Japanese and European surpluses are recycled to the United States to sustain higher rates of investment, while capital formation in Latin American countries cannot be financed.

Aggressive export growth is an obvious compensation to these adverse balance-of-payments effects. Projections of sustained and rapid export expansion have been repeatedly made by those eager to emphasize an optimistic scenario and the opportunities for better Latin American policy. The actual results have fallen short. Despite more realistic exchange-rate policies, export performance has not been able to carry all of the burden placed upon it. It is tempting, then, to argue that more real devaluation is necessary.

But at some point the strategy of reducing real wages as a means of greater competitiveness becomes self-defeating. Adjustment is intended to increase income, not to perpetuate losses. Market share is gained not only by price competitiveness but by quality and design. New investment and rising productivity must become the basis of increased export market share, and these can be prejudiced by exclusive reliance on price signals. Indeed, the pressure on Latin America to produce large and unprecedented trade surpluses has contributed to inadequate structural adjustment.

INTERNAL DISTORTIONS

An important lesson of the debt crisis has been the dichotomy between internal and external adjustment. Latin American countries had little alternative to making a radical adjustment in their balance of payments. The goal of sustaining the health of a suddenly precarious international financial system required the continuity of interest payments on the debt. That objective, despite the rhetoric to the contrary of the Baker Plan and more recently the Brady Plan, dominated. Economic growth was residual, and its shortfall credited to inadequate domestic policies.

In understanding why internal and external performance have not been more closely linked, as monetarist models of the balance of payments that underlie International Monetary Fund programs would suggest, a central part of the story relates to the domestic effects of the large resource transfers that Latin American countries have made. These have amounted to more than $180 billion since 1982 and have averaged something like 5 percent of regional gross product. This measure of the adjustment effort makes clear the countries' significant sacrifices.

The transfer has been made. In this respect, the classic international transfer problem, elaborated in the context of the German reparations question, is irrelevant. Then the question was whether German exports could be absorbed without an offsetting deterioration in the terms of trade that might make transfer impossible. In more modern phraseology, the trade surpluses associated with the transfer suggest that a foreign-exchange constraint is not binding. Export revenues have increased despite an unpromising world trade performance, and, even more important, imports have been dramatically reduced. Although actual trade surpluses exaggerate the freedom from external limits — because growth has also been kept down and imports restricted—the foreign-exchange constraint figures less prominently as a concern than the savings and fiscal limitations.

Inadequate foreign exchange has less weight in part because of more aggressive exchange-rate policy. But real devaluation has also contributed to acceleration of inflation. When economies are substantially indexed, changes in relative prices and incomes are difficult to achieve. One sector is always quickly catching up to another. Then the only way to achieve a decline in labor costs is by accelerating inflation to induce a lower average wage over the period when nominal wages are fixed.

An example may help. Suppose initial nominal wages are 100, inflation is 100 percent, and adjustments occur every year. Then the average real wage over the year is 75, midway between the initial 100 and the terminal 50. In the second year, nominal wages would start at 200—worth 100—and the average wage would be unchanged if inflation remained constant. But suppose it is necessary to reduce average wages to 60. Then inflation of 400 percent would be necessary, producing a terminal wage of only 20. Relatively small changes in average real wages require large changes in the rate of price increases.

It is no accident that the economies of Argentina and Brazil, where indexing was formal, experienced the largest inflationary impulses from devaluation or that Mexico achieved a larger reduction in real wages with less feedback on prices. Increases in the frequency of adjustment and the extent of nominal wage increase only serve to feed the inflationary process. Here, then, is a domestic cost corresponding to the favorable trade performance.

The resource transfer also has implications for the level of feasible domestic investment. If reduced domestic consump-

tion, public and private, does not finance the bulk of the payments of interest abroad, the only other alternative is a contraction in investment. Capital formation has to be crowded out to permit some part of domestic saving to be used for debt service. When private consumption is interest inelastic, as it seems to be, the high real interest rates that prevail in many countries serve to compress investment. The debt crisis has given new significance to the savings constraint as a factor contributing to poor performance in the Latin American countries. It has underlined the problem of reducing consumption in countries where income inequality is considerable. The poor do not have much option of cutting back, and those better off are the more unwilling to see their standards of living affected in the midst of economic decline.

That reluctance is reflected in the opposition to the obvious option of increased taxes as a way to generate larger public saving and to finance domestic investment. An expanded direct public command over resources is the more indicated route since the external debt in most Latin American countries is predominantly public; even where the debt was initially privately contracted, governments have been pressured to assume responsibility. Accordingly, the public sector must acquire the foreign exchange needed for interest payments principally from private exporters—although there is an exception when public enterprise exports are a major source of foreign-exchange earnings.

The fiscal constraint has turned out to be a very serious obstacle and perhaps the most important proximate cause of poor domestic performance. Reductions in taxation rather than increases have been the rule. Inflation is again a part of the story. Accelerating rates of inflation erode the real value of tax collections rapidly even when payments are indexed. In addition, limited economic growth has created pressure for fiscal incentives and subsidies to private economic activity and resistance to any larger collections as disincentives to investment and expanded production. Growth of informal-sector activity and simple evasion have led to further erosion of the tax base. On the other side of the ledger, expenditure reduction has not been sufficient to lead to larger public sector surpluses. One important reason is that mounting interest payments cancel out lower outlays for investment and social services.

Large public sector deficits thus continue. They can be financed only by issuing money or internal debt. The former feeds inflation and has to contend with progressively smaller holdings of money by the public that limit the collections of the inflation tax. The latter, bearing high rates of interest, attracts resources voluntarily but at the expense of applications in more productive assets. Growing internal debt, moreover, is subject to the danger of instability in the longer term. When the rate of interest is higher than the rate of increase of governmental receipts, the burden of debt-service payments relative to public sector revenues increases. Today's finance becomes tomorrow's larger problem, as it has for many Latin American countries.

In the end, therefore, we see a consistent, but undesirable, equilibrium of trade surpluses, high and accelerating rates of inflation, high real interest rates, rising shares of public expenditure devoted to interest payments, a reduced level of investment, and low rates of growth. Arguing for more outward orientation not only does not help but can even harm. Trade surpluses are too large and detract from effec-

tive domestic adjustment. It is fine to rely on exports when savings rates are high and public sector deficits under control; when they are not, the simplistic formula yields incorrect results. Indeed, large trade surpluses in the short term work against exports in the long term by reducing investment and making competitiveness depend upon cheap wages rather than productivity change.

Such domestic distortions as the counterpart to successful resource transfers are now better understood. In addition, there is recognition that a large debt overhang can create disincentives to the adjustment effort countries should make. If significant domestic efforts go simply to ensure continuing resource transfers, they are less likely to be made. Debt stands as a lien on the economy, providing fewer degrees of freedom for policymakers and provoking uncertainty and pessimistic expectations from potential private investors. One important counterweight, the prospect of renewed voluntary lending as a reward for performance, is realistically absent. That is one key reason why the current problem is different from historical debt crises before 1929, and why — as in the experience of the 1930s — attention necessarily turns to reduced debt service.

At a certain level, debt stands to become self-defeating. Its adverse effects actually reduce the probability of its repayment to the point where creditors, and not only debtors, could benefit from debt reduction. That perception lies behind the expanded menu of options developed to lower debt service, such as exit bonds for smaller banks in lieu of new money, debt buybacks, and debt-equity swaps. The latter, subsidizing as they do foreign exchange, are especially favored by the banks but are correctly resisted by countries as a further imposition upon an already depleted public treasury. The Brady Plan provides an official blessing to debt reduction, but only limited resources and weak leadership for effective implementation of that new strategy. Banks, while they may recognize the advantage of smaller resource transfers and debt levels for debtor-country performance and hence longer-term repayment prospects, will not find it in their individual interest to offer relief first; there is a collective-action problem. Moreover, there is profit in delay so long as high-yield loans continue to be serviced.

Debt reduction has, in the last analysis, gained in appeal because the other way of reducing net resource transfers, increased capital flows, failed to materialize under the Baker Plan. Banks voted with their balance sheets, preferring to avoid large and continuing commitments of future resources. Increasing debt was unattractive because of high real interest rates relative to realistic projections of export growth. So long as interest rates are greater than export growth rates, debt-export ratios will remain stable only if export surpluses are continuously generated. But such surpluses, while easily assumed in arithmetic exercises, take a toll in domestic economic performance, as we have seen.

Latin America's outward orientation in the 1980s, just as in the 1970s, has thus been flawed, but not in the simple fashion of inappropriate exchange-rate policy. First the countries of the region chose to integrate financially to excess and, more recently, to stress exports relative to imports. Asian emergence into world markets was initially characterized by import surpluses that assured the availability of capital and technology of the most recent vintage. Only later, because of export penetration and restrictions on agricultural and other imports, did export surpluses appear.

SOME POLITICAL CONSIDERATIONS

The principal economic task ahead for Latin America is to define a more effective, and domestically rooted, style of integration into the international economy. That objective is complicated by the simultaneous political opening in the region. In 1988 and 1989, elections will have been held in all the principal Latin American countries.

Democratization and debt, and economic performance more generally, have become intertwined. Debt problems helped to send the military back to the barracks, as authoritarian technocratic styles proved inadequate to cope. Now they favor critics of incumbents, whether more orthodox or more populist in their orientation. Ironically, at a time when there has been substantial convergence of economists around the kinds of policies that seem necessary to foster recovery, politicians offer too wide a range of choice to electorates. They promise too much, and they appeal to the weariness of voters eager for a change, but without much faith in the alternatives.

Increasingly, however, the issue is not the appropriate diagnosis of the problem but the inability to implement coherent and consistent policies. One has by now a reasonable idea of what has to be done and what has to be avoided. Neither populism nor straight orthodoxy seems to have worked. But in the absence of a dominant national commitment to economic growth as a first requirement of security — such as that found in Korea and Taiwan — and in the presence of substantial economic inequality that creates a multiplicity of elite interests on one side and mass pressures on the other — an inequality conspicuously absent in Korea and Taiwan — the unsatisfactory status quo emerges as a preferable option in many countries. It is easier to abide inflation than to raise taxes, easier to give credit subsidies than to reduce public sector employment, easier to grant wage increases than to liberalize imports, and so on. Even the prospect of losing popularity and office seems incapable of making better economic policy into good politics.

External relief adds a new and important degree of freedom to the equation set. Reduced debt service makes new resources available to the public sector and strengthens its depleted capacities. That favorable prospect should not be exaggerated, however, even under the best of circumstances. Debt-service reductions will apply only to the medium- and long-term commercial bank debt and not to short-term obligations or official loans. For Latin America as a whole, that exempts a third of the debt. In the second place, rising international interest rates in the past 18 months are becoming a considerable negative offset. Third, the onerous effects of the debt burden will not necessarily translate into equal and symmetric benefits when reduced: investment decline will not automatically be reversed.

It is only if debt relief is coupled with new domestic initiatives that it can serve as a firm basis for economic recovery. That, of course, is the logic behind the insistence upon conditionality and internal reform. But that logic is incomplete. Making governments enact unpopular policies will not lead to a durable resolution of the implementation problem. Successful stabilization is not a once-and-for-all dose of bitter medicine or a surgical intervention; it is a process of continuous policy adjustment that weights priorities and regulates economic activity. Implementation of a development strategy is no different.

Latin America's political deficiencies will not be so easily compensated for by a technocratic blueprint. The absence of an effective structure of political parties and the lack of sheer experience in governance are significant handicaps to sustained economic recovery. They render even more difficult the task of creating durable coalitions capable of consistent policy. What is sometimes seen as external coercion to pursue narrowly defined austerity programs can complicate rather than assist.

One appeal of a market-oriented strategy is that it apparently insulates against unproductive political intervention. That underlies the Buchanan prescription of an inviolable constitution to preclude rent-seeking distortions.[9] But one does not erase real interests by fiat; there is no capacity to enforce such a charter. Those who are prescribed from exerting their special influence through one sphere will spill over to another: instead of requesting administrative favors, large firms will exert monopoly power. There is no substitute but to construct the needed political consensus to implement policy on a continuing basis. That theme is too frequently absent in discussions of economic reform. Opportunities for self-enforcing policies that can narrow debate may be helpful, but automaticity will always be limited.

The correct conclusion is thus not the uniform application of orthodox remedies to promote the economic recovery of Latin America. That is to draw the wrong lesson from East Asia by focusing narrowly on specific exchange-rate, interest-rate, and other policy instruments. It is also to ignore the record of inadequate adjustment under International Monetary Fund auspices. The right question is how to reconstruct a Latin American developmental state that can

9. For this approach, see the contributions to J. M. Buchanan, R. D. Tollison, and G. Tullock, eds., *Toward a Theory of Rent Seeking Society* (College Station: Texas A&M University Press, 1980).

consistently implement the right policies, not just register the right prices. State direction is not enough; but substituting a minimal state is to treat symptoms rather than the problem. Reforms must have a domestic basis in a sustainable societal consensus. That is the challenge facing the new democracies in the region, made harder by the debt and its attendant domestic distortions.

ANNALS, *AAPSS*, **505,** September 1989

The East Asian NICs in Comparative Perspective

By STEPHAN HAGGARD

ABSTRACT: Purely economic analyses of the East Asian newly industrializing countries have overlooked the politics of their growth. Why were these countries able to pursue strategies that combined rapid growth with a relatively equitable distribution of income? The reason lies partly in external conditions, including expanding world trade, and, in the case of Taiwan and Korea, pressure from the United States for policy reform. Domestic social and political conditions were also auspicious, however. Export-led growth was facilitated by weak labor movements and the absence of leftist or populist parties. A relatively brief period of import-substitution policies prevented the development of strong protectionist business interests. Equity was advanced by land reforms in Korea and Taiwan and by the absence of a rural sector in Hong Kong and Singapore. No explanation is complete, however, without reference to the strength of the East Asian states, including their insulation from interest-group pressures and their cohesive, meritocratic bureaucracies. These political institutions facilitated coherent, decisive, yet flexible policy.

Stephan Haggard received his Ph.D. in political science from the University of California, Berkeley, in 1983 and is currently associate professor of government at Harvard University. His articles have appeared in World Politics, International Organization, The Bulletin of Concerned Asian Scholars, Latin American Research Review, *and a number of edited collections. He is now completing two manuscripts:* Pathways from the Periphery: The Politics of Growth in the Newly Industrializing Countries *and* The Transition to Export-led Growth in Korea.

ECONOMIC analyses of the East Asian newly industrializing countries (NICs) — Korea, Taiwan, Hong Kong, and Singapore — have foundered on a simple puzzle. Export-oriented development clearly contributed to their rapid growth. Yet if such a strategy is superior, why have so few developing countries successfully replicated it? The development experience of the East Asian NICs certainly has lessons for other countries, but it would be misleading to overlook the factors that explain why the East Asian countries opted for growth-oriented policies. This article explores why political leaders choose the development strategies they do, comparing the East Asian NICs with countries that have pursued more inward-looking policies, particularly Brazil and Mexico.[1]

Three historical patterns of Third World industrialization can be distinguished, each linked with important policy choices: an import-substitution trajectory, characteristic of Mexico, Brazil, Turkey, India, and other large less developed countries; an export-led growth pattern, of which Korea and Taiwan are the most successful cases; and an entrepôt path, of which Singapore and Hong Kong are examples.

Virtually all developing countries began their contact with the world economy as primary-product exporters; many remain dependent on commodity exports. In this stage of growth, the primary sector produces food for local consumption — the traditional sector — and raw materials or foodstuffs for export — the enclave sector. Exports generate local purchasing power and finance the import of consumer goods. In the typical colonial economy, government policy supported this pattern. Trade was relatively free and exchange rates were fixed. The nonprimary sector consisted mainly of commercial services and craft production.

One transition from an economy based on primary exports is usually toward import-substituting industrialization (ISI). In the first stage of ISI, the earnings from primary-product exports, supplemented with foreign borrowing and aid, finance the import of producer goods. These provide the foundation for local production of consumer goods, such as textiles. ISI may occur naturally, as the result of balance-of-payment problems or as a by-product of trade and exchange controls designed to manage them. ISI can also result from explicit policies designed to support manufacturing, such as protection and subsidized finance.

There is debate as to whether primary import substitution naturally reaches some point of exhaustion, when the domestic market for import substitutes is saturated.[2] Size is crucial here. Large internal markets present the temptation to forge backward linkages into intermediate and capital goods industries in which scale economies are important. The move into heavy industries raises policy choices about the appropriateness of different leading sectors and

1. For further reading, see Stephan Haggard, "The Newly Industrializing Countries in the International System," *World Politics*, (38)2 (Jan. 1986); Stephan Haggard with Tun-jen Cheng, "State and Foreign Capital in the East Asian NICs," in *The Political Economy of the New Asian Industrialism*, ed. Fred Deyo (Ithaca, NY: Cornell University Press, 1987); Stephan Haggard, *Newly Industrializing Asia in Transition: Policy Reform and American Response* (Berkeley: University of California, Institute of International Studies, 1987). The discussion of alternative development strategies is summarized in Bela Balassa, "The Process of Industrial Development and Alternative Development Strategies," in *The Newly Industrialized Countries in the World Economy*, by Balassa (Elmsford, NY: Pergamon Press, 1981).

2. See Albert Hirschman, "The Political Economy of Import-Substituting Industrialization in Latin America," in *A Bias for Hope*, by Hirschman (New Haven, CT: Yale University Press, 1971).

the role of foreign and state-owned firms, which are likely to be important in this new phase of growth.

A final stage of this growth path, seen in the 1970s and 1980s in Latin America, has been to supplement import substitution with the expansion of manufactured exports. Exports were pushed out by special incentives, but these efforts did not solve chronic payment imbalances and were accompanied by an expansion of foreign borrowing. With the evaporation of foreign credit in the 1980s and the need to repay past obligations, export efforts intensified.

The industrialization of countries pursuing export-led growth also began with a period of primary-product export and was similarly followed by a period of import substitution. The limitations of the first phase of ISI were met in part by continued import substitution in selected sectors, but primarily through a shift in incentives to favor the export of labor-intensive manufactures. This involved stable macroeconomic policies; devaluation, which signaled to domestic firms their comparative advantage; and selective import liberalization to give exporters access to needed inputs. It also entailed more targeted and discretionary supports to exporters. A third economic transition came in the 1970s and 1980s in the effort to promote the development of more technology- and capital-intensive sectors. Both Korea and Taiwan targeted particular industries for support, and the second phase of export-led growth thus bears some resemblance to the third stage of import substitution. The East Asian economies were more sensitive to developments in world markets, however, and this put limits on the pursuit of such industrial deepening.

Entrepôts, finally, have large service and commercial sectors to support their function as intermediaries between primary-product-exporting hinterlands and the world economy. Because entrepôts have no rural sector of their own, both food and labor are pulled from the hinterland. The first important transition is the diversification from purely commercial activities into manufacturing. With restricted domestic markets, trade is free, though the extent of direct government involvement in production varies between laissez-faire Hong Kong and Singapore's dirigism. The second transition, similar to that in the model of export-led growth, is toward industrial diversification, but with commercial and entrepôt functions continuing in importance.

EXPLAINING DEVELOPMENT STRATEGIES

Four sets of political factors can affect the choice of national strategies: pressures emanating from the international system, domestic political coalitions, domestic political institutions, and the influence of ideology.

*International constraints:
    Shocks, size, and
    major power influence*

The international system can constrain policy either through economic shocks and pressures or through the direct influence of dominant states. One would predict a shift from a model of primary-product export to ISI when commodity producers face price shocks or when access to markets, supplies, and capital is severed. Price shocks change the relative rates of return between agriculture and manufacturing activities. Incentives to substitute for imports will also increase when foreign exchange earnings and capital inflows dwindle and needed inputs become scarce.

Historical evidence supports these generalizations. The 1930s were a period of accelerated industrialization and increased government intervention across Latin America.[3] The two world wars also disrupted traditional trade and capital flows and were important catalysts to industrialization in Latin America. In Korea and Taiwan, severe balance-of-payments crises associated with war and reconstruction forced import substitution. In Hong Kong, the Chinese Revolution and the strategic embargo associated with the Korean War reoriented traditional trade patterns. In Singapore, the breakdown of association with Malaysia in 1965 forced a reorientation of growth strategy toward world markets.

Negative shocks have much stronger effects than positive ones. A positive shock of expanding world trade will not provide a sufficient incentive to launch export-oriented policies. Once the strategy of protection is chosen, it entrenches the interests of policymakers and business in the domestic market. Once manufactured export-oriented growth is launched, by contrast, firms acquire a stake in the outward-looking strategy.

This strategy exposes firms to new international pressures, though. The East Asian NICs all faced problems of adjustment in the 1970s and 1980s as a result of shifting comparative advantage, protectionism, and slowed growth in their major markets. The response to these pressures varied, however. Korea responded with an aggressive, state-directed push into heavy industries; Hong Kong barely budged from its tradition of laissez-faire. These differences cannot be explained with reference to the external environment alone.

3. See Fernando Enrique Cardoso and Enzo Faletto, *Dependency and Development in Latin America* (Berkeley: University of California Press, 1979).

The second way in which the international system acts on state choice is through direct political pressures. The greatest influence is exercised by formal empire or military occupation, since control of the colony's economic activity is directly in the hands of the metropole. A lesser but still significant degree of influence is exercised by an alliance leader that can link military and economic support to policy reform. Finally, the least degree of political influence can be expected where there are asymmetrical economic relations but no imperial controls, security links, or aid ties.

This distinction between formal empire, military alliance, and economic hegemony is useful in distinguishing the degree of influence exercised by the major powers in East Asia and Latin America. The United States controlled an informal empire in the Caribbean and Central America, but by the 1930s, the large Latin American countries had been independent for over a century and frequently adopted policies at odds with U.S. preferences. Security considerations had some role in economic developments in Mexico and Brazil in the late 1930s and during World War II, but these worked to increase the freedom of maneuver of the large Latin American states. The United States was more concerned about their stance in the global conflict than the Latin American nations were dependent on the United States for their security.

The East Asian NICs, by contrast, have all been colonies in this century. The early development of Singapore's and Hong Kong's economic policy to this day has been overseen by the British. The early stages of Korean and Taiwanese development were shaped by Japan's conception of regional autarky that combined production of raw materials and foodstuffs with investment in infrastructure and industry in its colonies. The defeat of Japan in World War II was followed by the occupation of Korea, war, and the emergence of separate regimes in north and south. The Chinese Revolution pushed the Nationalist Party, or Kuomintang (KMT), to Taiwan. By 1950, the divided Republics of China and Korea were integrated into a U.S. security complex in Asia. U.S. aid was important not only materially but also because of the political support it rendered to the two new regimes. In both cases, the United States financed ISI based on a significant array of state controls. The United States did have a significant tool for influencing policy in the threat to terminate aid. It was not wielded until aid policy was reassessed in the late 1950s and under the Kennedy administration. The move to reduce aid commitments increased the influence of American advisers, who became important transnational allies of domestic economic reformers.

Society as an explanation

A societal approach rests on several simple assumptions. Policies have distributional consequences. Groups will mobilize to advance their interests. Politicians will respond to these pressures to achieve their own personal and political aims. Policies will thus be exchanged for support and will reflect the interests of dominant coalitions, whether seen as ruling parties, sectors, classes, or interest groups. The state is seen as the arena in which coalitional battles are waged.[4]

4. Among prominent societal approaches to development strategies are Markos Mamalakis, "The Theory of Sectoral Clashes," *Latin American Research Review,* 4(3) (1969); Robert Kaufman, "Industrial Change and Authoritarian Rule in Latin America: A Concrete Review of the Bureaucratic Authoritarian Model," in *The New Authoritarianism in Latin Amer-*

There are problems establishing the connection between coalitions and public policies in the NICs. The easily identifiable electoral and legislative coalitions that influence public policy in the advanced industrial states are not relevant in the authoritarian NICs. Even during democratic periods in Singapore, Korea, and Brazil, the link between electoral politics and economic policy is weak. Are the relevant groupings, therefore, those based on sector, class, factors of production, firms, or interest groups? One approach is to begin with some simple expectations about how the power and interests of agriculture, the industrial working class, and business affect national strategy. These sectors correspond roughly to the factors of land, labor, and capital, though it is clear that none of these groups constitute a homogeneous set of interests.

The legacy of the countryside

The trade and exchange-rate policies supporting ISI are biased against agriculture, and the cheap-food policies favorable to industrialization are detrimental to the countryside. One might therefore expect more balanced trade, exchange-rate, and pricing policies where agricultural interests are strong or where political elites have a concern about the allegiance of the peasantry.[5] There is no evidence in either Korea

ica, ed. David Collier (Princeton, NJ: Princeton University Press, 1979); Michael Lipton, *Why Poor People Stay Poor: The Urban Bias in World Development* (Cambridge, MA: Harvard University Press, 1977).

5. See Jeffrey Sachs, "External Debt and Macroeconomic Performance in Latin America and East Asia," *Brookings Papers on Economic Activity,* no. 2 (1985). On the role of agriculture in East Asian development, see Kym Anderson and Yujiro Hayami, *The Political Economy of Agricultural Protection: East Asia in Comparative Perspective* (Winchester, MA: George Allen & Unwin, 1988).

or Taiwan that concern with the rural sector was a direct influence in the transition to an outward-oriented strategy, however. More important was the absence of a natural resource base generating export earnings. This, coupled with the impending decline in U.S. aid, left few options for financing a costly ISI strategy.

As colonies, Korea and Taiwan were agricultural appendages to Japan, though Japan invested heavily in agricultural modernization in both cases. Decolonization was followed by land reform, motivated in Taiwan by the debacle on the mainland and in Korea by the political pressures associated with the division of the peninsula. Hong Kong and Singapore did not have to contend with the thorny problem of agricultural transformation. Gauging the importance of the land reforms — and the absence of an agricultural sector in the entrepôts — for subsequent industrialization demands posing some hypotheticals. The reforms enhanced the state's freedom of maneuver by eliminating a potential source of opposition to industrial initiatives.

The redistribution of assets in land had a broadly equalizing effect on development in Korea and Taiwan.[6] The absence of a rural sector in Singapore and Hong Kong had the same effect, since agricultural productivity and incomes tend to be lower than those in the modern sector. This, in turn, had political consequences. Despite the squeeze on agriculture that followed the reforms in Korea and Taiwan,

they created at least tacit rural support for both regimes.

The shock to the agriculture- and mining-based economies of Latin America in the 1930s strengthened the political and economic position of manufacturing interests. The political transition to a national strategy favoring industry showed a wide variation of coalitional patterns, however.[7] In Brazil, the transition was accompanied by political compromises with rural elites, and the state's penetration of the countryside remains limited. Mexico's social revolution legitimated redistribution of land. This project was pursued under Cárdenas in the 1930s but faltered as a result of a variety of political pressures, including the creation of new landed interests out of the "revolutionary family" itself. Despite recurrent pressures for redistribution of land, ownership remains highly skewed. The Cárdenas period had an unexpected political consequence, however: the creation of a party organization that ensured political support from, and control over, the peasantry.

ISI may be disadvantageous to the rural sector as a whole, but the importance of agriculture in generating foreign exchange resulted in support of export-oriented and modern agriculture in both countries. A new stratum of commercial agricultural interests was created through the extension of irrigation, infrastructure, and credit, but at the expense of the peasantry.[8]

In both the East Asian and Latin American NICs, the pursuit of industrialization was accompanied by a relative political weakening of agricultural interests, but it is difficult to tie industrial policy to the

6. For comparative analyses of the equity issue, see Joel Bergsman, *Growth and Equity in Semi-Industrialized Countries,* World Bank Staff Working Paper no. 351 (Washington, DC: World Bank, 1979); Gary S. Fields, "Employment, Income Distribution and Economic Growth in Seven Small Open Economies," *Economic Journal,* vol. 94 (Mar. 1984). See, however, Hagen Koo's skeptical view, "The Political Economy of Income Distribution in South Korea," *World Development,* 12(10) (1984).

7. Kaufman, "Industrial Change and Authoritarian Rule in Latin America."

8. See Merilee Grindle, *State and Countryside: Development Policy and Agrarian Politics in Latin America* (Baltimore, MD: Johns Hopkins University Press, 1986).

outcome of an overt sectoral clash. Nor is there evidence that the strength of, or concern for, rural interests was important in the transition to export-led growth. The transformation of agriculture is of significance in explaining the consequences of different industrial strategies, however, particularly the high levels of inequality characteristic of Latin American industrialization. Neither Mexico nor Brazil experienced the equalizing reforms of Korean and Taiwanese development, and ISI further skewed the unequal distribution of income.

Labor

The political weakness of the industrial working class appears common to all the NICs. Analysts of Brazilian and Mexican labor have stressed the importance of state and party corporatist controls. While there are differences in the political organization of labor in the East Asian NICs, labor movements have either been weak — Taiwan and Hong Kong — or where active, either drawn under state corporatist control — Singapore — or repressed, as in Korea. The organization of labor occurred at a relatively early stage of Latin America's development and was tied to the development of leftist parties and ideologies that supported an economically nationalist project. Despite a variety of subsequent controls and struggles between capital, the state, and labor, organized labor benefited from ISI. The longer ISI was pursued, the greater the constraining weight of its urban political constituency, of which labor was a part.

Drawing primarily on the Argentine and Brazilian cases, Guillermo O'Donnell has argued that the second phase of ISI "demanded" new controls on labor.[9] There is

no compelling reason why this should be so, and the argument sits poorly with historical fact. In Mexico, government organization of labor predates the self-conscious adoption of ISI. In Brazil, secondary ISI was part of a populist political project that antedates the military coup in 1964.

Variations in the political organization of labor in Brazil and Mexico do help explain differences in the way ISI was pursued. In Mexico, corporatist control over labor allowed the Institutional Revolutionary Party to weather a sharp and painful devaluation in 1954, beginning the period of so-called stabilizing development that remained intact until populist pressures resurfaced in the 1970s. In Brazil, the competitive bidding for support associated with a multiparty system contributed to inflationary pressures over the 1950s and early 1960s. The repression of the labor movement that followed the military coup in 1964 resulted from political considerations as much as economic strategy, but the new political order granted market-oriented technocrats a new degree of freedom. Over the late 1970s, the effort to compress wages in both Brazil and Mexico had another source: the effort to adjust to huge external debt burdens.[10]

A plausible connection can be said to exist between the pursuit of a strategy based on exports of labor-intensive manufactures and labor weakness.[11] The weak form of the argument is that the absence of a mobilized labor movement expanded the

9. Guillermo O'Donnell, *Modernization and Bureaucratic Authoritarianism* (Berkeley: University

of California, Institute for International Studies, 1973); Collier, ed., *New Authoritarianism in Latin America.*

10. Robert Kaufman, "Democratic and Authoritarian Responses to Stabilization in Latin America," *International Organization,* vol. 39 (Summer 1985).

11. See Fred Deyo, *East Asian Labor in Comparative Perspective* (Berkeley: University of California Press, forthcoming).

freedom of government and business. Weak labor movements help explain the absence of leftist and nationalist coalitions and allowed the state to impose relatively free labor markets, keeping wage pressures down and increasing profits and managerial flexibility. A stronger form of the argument asserts that labor was controlled for the purpose of pursuing export-led growth. This hypothesis cannot be sustained. In Taiwan and Korea, labor controls had political roots, and in Hong Kong a steady stream of refugees and peculiar features of the union structure kept labor weak. Only in Singapore does control of labor appear to be tied directly to economic strategy, though during the late 1970s, this meant allowing wages to rise to force firms to adopt more technology-intensive practices.

Despite extensive controls on trade union activity in Taiwan, Korea, and Singapore, export-led growth contributed to a relatively egalitarian distribution of income. The East Asian NICs have seen a decline in poverty, increases in real wages, and sustained state interest in the development of human capital. Real wages have lagged increases in productivity, and there is clearly urban marginalism in all of the NICs. Overall, however, East Asian labor markets do not appear to be characterized by the same degree of dualism visible under ISI in Latin America.[12]

The interests of business

In both East Asia and Latin America, the protectionist policies associated with the first stages of ISI favored local entrepreneurs, but when these policies were

12. See Alejandro Portes, "Latin American Class Structures: Their Composition and Change during the Last Decades," *Latin American Research Review*, 20(3):7-39 (1985).

launched the domestic industrial bourgeoisie was politically and economically weak. In Taiwan, and to a lesser extent Korea, it might be more accurate to say that protection fostered the local bourgeoisie rather than the other way around. In Mexico and Brazil, the adoption of a coherent policy toward industrial development was very slow in coming and, while the evidence is controversial, resulted as much from state interest and adjustment to international shocks as from business influence.

Explaining the shift to secondary ISI, and particularly to export-led growth, in terms of business interests is particularly difficult. Export-led growth poses a threat to firms oriented toward the domestic market. There is no evidence in Korea or Taiwan that local industry was the driving force behind export-oriented policies. In Singapore, local manufacturing was particularly weak and was further marginalized by a strategy based largely around multinational corporations. In Hong Kong, there is a more plausible case that business influence mattered, but it was not the influence of manufacturing interests that was important but rather the commercial and financial establishment, which pushed laissez-faire.

There were characteristics of local business that favored the adoption of export-oriented policies in Korea and Taiwan. With relatively small internal markets, surplus capacity in light manufacturing could be turned to production for international markets. The period of ISI was relatively short, and the state was able to both force and ease the transition into international markets. Rather than reflecting business interests, however, the ability to shift policy toward a more outward-looking growth strategy rested on a certain political autonomy from the short-term interests of the private sector.

This does not mean that government was oblivious to business concerns. The risk and uncertainty associated with an export-oriented course helps explain the extensive state intervention characteristic of economic growth in Korea, Taiwan, and Singapore. The turn to export-led growth in the larger Asian NICs was a two-tiered process. At one level, the state shifted incentives to promote exports, signaling potentially competitive firms of their advantages. This incentive reform was supplemented by state interventions through targeted loans, selective protection, the provision of information, and the organization of business itself. These institutional reforms reduced the risks associated with the transition.

In the large Latin American NICs, the longer duration of ISI produced entrenched protectionist interests that constrained the freedom of government maneuver. As protection was extended upstream into new industries, the coalition supporting inward-looking policies broadened. Domestic end users of protected intermediates and capital goods were naturally disadvantaged in efforts to penetrate foreign markets. When the Latin American NICs did adopt liberal policies — after 1964 in Brazil and in the 1970s in Argentina and Chile — the experiments came under authoritarian regimes with significant independence from local manufacturing interests.

One hypothesis common to recent studies of Latin America is that multinationals have been key actors in determining patterns of industrialization.[13] The incentives

13. Peter Evans, *Dependent Development: The Alliance of Multinational, State and Local Capital in Brazil* (Princeton, NJ: Princeton University Press, 1979); Richard Newfarmer, *Profits, Progress and Poverty* (Notre Dame, IN: Notre Dame University Press, 1985); Stephan Haggard, "The Political Economy of Foreign Direct Investment in Latin America," *Latin American Research Review,* 29(1) (1989).

associated with secondary ISI and export-led growth certainly provided new opportunities for multinationals, adding them to the coalitions favoring the new policy courses. Two caveats are important, however. First, multinational corporations seeking to exploit the new incentives, whether export oriented or import substituting, generally entered after the change in policy. Second, the positive and negative effects attributed to foreign investment can also frequently be attributed to the nature of policies themselves.

In all cases except Singapore, where the local private sector was weak, export-led policies provided opportunities for national firms. Given their external orientation and rapid world trade growth, multinationals and local firms could coexist side by side without the threat of denationalization. In Latin America, the role of foreign direct investment involved greater potential for political conflict. The shift to a secondary phase of ISI demanded an opening to foreign firms, which quickly came to occupy a dominant position in the new ISI industries, such as the automobile industry.

The state as actor and organization

A third perspective on policy reform focuses on the legal and institutional setting in which social forces operate. Changes in strategy are generally accompanied by broader institutional changes, and as Douglass North has noted, "institutional innovation will come from rulers rather than constituents since the latter would always face the free rider problem."[14] While a coalitional approach to policy looks at the interests and organization of social actors, an institutionalist ap-

14. Douglass North, *Structure and Change in Economic History* (New York: Norton, 1981), p. 32.

proach explains policy in terms of the preferences and organizational power of state actors.

Three aspects of the state affect the ability of political elites to realize their goals. First, different political arrangements can increase political elites' insulation from societal groups seeking particularistic benefits, thus expanding their leeway to act.[15] Second, the coherence of policy is affected by the internal cohesiveness and centralization of decision-making authority. Finally, the ability of government leaders to achieve their objectives, and the way in which they pursue them, is affected by the range of policy instruments they have at their disposal.

The economic history of the NICs suggests repeatedly that state-society linkages limiting the level of independent organization of interests were crucial for policy reform, including the move from the primary-product phase to ISI in Latin America, the move to so-called stabilizing development in Mexico after 1954, and the move toward market-oriented policies in Brazil after 1964 and in the Southern Cone in the 1970s. Insulated political leaderships also help explain the turn to export-led growth in the East Asian NICs. In Korea, crucial economic policy changes were launched following the military coup in 1961 that brought Park Chung Hee to power. Park was able to cut through the rent-seeking that had characterized the presidency of his predecessor, Syngman Rhee. Chiang Kai-shek's KMT enjoyed virtually complete political autonomy through its extensive penetration of Taiwanese society.

15. This is an unstated implication of Mancur Olson, *The Rise and Decline of Nations* (New Haven, CT: Yale University Press, 1982). See the discussion of "soft" and "hard" states in Gunnar Myrdal, *The Challenge of World Poverty* (New York: Vintage Books, 1970).

Singapore's pursuit of a strategy based on multinationals came after Lee Kuan Yew consolidated one-party rule. Even Hong Kong fits the East Asian political pattern. Economic policy remains in the hands of a powerful financial secretary.

The cohesiveness and centralization of decision making will also affect the ability of the state to inaugurate reforms. Factions in an internally divided state are more likely to seek clients and pursue their independent visions of the public good. An internally cohesive state, by contrast, is more likely to pursue consistent and credible policies. Brazil and Mexico have experienced periods of relatively coherent policy—in Mexico from 1954 through 1970 and in Brazil following the coup in 1964—that reflected such internal bureaucratic consistency. On the whole, however, the larger states of Latin America have had greater difficulty maintaining their internal coherence.

Korea in the 1950s also provides a case study in internal fragmentation. This was reversed following the military coup of 1961, however. While intrabureaucratic conflict is certainly not absent from the East Asian NICs, the period of export-led growth in all four has been characterized by a relatively centralized and concentrated economic decision-making apparatus.

Finally, political elites view the solutions to particular problems through the lens of the instruments available to them. Their options are limited or expanded by the tools they have at hand. This fact is important in explaining the way particular strategies are pursued. In Brazil, Mexico, Korea, and Taiwan, the turn to import substitution corresponded with a period of state building and the accretion of new policy instruments. A number of variations in national policy can be traced to this early period of national consolidation. For example, strong and conservative central banks developed early in Mexico and Taiwan, compared to Korea and Brazil, where central banks have been subordinated to finance and planning ministries.

An interesting example of the importance of the instruments available to state elites is provided by the way the East Asian NICs adjusted to the shocks of the 1970s and 1980s. The Korean leadership turned to its control over the financial system to direct a second round of import substitution. Taiwan relied to a greater extent on fiscal measures and particularly on state-owned enterprises, which had been a feature of the KMT's management of the economy since its rule on the mainland. Lee Kuan Yew's consolidation of political power hinged critically on wooing key segments of the labor movement into state-affiliated unions. Ever since, Singapore's development strategy has hinged centrally on the control of wages. Hong Kong, by contrast, developed few instruments of intervention and has consistently relied on a market-oriented system of adjustment.

Policy must always be viewed through the lens of what Barry Ames has called the "survival interests" of politicians.[16] Policies will reflect the effort to build and sustain coalitions. But the ability to do so also rests on characteristics of the state as an institution: the degree of autonomy from social forces; the cohesion of the policy-making apparatus, and the instruments state elites have at their disposal.

*Ideas: The transmission of
policy-relevant knowledge*

If international constraints, societal interests, and state capacities could be shown

16. Barry Ames, *Political Survival: Politicians and Public Policy in Latin America* (Berkeley: University of California Press, 1987).

to determine policy choice, an ideational perspective would be superfluous. Yet the range of options open during a time of crisis is not entirely determined by these factors. The economic ideologies available to political elites often loom large as an explanation of state action. By "economic ideologies" I mean more or less coherent frameworks of policy-relevant knowledge. These ideas originate among professional economists and policy analysts and are transmitted through international organizations, bilateral aid missions, the training of professional economists, universities, research centers, and think tanks.

The ideas of the United Nations Economic Commission on Latin America in the 1950s and 1960s and various forms of thinking that grew out of it provided a theoretically elaborated rationale for inward-looking policies. It is plausible that these ideological currents shaped the direction of economic policy in a number of Latin American countries, but since size, external shocks, and domestic political interests also pushed in the same direction, it is difficult to establish the independent role of ideas. The shift to export-oriented growth in East Asia, by contrast, provides a somewhat better testing ground since the structural constraints appear somewhat less binding, at least for the two larger NICs. Both faced declining U.S. aid commitments, but various ideas existed about how to respond. In the mid-1950s, more conservative KMT members championed a statist adjustment strategy, while young colonels in the Korean junta in 1962 and 1963 were advocating so-called self-reliant policies. In both cases, the American Agency for International Development had influence on development thinking. Similarly, Hong Kong's economic orientation has been institutionally entrenched in a succession of financial secretaries for whom laissez-faire constituted a virtual article of faith.

CONCLUSION

I began by tracing three growth trajectories and identifying critical transitions within them. Policy played an important role in these transitions. I outlined a series of causal variables aimed at explaining the salient differences between the Latin American and East Asian development paths. External shocks, whether from war or depression, played a critical role in the development of local manufacturing capabilities. Outside of the entrepôts, the controls instituted to manage balance-of-payment crises strengthened local manufacturing interests both politically and economically.

The crucial puzzle is why the East Asian NICs abandoned the strategy of import substitution to launch a new industrial course. Part of the answer is that they did not wholly abandon ISI; protection remained in place and the government played a role in developing new industries. Yet in comparative perspective, East Asian development does differ sharply from that of other developing countries. A second explanation is size and resource endowment. The East Asian NICs were too small and too poor in resources to rely on the domestic market. Market size helps account for the lure of continuing import substitution in the larger Latin American NICs, but a number of developing countries have pursued policies quite at odds with their comparative advantage. The deeper question is why these countries pursued growth-oriented policies at all.

There are a number of factors that have not been considered here: the emphasis East Asian societies place on education; the role of Confucian culture; the proxim-

ity of Japan and the Japanese model. I have stressed three different pieces of the puzzle, however. First, all of the East Asian NICs adopted a manufacturing-oriented growth strategy in the wake of external pressures: aid cuts for Korea and Taiwan, the severing of political relations with Malaysia for Singapore, and the interruption of trade with China for Hong Kong. Second, government institutions granted political elites a high degree of autonomy in pursuing their developmental goals. Freed to some extent from short-run political pressures, and controlling strong bureaucracies and decision-making structures, state elites could formulate and implement coherent strategy. Finally, some attention must be paid to the diffusion of ideas through transnational networks, even though they were ultimately filtered through distinctive national institutions.

This analysis suggests the need for some caution in drawing lessons from the East Asian cases. Some factors, such as external shocks, are beyond control, though their importance has hardly waned. The debt crisis is currently producing profound changes in economic policy and political structures throughout the developing world. Strong states cannot be created overnight, nor should we forget the underside of authoritarian rule in East Asia. Political development has clearly lagged economic growth.

Yet there are also some lessons to be learned. It is worth underlining, as other pieces in this volume do, that East Asian success did not spring from a blind faith in the market. While Hong Kong pursued a laissez-faire course, this was but one route to rapid growth. In the other NICs, state and market were viewed as complementary. Second, economists give particular attention to specific policy reforms, such as devaluation or trade liberalization. My account suggests that equal weight must be given to institutional development. The NICs' success is attributable in no small measure to bureaucracies and decision-making structures that generated consistent and credible policy. In supporting policy reform, aid donors and international agencies could pay greater attention to creating the institutional infrastructure that would generate informed, even if politically constrained, policy decisions in the future.

ANNALS, *AAPSS*, **505**, September 1989

Tigers in Latin America?

By LAURENCE WHITEHEAD

ABSTRACT: This article discusses the contrasting trade orientations of the East Asian newly industrializing economies — the four tigers — and Latin America. It questions some myths about the ingredients of East Asian policy success and draws attention to the underlying geopolitical factors that help to account for the contrasting trade performance of the two regions. It concludes that the East Asian experience is at least as aberrant as that of Latin America and that to call the former a model is a misnomer since the most essential ingredients are not transferable.

Laurence Whitehead is an official fellow in politics at Nuffield College, Oxford, and an editor of the Journal of Latin American Studies. *His recent publications concern the Latin American debt crisis and democratization and include* Transitions from Authoritarian Rule *(1986), which he edited with Guillermo O'Donnell and Philippe Schmitter. He is also writing several sections of the* Cambridge History of Latin America.

TWENTY-FIVE years ago no one would have dreamed of studying the four tigers—Hong Kong, Singapore, South Korea, and Taiwan—as a group, and still less of deriving lessons from their economic performance for transfer to Latin America. One British colony; one newly independent island state; one military-dominated product of the partition of an ancient Asian state; and one off-shore province of the celestial empire provisionally occupied by the defeated side after a Communist revolution—what worthwhile generalizations could apply to these four, and even if such generalizations could be found, what likelihood was there that they would apply also to the twenty long-established Ibero-American republics? At a stretch someone might have attempted a political analogy: that in their different ways the four East Asian communities—they could hardly be called nations—were all reeling under the world historical upheaval embodied in the Chinese Revolution of 1949, while 19 of the Latin American nation-states were to some extent responding to the trauma of the Cuban Revolution of 1959. Perhaps something could have been made of this argument but not too much, for Cuba is but an outpost of Latin America, overshadowed by the North American landmass, whereas China is the cultural, demographic, and geographical core of Asia. If it was accepted that Latin America needed lessons in economic management from elsewhere, then, of course, it was assumed that such lessons would come from Europe or North America. Thus the Marshall Plan was invoked as the model for the Alliance for Progress, and critics of the Alliance turned not to Seoul or Taipei but to Chicago or Moscow for their alternative sources of inspiration. In this article I explore (1) the contrasting trade orientations of East Asia and Latin America; (2) the apparent ingredients of East Asian policy success; and (3) the underlying geopolitical factors that help to account for the contrasting trade performance of the two regions and that limit the transferability of East Asian experience.

THE RISE OF THE
SUPER EXPORTERS

How different is the geopolitical—and ideological—climate of the 1980s! The World Bank's *World Development Report* for 1987 illustrates the transformation. It classified 43 developing countries into four categories according to their trade strategies between 1963 and 1985, namely: (1) strongly outward oriented; (2) moderately outward oriented; (3) moderately inward oriented; and (4) strongly inward oriented. Only three countries appeared in the first category: Hong Kong, South Korea, and Singapore. No doubt Taiwan would also have figured here if its diplomatic isolation since 1979 had not extended to its removal from official international statistics and world economic reports. By contrast, of the 14 Latin American countries in the study, 11 were classified as either moderately or strongly inward oriented, and only 3 were said to be moderately outward oriented. On the basis of this rather crude and arbitrary classification, the *Report* went on to observe that "total factor productivity increased much faster in the strongly outward-orientated economies than in the strongly inward-orientated economies," which "suggests that rapid economic growth and efficient industrialization are usually associated with outward-orientated policies on trade." The deduction that Latin America should adopt East Asian trade policies in the hope of then achieving East Asian rates of growth and export expansion was fairly unmistakable, although the *Report* did enter the significant qualification that "the evidence in favour of outward-orientated over inward-orientated policies may be convincing, but the issue of *how* an economy may be successfully moved from one to another is a separate question. Recent experience in Argentina, Chile and Uruguay suggests that the transition to outward-orientated policies should be carefully phased."[1] So *caveat emptor.*

Internal World Bank documents can be much more forthright, with phrases like "the extraordinary performance of the four low-income Far Eastern countries towers over and contrasts sharply with the inadmirable performance of many middle income Latin American countries. Today (March 1988) the East Asian lessons take on a sense of urgency since many Latin American countries desperately need to grow out of their existing debt." Comparing the 1980s with the 1950s, influential Latin American economists have documented the same unflattering comparison: "There can be no doubt that Latin America has fallen dramatically behind Europe and East Asia. . . . There is simply no reason to believe that 'the Confucian work ethic' or 'the Spanish heritage' mean that East Asia

can make it while Latin America cannot."[2] Whereas real per capita income rose 7.6 percent per annum between 1965 and 1985 in Singapore and 6.6 percent per annum in South Korea, it grew only 4.3 percent per annum in Brazil over the same period and only 2.7 percent per annum in Mexico — not to mention just 1.7 percent per annum in the United States. The strongest indicator of divergence between East Asia and Latin America comes from the most recent forecast of the world economy from 1986 to 1992, just published by a respected London-based economic team. This envisages a 135 percent rise in the volume of exports from the four tigers over the seven years, during all of which time these Asian developing countries will be running large current-account surpluses on their balance of payments. By contrast, the volume of Latin American exports is forecast to grow by only 20 percent over the same period, during which world trade in general will grow by 46 percent. In this view, Latin America will still be facing severe balance-of-payments deficits and will be acutely burdened by debt in the middle of the next decade.[3]

1. World Bank, *World Development Report 1987* (New York: Oxford University Press, 1987), pp. 92, 94. The evidence described here as "convincing" is, in fact, extremely thin: (1) the trade regimes of Hong Kong and South Korea are profoundly divergent both in history and in content; (2) correlation does not establish causation; (3) in a causal association the time lags should be indicated; (4) a sample of three countries is too small to establish a general rule, especially when one of the three — Singapore — has to be excused as an exception (see ibid., p. 92); (5) the sample omits the fastest-growing developing country, which was not an East Asian super exporter. Botswana's per capita income grew by 8.3 percent per annum between 1965 and 1985, compared with 6.6 percent per annum for South Korea and 6.1 percent for Hong Kong.

2. Bela Balassa et al., *Toward Renewed Economic Growth in Latin America* (Washington, DC: Institute for International Economics, 1986), pp. 19, 21. For a more solid discussion, see Gustav Ranis and Louise Oppock, "Latin America and the East Asian NICs: Development Strategies Compared," in *Latin America and the World Recession,* ed. Esperanza Durán (New York: Cambridge University Press, 1985), pp. 48-66.

3. *National Institute Economic Review,* no. 25, p. 35 (Aug. 1988). Similarly, *OECD Economic Outlook,* no. 44, p. 59 (Dec. 1988), foresees a rise from 7.7 percent to 8.8 percent in the four tigers' share of world exports between 1987 and 1990, during which period Latin America's share seems certain to languish at around 4.0 percent, the lowest level this century. The United States' share is expected to remain below 12.0 percent.

LESSONS AND THEIR NONTRANSFERABILITY

What lessons might be learned in Latin America from the economic policy successes of the four tigers? And what would Latin America look like if it successfully borrowed from these East Asian examples? The answer to the second question is rather odd and suggests that perhaps there were unusual geopolitical conditions that helped generate such a strong outward orientation in the four Asian economies, conditions that cannot easily be replicated elsewhere. In fact, these small overcrowded territories were all artificially truncated from their respective hinterlands by the political conflicts of the 1950s and 1960s, with the result that for national security, as much as for economic reasons, they were constrained to seek commercial outlets in distant and unfriendly markets. In the absence of equivalent political traumas in Latin America, it may be doubted whether it makes any sense to imitate such an extreme degree of outward orientation as the tigers have achieved. On the contrary, with the passage of time, the initiating spur to East Asia's outward orientation could be expected gradually to fade.

First, though, what are the lessons of the East Asian experience? To answer this question we should look carefully at the policies actually implemented there, rather than at the stylized policy package many international advisers have rather casually invoked to explain the region's remarkable economic success. Looked at in this way, it turns out that there is a surprisingly wide range of policies the Latin American might choose between, reflecting the considerable variation of conditions between the four territories and over time. There is therefore considerable room for differences of interpretation over what consti-

tuted the decisive ingredients of policy success in East Asia, and no single prescription emerges as the one sure path to rapid growth. Nevertheless, there are some strong and recurrent patterns.

THE INGREDIENTS OF POLICY SUCCESS

These were all, for example, highly centralized, relatively well educated, and well-disciplined societies without extreme inequalities of rural landownership, governed by regimes with a clear sense of direction and the ability to take a long view, if necessary overriding temporary resistance or sectional protest. Various labels have been proposed for this condition: hard states; modernizing authoritarian regimes; developmental dictatorships; national security regimes.[4]

One lesson for Latin America, then, could be that the four tigers have shared in a particular style of policymaking: centralized, disciplined, and long-term. That style could have contributed as much as the actual content of the policies to East Asia's remarkable economic success. Indeed, there are some policies that may only succeed at all on condition that they are implemented in such a style. If so, then Latin American economic managers who do not happen to command a so-called hard state might have to practice a more consultative and incremented style of policymaking, and that in turn might require a somewhat different mixture of policies.

4. The seeming uniqueness of the British colonial regime in Hong Kong may preclude its inclusion under these headings. In fact, power is shared between the formal political authorities, some business interests, and the representatives of Beijing, but this tacit condominium rules over a highly disciplined and centralized society and can adopt a relatively long view, that is, at least to 1997.

The content of the policies is also critical, however. Because South Korea alone accounts for about half the gross national product and over half the population of the four tigers, it is appropriate to concentrate on the history of Seoul's development strategy, even though it cannot be taken as representative of the entire group. The following key points can been extracted from a recent World Bank country study.

Korea's export "takeoff" . . . would not have been possible without decisive and innovative policies. These included a rationalized exchange rate regime, selective import liberalization, directed credit, and a host of finely-tuned, export-promoting instruments. . . . Korean strategy did not wholly conform to theoretical prescriptions. Government intervention exceeded the level generally held to be appropriate. And while some crucial prices were "gotten right", others remained distorted. . . . The 1961-73 period represented a unique combination of aggressive orientation and classic import protection. Korean policymakers had a clear control over trade, exchange, and financial policy, as well as aspects of industrial decision-making. . . . [Until 1975 Korean companies] continued to have to meet export performance requirements in order to qualify as an importer. . . . Before 1967 most commodities could not be imported into Korea. . . . unless the industry association representing import-competing firms certified the absence of adequate domestic substitutes. . . . [Thereafter] Korea's trade policy was marked not by the absence of protection in general, but by its absence in those industries that had strong export potential. . . . protection of the domestic market was high in industries in which Korea did not face strong export prospects. . . . Support for exports was pervasively channeled through the state-controlled banking system. . . . Following explicit priorities of Government, banks increasingly used export performance as the criterion of credit-worthiness. Access to bank credit was extremely important, since the bank lending rate was substantially below the cost of borrowing in the alternative

curb market. . . . Institutions such as trade promotion meetings, industry and firm level export targets, close surveillance of export performance, and special awards for export achievements are legendary. . . . These instruments, backed by high-priority lending to exporters, gave trade performance extraordinary visibility and doubtless helped to focus the efforts of all economic institutions — firms, banks, and the bureaucracy. . . . A new Tax Exemption and Reduction Control Law [1975] gave five-year tax holidays, investment tax credits and accelerated depreciation to designated "key" industries. At the same time other businesses faced higher taxes. . . . Since 1979 Korea has pursued a slow, but deliberate policy of [import] liberalization. In contrast to the liberalization experiences in South America, there is little urgency or drama to this effort. The government is withdrawing slowly, although unevenly, in the policy areas of domestic finance, import barriers and domestic export promotion. . . . To understand the importance of the reform program, it is worth noting that there is no strong constituency for liberalization in Korea, in part because consumption goods, the items most heavily protected, account for only about five percent of the current import bundle, but also because there is also a strong Korean sense of self-reliance. Liberalization *per se* is only seen as a useful process if it: (i) improves external competitiveness. . . . or (ii) is necessary to appease trade partners.[5]

MORE GOVERNMENT OR LESS

Latin American governments seeking to emulate South Korea's remarkable trade performance might therefore consider giving the minister of finance the power to appoint commercial bank presidents and to order the priority allocation of subsidized

5. *Korea: Managing the Industrial Transition* (Washington, DC: World Bank, 1987), pp. 29, 31, 36, 42, 60. Cf. Robert Wade, "East Asian Financial Systems as a Challenge to Economic Orthodoxy: Lessons from Taiwan," *California Management Review,* 27(4) (Summer 1985).

credit to those firms and sectors that fulfill centrally planned targets of export expansion. Rapidly rising levels of agricultural protection could be introduced as the industrial sector expands. Automobile imports could be precluded either by an outright ban or through penal levels of taxation. In Korea, although the domestic automobile industry was producing negative value added at world prices as recently as 1982, this was no bar to an aggressive export drive that increased passenger vehicle output tenfold in the ensuing six years. Direct foreign investment by multinational corporations could be downplayed and foreign portfolio investment via the stock market could be carefully restricted to a handful of locally managed funds. In Korea, the law forbids direct foreign ownership of local equity and stipulates that foreign holdings must not exceed 10 percent of total market capitalization or 10 percent of the voting rights in any Korean private company. Strikers could be threatened with the death penalty. Latin American governments that adopted such measures could point to the Korean example to show that they are compatible with a strongly outward orientation of trade policy.

TRADE INTENSITY

What would the economy of Latin America look like if the emulation of the policies of the largest Asian tiger resulted in Korean-style export dynamism? South Korea's exports have reached 45 percent of national income, compared with 60 percent for Taiwan, well over 100 percent in the case of Hong Kong, and over 150 percent for Singapore. At the current level of national income, Latin American exports would have had to rise more than threefold to reach the Korean ratio of openness. If

such trade expansion raised Latin America's national income above the present depressed level, as it surely would, then to reach Korea's level of openness would require that much more in additional exports.

The least one can say is that if Latin America were now to emulate Korea's current ratio of exports to gross national product, the subcontinent would be exporting substantially more than the United States presently sells abroad. If Latin America were also to replicate the trade and current-account surpluses presently achieved by the four tigers, this could destabilize the world economy as did the Organization of Petroleum Exporting Countries' surplus of the 1970s, or the Japanese so-called structural surplus of the 1980s.

These may seem far-fetched thought experiments, but they point to a significant practical conclusion. Not all countries — not even all Latin American countries — can be tigers at the same time. Latin America currently has almost 5 times the population, 3 times the gross national product, and over 100 times the territorial extension of the four East Asian territories, all of which limit the extent to which the latter's extreme trade orientation can be imitated. Both the demands of internal development and the international constraints on super exporting would act to limit Latin America's outward orientation long before the region could reach current East Asian levels of trade dependence. None of this is to argue against greater Latin efforts at export promotion, but it does cast doubt on whether the four tigers offer an appropriate model.

The East Asian trade experience has been at least as aberrant as the Latin American counterpoint. One indicator of this is that the long-term growth of East Asian exports has been around three times as fast as world trade, whereas that of Latin American exports has been around two-thirds as fast.[6] Economists have rightly rejected cultural explanations for this divergence and have stressed the impact of policy, but then they have tended to view the policy choices as if they were entirely voluntary. The main structural explanation for policy divergence that has been offered is that East Asia is resource poor, whereas Latin America is resource rich. But this generalization is too loose and too ahistorical to explain much.

A GEOPOLITICAL EXPLANATION

A geopolitical explanation has more precision and helps to clarify how far the experience of the tigers is transferable elsewhere. To begin with, three of the four East Asian territories have, almost from the original moment of settlement, been exceptionally outward oriented. Hong Kong and Singapore were, of course, founded in the nineteenth century as international trading posts within the British empire, and since the sixteenth century Taiwan has been occupied successively by the Portuguese, the Dutch, the Spanish, the French, and the Japanese. The arrival of 2 million Chinese refugees from the Communist mainland in 1949 was just the last in this succession of impositions from abroad. Korea is the only country with a predominantly indigenous history, but from 1910 to 1945 Korea was a colony of Japan, which forbade teaching in the Korean language, and it has been partitioned by the super-

6. Paradoxically, both deviations from the mainstream of world trading practices have been blamed for contributing to the U.S. trade deficit. The four tigers hurt the U.S. trade balance by their lopsided emphasis on exporting, while poor Latin American export performance causes them debt-servicing problems and thus an inability to finance imports from the United States.

powers since 1953. In Latin America, only Cuba, Panama, and Puerto Rico have remotely comparable histories of outward orientation.

The Chinese Communist victory of 1949 and the Korean War of 1950 severed three of these territories from their respective economic hinterlands. Singapore was expelled from the Malaysian Federation in 1965 with milder but to some extent comparable psychological effect. Consider the impact of these political events on the preexisting trade and investment regimes. Obviously, the Kuomintang government in Taiwan allowed no commercial or financial relations with the Chinese mainland, which it considered occupied by usurpers. To this day Taipei formally claims to be the legitimate government of all China — those elected in 1948 still constitute the national Congress seated in Taiwan — and still forbids direct economic exchange with the mainland. The Taiwanese attempted to compensate for their international political isolation by very active economic exchange with the non-Communist world. Taiwan is not a conventional member of the multilateral trading system in that it grants preferential tariff rates to U.S. suppliers, thus contravening the most-favored-nation provision, and accumulates huge gold reserves. About 40 percent of its exports go to the United States, although diplomatic relations have been broken since 1979.

The international political status of Hong Kong is equally anomalous. A British colony until 1997, it will revert to Chinese sovereignty under a "one country, two systems" formula thereafter. Much of the capital located in Hong Kong originated in refugee flight in the late 1940s. Shipowners from Shanghai, for example, literally brought their ships with them to the British colony at that time. Then, when Beijing entered the Korean War, the West imposed a trade embargo against the mainland, and, of course, Hong Kong as a colony had to comply. This forced the entrepôt to switch into manufactured exports targeted at distant markets. As 1997 draws near, however, Hong Kong's economic orientation is swinging back toward the Chinese interior.

Whereas Kuomintang forces occupy Taiwan and British troops are for the time being garrisoned in Hong Kong, it is the U.S. military that underpins the Seoul regime's international orientation. Obviously, trade with the North and with China was precluded by the Korean War. After an unpleasant 35 years as a Japanese colony, the South Koreans were not keen to continue a semicolonial economic relationship with Tokyo. Various restrictions concerning foreign investment and the protection of the home market can probably be viewed as defenses against renewed Japanese domination. The relationship between South Korea and Japan is, of course, quite complex and includes substantial Japanese assistance for South Korea's export drives as well as a strong sense of rivalry.[7]

Seoul's centralized and disciplined approach to the conquest of foreign markets demonstrates that if war is the continuation of politics by violent means, trade can be the continuation of war — a military struggle for survival — by economic means. Here, for example, is how the World Bank country study on Korea interprets the heavy-chemicals-industry drive of 1973-79: "The opening of US relations with China and the fear of a possible withdrawal of American troops prompted the Government to seek an industrial base for an inde-

pendent defence effort."[8] The South Koreans may now conclude that they have won their battle for survival, in which case their military approach to international trade could start to relax.[9] Moreover, if the two Koreas were ever to be reunified, then the conquest of distant markets would become a lesser priority.

In fact, all of the four tigers are currently seen on the verge of drastically reconsidering their external orientations. No doubt their huge economic successes contribute to these reassessments, but the root cause is a profound change in the geopolitical conditions that first spurred them into super exporting. In the future they will have far better prospects of commerce and investment in adjoining less developed hinterlands than has been the case over the past forty years. East Asia's tigers may well become more herbivorous, just as their example is being invoked to spur Latin America to greater aggressiveness in economic matters.

This geopolitical interpretation of the tigers underscores factors that would tend to limit the relevance of their experience for Latin America. A longer discussion would be needed to analyze the patterns of inward-looking development in Latin America; the role of the hinterland in diverting energies away from external markets; the regional consequences of being sheltered for so long from the wars and

7. See Dal-joong Chang, *Economic Control and Political Authoritarianism: The Role of Japanese Corporations in Korean Development, 1965-79* (Seoul: Sogang University Press, 1985).

8. *Korea: Managing the Industrial Transition,* pp. 38-39.

9. With the establishment of democracy, South Korea's military attitude toward social discipline could also begin to ease. In 1988, the Ministry of Defense admitted that over 6400 military personnel had died since 1980, including 2200 reported suicides and 299 killed in assaults by superiors on juniors. The major parties have called for a thorough investigation. Similarly, some large firms that employed armed gangs to intimidate labor activists are now under pressure to reconsider their employment practices.

revolutions that have wracked the Old World; the problems of too much continuity with an oligarchic and seignorial past. Here it must suffice to say that the characteristic conditions of Latin America are not confined to that continent; the Philippines seems more Latin American than East Asian, for example.

No doubt there are some limited lessons that can be borrowed from the experience of the Asian super exporters, just as there are lessons that can be derived from comparing one Latin American country with another. It is far from clear, however, that the cause of economic recovery in Latin America is well served by exaggerating the applicability of East Asian models or by serving up policy packages based on highly selective — and often downright misleading — interpretations of what the tigers have been doing and why. Viewed in a proper historical and geopolitical context, these Asian experiences seem quite sui generis, not readily transferable, and not even problem free for those most directly involved. It should be borne in mind, for example, that nearly all the inhabitants of the four territories are Chinese and Korean speakers, whereas the elite controlling the outward orientation has to be fluent in English.

CONCLUSION

It is worth recalling that, with a sixth of the population of Latin America, the four tigers require an equal number — 1.1 million men — to serve in the armed forces. The East Asians spend about 6 percent of their national income on defense, compared with the little more than 1 percent spent by the South Americans. Given their recent history and geopolitical location, it is hardly surprising that the inhabitants of these four Asian territories feel vulnerable and seek both strong defenses and close ties with distant protectors. With a total population of about 70 million people, many of them first- or second-generation refugees from the political upheavals of the hinterland, they are crowded into a total land surface — for the four territories — of only 53,000 square miles, which is about the area of Arkansas, or only three-quarters of the space occupied by the 3 million inhabitants of Uruguay. Their territory is more densely populated than Holland and far less fertile. This background should help to explain why their economies are so strongly outwardly oriented, although with the normalization of relations with their neighbors, the urgency of this priority may gradually fade. It should also underscore the reason why the four tigers hardly constitute an adequate model of economic and social organization for transfer to Latin America.

To say this is not to argue that export promotion is unimportant for Latin America or that Latin Americans are in any way inevitably condemned by their geographical location to their present marginal position in world trade. On the contrary, at various periods in world history a variety of different regions and sectors within the subcontinent have risen to positions of prominence in world trade comparable to that of the East Asian countries today. The silver mines of Peru played such a role in the sixteenth century, as did those of Mexico in the eighteenth. Argentina made a vital contribution to the world food trade in two world wars; first Mexico and later Venezuela occupied the role of foremost oil-exporting nation in the 1920s and 1950s, respectively. Even in the 1980s there are scattered pockets of the Latin American economy that are as intensely engaged in some form of international trade as the archetypal East Asians: the small island of Puerto Rico with 3 million inhabitants, a per capita income similar to that of Taiwan, and a comparable ratio of exports to gross national product; also some cities on the northern border of Mexico, not to mention certain narcotics-exporting enclaves. What these examples suggest to many Latin Americans, however, is that super exporting can be achieved at too heavy a price — in national sovereignty, in interregional imbalance, or in overspecialization.

Latin America's current trade problems are serious and therefore the region will require a long period of systematic effort to regain world market share. But export promotion will have to be reconciled, as will other urgent social demands including democratization, disinflation, and the tempering of acute regional and social inequalities. There is little prospect of any Latin American society's achieving the single-minded unity of purpose that has characterized the trading conquests of the four tigers.

The only part of East Asia sufficiently similar to offer a basis for realistic comparisons with Latin America is the Philippines, whose trade performance is very different from the four super exporters. In the Philippines, as in most of Latin America, the appropriate trade goal for the 1990s would be a modest and orderly shift of resources into the internationally traded sector; for example, a rise in exports to 25 percent of national income might be appropriate, rather than to 70 percent. This economic shift needs to be accompanied by a progressive strengthening of the rule of law and the institutions of representative government and by the incorporation of ex-cluded sectors and neglected regions. This is hardly a description of the development strategy that was adopted by the super exporters.

According to the Argentine writer Jorge Luis Borges, to see one's first tiger in the zoo is one of the most universal pleasures of childhood.

Plato (if he were invited to join in this discussion) would tell us that the child had already seen the tiger in a primal world of archetypes, and that now on seeing the tiger he recognizes it. Schopenhauer (even more wondrously) would tell us that the child looks at the tigers without fear because he is aware he is the tigers and the tigers are him or, more accurately, that both he and the tigers are but forms of that single essence, the Will.[10]

The child within us empathizes with the tiger.

A little empathy and a passing acquaintance with their recent history should help us to understand what has made the four tigers so aggressive in the pursuit of distant outlets for their products. But both history and empathy would also suggest that after a generation or two, even the most single-minded of super exporters would begin to doubt whether this was the only worthwhile objective to pursue. As Borges sought to demonstrate, we all carry within us not only the tiger but also a great many other beasts, both real and imaginary. It may be salutary to remind Latin Americans of their neglected internal tigers, but it is surely the East Asians who most need to reestablish contact with the rest of their subconscious bestiary.

10. Jorge Luis Borges, *The Book of Imaginary Beings* (New York: Penguin, 1974), p. 13.

Labor and Development Policy in East Asia

By FREDERIC C. DEYO

ABSTRACT: The rapid industrial transformation of South Korea, Taiwan, Singapore, and Hong Kong has in part been sustained by state development strategies oriented exclusively toward the needs of capital. Less often have criteria relating to the welfare of workers entered directly into state policy except insofar as such criteria are supportive of growth. Underlying this pattern of strategic priorities is the insulation of development planners and corporate executives from the political demands and opposition of workers. While political controls go some distance in explaining the political weakness of East Asian workers, the more fundamental causes are to be found, first, in the nature of employment relations in these countries and, second, in the sequencing of political and economic changes during the course of industrialization.

Frederic C. Deyo is associate professor of sociology at the State University of New York, Brockport. He received his Ph.D. in sociology from the University of Chicago and subsequently taught at Bucknell University and at the University of Singapore. He has published three books on East Asia: Dependent Development and Industrial Order: An Asian Case Study; The Political Economy of the New Asian Industrialism, *which he edited; and, most recently,* Beneath the Miracle: Labor Subordination in the New Asian Industrialism.

INDUSTRIALIZATION in Western Europe and the United States was shaped and conditioned by a need on the part of economic and governmental elites to accommodate popular-sector demands in economic decision making. These class compromises were reflective of emergent political influence on the part of farmers, urban workers, and a dynamic middle class. In Latin America, labor movements entered into populist coalitions that provided the basis for industrial development. In East Asia, by contrast, labor and other popular-sector groups were entirely excluded politically from the developmental coalitions and economic decision making that fostered industrialization. In Japan, from the early state industrial initiatives of the 1880s and 1890s through war mobilization and defeat in World War II, workers achieved little enduring political influence in economic policy. Following a period of heightened postwar labor militancy, Japanese elites reestablished effective control over workers during the 1960s.

The Japanese pattern of narrow developmental elite coalitions and the political exclusion of popular-sector groups from economic policy was followed closely by the so-called new Japans: South Korea, Taiwan, Hong Kong, and Singapore. In these countries, industrial policy through the 1960s and 1970s flowed directly from the economic and developmental priorities of corporate and state elites. To the extent that elite priorities incorporated distributionist and welfare considerations, such considerations were directed by the needs of long-term development or in order to preempt and forestall future political opposition, rather than in response to policy demands from popular-sector groups.

This article seeks to explain the political insulation of East Asian technocratic planners and corporate elites during the period of rapid industrial transformation in the 1960s and 1970s, as well as the compromised political position of these elites in some countries during the democratic opening of the mid-1980s. It is argued that the nature of political regimes, while important, fails fully to explain labor's political exclusion and that considerations both of economic structure and of the sequencing of political and economic change provide further keys to an adequate understanding of this unique development experience.

INDUSTRIAL POLICY AND THE POLITICAL EXCLUSION OF LABOR

There are two very different explanations for rapid economic growth in Singapore, Hong Kong, Taiwan, and South Korea, the newly industrializing countries (NICs) of East Asia. The first and better-established of these explanations holds that export-oriented industrialization (EOI) is a product of liberal trade regimes, private-sector decision making, and the free play of markets, with government action confined to the creation of a modern infrastructure and provision of a stable incentive system. Where more extensive government intervention has occurred, it has been more of an obstacle than a stimulus to growth.[1] This view is best confirmed by the rapid industrialization in Hong Kong under a regime of minimal state controls over trade and investment. To a somewhat lesser extent, it models the early EOI period of the 1960s in Singapore, Taiwan, and South Korea, where trade liberalization and reduced state intervention encouraged new investment in light export manufacturing.

1. Bela Balassa, "The Lessons of East Asian Development: An Overview," *Economic Development and Cultural Change,* supp., 36(3) (Apr. 1988).

The liberal explanation of East Asian development is challenged by a statist model, which emphasizes the developmental role of strong states in fostering and guiding rapid economic growth in this region.[2] At the center of this model are powerful state economic agencies that intervene directly in economic affairs, guiding investment into priority industries, establishing direct ownership or control in strategic sectors, and using their power during times of economic crisis to restructure the economy. The statist view best models the experience of the 1970s in South Korea and, to a somewhat lesser degree, Taiwan and Singapore.[3]

Beyond such cross-national and temporal variation in the applicability of liberal and statist views, these otherwise opposed positions do share important common ground. Each presupposes the virtual elimination of broad political debate of developmental alternatives, and the exclusion of nonelite groups from politics. In all four

cases, rapid industrialization has reflected an overwhelming priority given to economic expansion and the needs of capital, with a corresponding neglect of the redistributional and welfare demands of workers and farmers. In Taiwan, Singapore, and South Korea, such popular-sector political exclusion permitted rapid strategy shifts that initiated structural responses to the successive crises facing these economies over the 1960s and 1970s. In Hong Kong, colonial authorities both resisted popular demands for expanded welfare services and shielded private-sector economic elites from leftist political agitation.

This is not to argue that social welfare was entirely ignored. Indeed, a labor-intensive industrialization strategy was in part adopted to alleviate high and politically unacceptable levels of poverty and unemployment. Nor is it to assert that industrial transformation has not had beneficial social consequences. East Asian development has been associated with egalitarian income distribution, full employment, and dramatic gains in social welfare.[4] Rather it is argued that to the extent that welfare issues have been addressed, their importance has derived less from political necessity than from the requirements of continued growth itself. A useful illustration of this point is to be found in the substantial wage increases instituted by Singapore's National Wages Council in the years 1979-81. These increases were prompted not by the demands of workers, whose unions typically support government calls for wage constraint. Rather, they were but part of a larger program to discourage further investment in light, labor-intensive manufacturing in favor of higher-value-added industry.

2. Chalmers Johnson, "Political Institutions and Economic Performance: The Government-Business Relationship in Japan, South Korea, and Taiwan," in *The Political Economy of the New Asian Industrialism*, ed. Frederic C. Deyo (Ithaca, NY: Cornell University Press, 1987); Chung H. Lee and Seiji Naya, "Trade in East Asian Development with Comparative Reference to Southeast Asian Experiences," *Economic Development and Cultural Change*, supp., 36(3) (Apr. 1988); Peter Evans, "Class, State, and Dependence in East Asia: Lessons for Latin Americanists," in *Political Economy of the New Asian Industrialism*, ed. Deyo. See also the excellent collection of articles in Robert Wade and Gordon White, eds., *Developmental States in East Asia: Capitalist and Socialist*, IDS Bulletin 15 (Brighton, England: Institute of Development Studies, 1984).

3. Paul W. Kuznets, "An East Asian Model of Economic Development: Japan, Taiwan, and South Korea," *Economic Development and Cultural Change*, supp., 36(3) (Apr. 1988); Thomas Gold, *State and Society in the Taiwan Economic Miracle* (Armonk, NY: M. E. Sharp, 1986).

4. Frederic C. Deyo, *Beneath the Miracle: Labor Subordination in the New Asian Industrialism* (Berkeley: University of California Press, 1989).

The relative neglect of welfare criteria in economic policy is readily documented. The global competitiveness of East Asian light-industry exports during the 1960s and early 1970s derived in large measure from low wages, a very long workweek, and an absence of minimum-wage or social security legislation. As late as 1980, hourly compensation costs for production workers in manufacturing remained lower in South Korea and Taiwan than in Mexico and Brazil, the two major Latin American NICs. Even today, despite increased attention to worker welfare, the percentage of total government expenditure for health, social security, and welfare remains about one-third that of the Latin American NICs.[5] The average workweek remains extremely long, especially in South Korea and Hong Kong; work safety records are bad, especially in Taiwan; and minimum wage and social security provide little protection to workers, especially in light industries. In Hong Kong, state provision for housing, education, and health facilities, all justifiable as investments in human capital, were not accompanied by social security systems or unemployment compensation. More generally, the often remarked-upon welfare gains of East Asian workers have flowed less from welfare-oriented policy than from the long-term consequences of sustained industrialization itself. In the shorter run, workers endured the sacrifices demanded of them for the sake of future development.

If state policy priorities necessitated the political exclusion of the working classes, so did the speed with which such policy was periodically reoriented. Taiwan, Singapore, and South Korea have displayed a remarkable capacity to respond quickly and flexibly to emergent economic crises.

5. Ibid.

The policy responses to these crises, especially the shift to EOI in the 1960s and the subsequent turn to capital- and technology-intensive industry in the 1970s, entailed fundamental changes of economic strategy and structure. These shifts, while subject to debate at top policymaking levels, were subject to little open political discussion. Legislative deliberation was abbreviated and primarily reactive, and industrial associations were consulted at best, and more in matters of implementation than of basic policy formulation. Above all, there was virtually no inclusion of popular-sector leadership at any stage. To what, then, can we attribute the extreme political insulation of economic decision makers from popular political pressure during the 1960s and 1970s? Authoritarian political controls provide a partial answer. The impact and success of these controls, however, are strongly contingent on additional and relatively neglected consequences both of economic structure and of the sequencing of economic and political change.

THE WEAK POPULAR SECTOR: THE POLITICS OF EXCLUSION

The shift to light export manufacturing in the 1960s centered on the mobilization of labor, the major development resource available to these small and otherwise poorly endowed countries. That the competitive international position of East Asian economies was predicated on the maintenance of low labor costs, industrial peace, and worker reliability and productivity was explicitly recognized in state planning. In cases where labor demands jeopardized or compromised the new strategy, as in Singapore at the very outset of the new strategy in the mid-1960s and in South Korea in the late 1960s, repressive labor legislation backed by police coercion stifled dissent. In Taiwan, martial law, established some years earlier and for largely political reasons, had already effectively silenced erstwhile popular-sector critics of state policy.

While government controls clearly enhanced the political insulation of state planners, the very effectiveness of those controls over many subsequent years of development must itself be explained. Tight authoritarian controls over popular-sector opposition have been attempted throughout the Third World. The effectiveness of those controls, however, especially in Taiwan and Singapore, cannot alone be explained by the characteristics of labor regimes themselves. Rather, the sources of effectiveness are rooted as well in circumstances that undercut political and oppositional organization among subordinated groups. Of particular importance in East Asia are characteristics of employment systems associated with the period of rapid expansion in export manufacturing.

THE IMPACT OF EMPLOYMENT SYSTEMS

Characteristics of employment relate closely to the pervasive weakness of East Asian popular sectors with respect to injecting a working-class agenda into economic decisions taken by employers and state policymakers.[6] EOI, in contrast to the more limited import-substituting industrialization during colonial and postwar periods, created a vastly enlarged industrial work force. Whereas manufacturing workers had comprised 8-15 percent of the total work force in these countries during the mid-1960s, by 1985 manufacturing workers comprised roughly one-quarter of all workers in South Korea and Singapore and

6. Much of this section draws from ibid., chaps. 6-7.

one-third in Taiwan. But to conclude from such statistics that the organizational and political capacity of the now transformed labor force was thereby enhanced is to ignore important differences in the manner in which the emergent industrial work force was harnessed to the requirements of industrialism. Indeed, even to speak of the proletarianization of the work force obscures more than it reveals. In point of fact, the industrialization process in East Asia had a very uneven impact on the political capacity of workers, and only in South Korea has it generated a strong proletarian challenge to ruling groups.

Beginning in the early years of EOI in the 1960s, multitudes of young female workers have migrated to urban areas and to export-processing zones and industrial parks to find employment in the large light-industry factories that produce labor-intensive consumer goods for world markets. These workers often migrate in search of temporary work in order to achieve temporary independence, purchase a few luxury consumer goods, and send remittances home to help support parents and siblings. This pattern of short-term job commitment is especially pronounced for the young unmarried women who expect to marry and establish a family, withdrawing from factory employment upon the birth of their first child. Among these workers, turnover rates are high, and coworker and union loyalties tenuous. While these workers frequently protest their low pay, minimal job security, and periodic retrenchment during times of slack market demand, they rarely mount effective organized pressure on employers or the state, and they remain politically impotent to intrude in state policy.

Nor are the residential communities of these workers able to support effective worker organization and collective action. Typically, young female workers live either in dormitories owned and supervised by employers or in temporary households with other short-term workers. Lacking is the dense network of working-class associations and organizations that, in more stable proletarian sectors, provide leadership, sanctuary, and support to oppositional workers' movements. By consequence of both job instability and community atomism, relatively high rates of industrial protest are not accompanied by effective organization.

In Taiwan and Hong Kong more than elsewhere, EOI favored expansion in a second numerically important employment sector: that defined by small to medium-sized enterprises, dispersed in Taiwan to rural towns and regions. In small, family-based firms, workers are enmeshed in webs of family obligation and loyalty, while in the medium-sized firms, paternalism and diffuse loyalty, defined and enforced by community expectations and associations, constrain independent organization or interest advocacy by workers. In addition, the vitality of kin-based small firms provides continuing encouragement for workers to establish small firms of their own, thus discouraging group-based opposition in favor of individual mobility efforts.[7] To the extent that protest does occur, it is largely confined to politically inconsequential conflicts in kitchens and the back rooms of small firms.

The potential for effective class action has been confined primarily to a third East Asian employment sector: that of heavy-industry workers in the large-scale, capital-intensive chemical, mining, auto, ship-building, and petroleum industries. Here, large concentrations of male workers, accompanied often by their families, settle in more stable working-class communities in the expectation that despite periodic layoffs, they will remain employed in a partic-

7. Gold, *State and Society.*

ular industry, or at least in related work, until retirement. Wage ladders and seniority systems encourage occupational commitment, social solidarity among workers, and stronger union loyalties. Stable proletarian communities foster class-based ideologies and leadership while providing sanctuary and support to militant workers during times of protracted industrial conflict. In South Korea, it is among these workers that a sustained proletarian challenge to employers and state policy has been most pronounced.

These differences in capacity for effective collective action are readily seen in cross-national and cross-industry patterns of labor conflict. In Hong Kong and Taiwan, labor conflict has been minimal and inconsequential by international standards. South Korean unions have been relatively ineffectual as well. During times of political crisis, however, as in 1979-81 and 1985-88, labor militancy escalated sharply. During these periods, workers everywhere sought to use their new political leverage to challenge established employment and wage policies. But marked variation in the organizational capacity of these workers to mount effective demands shows clearly the differential power of workers across employment sectors. Among light-industry export-production workers, high levels of militancy were accompanied by extreme vulnerability to police action and employer intransigence. Two well-publicized strikes during 1979 exemplify the more general pattern. A work stoppage by female workers at the Tongil Textile Company resulted in a quick dismissal of 124 activists and an early return to work by the others. Later that year, workers dismissed from the Y. H. Trading Company sought refuge and assistance in the headquarters of the oppositional New Democratic Party. Police broke into the headquarters and beat and arrested many of the demonstrators. In neither case did workers succeed in influencing management decisions.

These short-lived protests may be contrasted with those among heavy-industry workers. In April of 1980, coal miners at the Tongwon Coal Mine were able to blockade and occupy the town of Sabuk-up for several days and to bring all local business to a halt for the duration. This strike for a substantial pay boost ended in significant gains for workers, including a large wage increase, a doubling of the annual bonus, resignation of the president of the local union, who had been accused of siding with management during the dispute, and government commitment to expanded local expenditures for housing, roads, and other public works. Similarly, a major strike at the Dongkuk Steel Mill in May, involving violent confrontations between workers and police, resulted in a final settlement that met most worker demands.

The South Korean strike surge of the mid-1980s displays the same interindustry pattern. While in this politically charged climate strikes everywhere gained significant pay increases, such increases among textile, apparel, and footwear workers were roughly half those earned by other manufacturing workers. In 1987, strikes by workers at Daewoo Shipbuilding and Heavy Industry and at Daewoo Motor Corporation eventuated in very substantial wage increases. That same year, Hyundai Heavy Industry workers rejected their union as pro-management and insisted on establishing their own independent union. This dispute culminated in nonviolent street demonstrations by 40,000 workers from various local firms, followed by a rally at a local sports stadium. Following recognition of the new union there, the Hyundai Engine Corporation was shut

down for two months over a similar wage dispute. The protracted nature of these disputes, as well as their favorable outcomes for workers, encouraged managers at a Hyundai dockyard to reach a quick settlement with their own workers when a strike was called in April of 1988.

A paradox arises at this point. In both Singapore and Taiwan, large numbers of workers are employed in oil refining, shipbuilding, and other heavy industries. Why have these workers and their unions failed to achieve the political strength of their South Korean counterparts? In order to explain this cross-national difference, it is necessary to examine the variation in the sequencing of political and economic change in these three countries.

THE DIVERGENT SEQUENCING
OF POLITICAL REGIMES
AND ECONOMIC CHANGE

In Singapore and Taiwan, tight authoritarian regimes preceded rapid industrialization and remained in place through the 1970s. In both cases, early political repression was followed quickly by an effective and pervasive preemptive organization of economic, political, and community life prior to the economic and social transformations attendant upon rapid industrialization. Following the elimination of the oppositional Socialist Party — Barisan Socialis — and its union affiliates in the 1960s, Singapore's ruling party, the People's Action Party, established a vigorous, tightly controlled National Trades Union Congress. As important, the ruling party instituted a system of state-controlled neighborhood associations and community centers throughout its comprehensive public housing projects. Similarly, Taiwan's Nationalist Party, the Kuomintang, organized a state-controlled national trade union federation, the Chinese Federation of Labor. In addition, the party extended and deepened the colonial Japanese pattern of sponsoring a vast network of state-controlled social organizations. Following a ruthless liquidation of oppositional groups during the years 1947-49, virtually all remaining social groups — women, youth, residential communities, schools, professional and business associations — were harnessed to and often subsidized by the ruling party.

Quite different were the nature and sequencing of change in South Korea. Following the collapse of the corrupt Syngman Rhee regime in 1959 and the short-lived democratic interlude in 1960, Park Chung Hee imposed martial law. In subsequent years, however, in response to U.S. pressure, he instituted democratic reforms that permitted some freedom to workers and other groups. During this same period, he also launched the export-manufacturing strategy already adopted in Taiwan and urged on him by the U.S. Agency for International Development and the World Bank. Then, in response to labor strikes against foreign firms in the late 1960s, Park imposed tight new restrictions on workers, thus initiating what became progressively more repressive labor controls during the 1970s.

That the effectiveness of these controls relied to an ever greater degree on police and military coercion derived from two factors that clearly differentiate the South Korean experience from that in Singapore and Taiwan. First, they did not precede, but rather followed, the early phase of rapid industrialization. Second, they did not penetrate society as deeply as did those in Singapore and Taiwan. They were directed primarily at unions and at strikes, political demonstrations, and other forms of collective action rather than at the broader social foundation for such action in working-class community and associational networks outside the formal political arena. This failure to preempt the deeper political and organizational sources of dissent eventuated in a continuing and increasing need to rely on repressive police controls to contain the growing oppositional power of labor. This escalation of opposition culminated in the violence of the early years of the Chun regime (1980-84), best symbolized by a tragic confrontation in 1980 in which police killed hundreds of students and workers in the industrial port city of Kwangju.

It should finally be noted that despite these differences in the brutality and degree of public acquiescence to state controls, in all three countries, political elites remained effectively shielded from popular-sector demands until the late 1970s, at which point South Korea departed from the experience of the other East Asian NICs.

THE 1980s: REGIME SHIFTS, EMPLOYMENT SYSTEMS, AND LABOR

Throughout the Third World, the decade of the 1980s saw a pervasive relaxation of political controls over popular-sector groups and increased pluralism in political arenas. In East Asia, demands for political change on the part of an increasingly numerous and vocal middle class have, to varying degrees, eventuated in democratic reforms. These reforms have in turn enhanced the political position of labor.

Students, intellectuals, and some other segments of the middle class precipitated a successful challenge to military rule under Chun Doo Hwan, prompting direct presidential elections and open party competition for legislative seats. In Taiwan, growing disaffection with martial-law restrictions on political activities, culminating in political demonstrations in the late 1970s, has induced more gradual political reforms, including tacit permission for the organization of oppositional political parties and replacement of martial law by a somewhat less restrictive national security law.[8] Far more limited has been political opposition to restrictive single-party rule in Singapore. There, the ruling party has thus far successfully contained such opposition through minor preemptive reforms.

The varying extent of political opposition and its regime consequences is primarily attributable to corresponding variation in the extent to which it has, on one hand, been associated with exploitable fissures among elite groups, and, on the other hand, has generated broader oppositional class alliances. In some cases, an increasingly resourceful corporate elite has sought greater freedom from state intrusion. In South Korea, for example, the giant corporate business groups have become ever more restive under blunt state controls and have pushed hard for economic liberalization. Similarly, the growing political influence of business is suggested by the prominence of business representatives in Taiwan's Economic Revitalization Committee, established in 1985 to suggest reforms in economic policy. Such elite opposition is less apparent in Singapore's foreign-investment-dominated industrial economy or in Hong Kong's more liberal economic regime.

More important for the success of middle-class demands for political liberalization have been coalitions with other popular-sector groups. In both South Korea and Taiwan, farmers' groups have become an

8. Ibid.

important wing of political opposition, reflecting growing concern about reduced protection from U.S. agricultural imports and, in Taiwan, increasingly alarming environmental pollution. Beyond this commonality, the greater strength of the political opposition in South Korea than in Taiwan derives in part from differences in the extent of political activation on the part of labor. In South Korea, more than elsewhere, workers have been better able to exploit the political opportunity afforded by middle-class dissent. By contrast, the very weak response of Taiwanese workers to new political possibilities is suggested by failure of the Chinese Federation of Labor to accept an official invitation to participate in deliberations preceding the revision of existing labor legislation. While the 1984 Labor Standards Law, which emerged from these deliberations, offered improved pension and severance benefits to workers, these improvements were made primarily at the insistence of the Department of Interior and in the face of significant business resistance.[9] More recently, efforts to establish a labor party in Taiwan have been led by middle-class groups and professionals rather than by labor leaders themselves. Similarly, Singapore's National Trades Union Congress has continued to support official calls for wage restraint during recent years. By consequence of these differences both in the extent of political reform and in labor's response to such reform, South Korean workers have been able to achieve far greater political voice in national and local affairs in recent years than their counterparts in the other countries.

9. Tun-jen Cheng, "Democratizing the KMT Regime in Taiwan" (Paper delivered at a conference on economic growth and political change in the Asia-Pacific region, Hua Hin, Thailand, 20-23 June 1988).

CONCLUSION

Authoritarian political controls across all four East Asian NICs have powerfully constrained labor movements and their capacity to influence enterprise or governmental decision making. Labor's political exclusion, which has encouraged rapid capital accumulation and economic growth over a period of nearly three decades, is rooted in large measure in the employment systems through which labor has been mobilized for export production. Workers in light export industries have lacked the occupational stability to organize effectively. Small-enterprise and rural industry workers have been tightly ensnared in paternalistic controls at work and in their communities. Only heavy-industry workers, especially in South Korea, have been able to capitalize on their relative job stability and community resources to organize independent oppositional movements.

That heavy-industry workers in Taiwan and Singapore have not been similarly successful in organizing politically is attributable to early efforts on the part of ruling elites to preemptively organize workers, farmers, and community residents into state-controlled associations. In South Korea, authoritarian political controls in the late 1960s followed rather than preceded early industrial expansion, were largely repressive rather than preemptively corporatist, and failed to extend beyond unions, political parties, and the mass media to community and informal arenas. These differences in economic structure, regime type, and developmental sequencing go far in explaining the greater capacity of workers in South Korea than in Taiwan and elsewhere to exploit the political opportunities afforded by middle-class-initiated political reforms in the 1980s.

Report of the Board of Directors to the Members of the American Academy of Political and Social Science for the Year 1988

MEMBERSHIPS AND SUBSCRIPTIONS
AS OF DECEMBER 31

Year	Number
1978	12,816
1979	10,884
1980	10,059
1981	9,874
1982	9,536
1983	8,904
1984	6,564
1985	5,704
1986	5.606
1987	5,151
1988	4,674

PUBLICATIONS
NUMBER OF VOLUMES OF *THE ANNALS* PRINTED
(6 PER YEAR)

1978	85,605
1979	71,513
1980	65,153
1981	69,313
1982	74,211
1983	68,236
1984	52,154
1985	52,800
1986	53,201
1987	43,629
1988	53,497

FINANCES
SIZE OF SECURITIES PORTFOLIO
MARKET VALUE AS OF DECEMBER 31

1978	385,795
1979	377,915
1980	368,926
1981	351,886
1982	390,119
1983	485,809
1984	384,312
1985	369,389
1986	373,320
1987	387,997
1988	350,617

NUMBER OF VOLUMES OF *THE ANNALS* SOLD
(IN ADDITION TO MEMBERSHIPS AND SUBSCRIPTIONS)

1978	8,124
1979	5,907
1980	8,751
1981	5,884
1982	7,562
1983	5,877
1984	5,230
1985	5,910
1986	5,119
1987	5,314
1988	13,283

STATEMENT OF INCOME AND RETAINED EARNINGS FOR THE YEAR ENDED DECEMBER 31, 1988

Income
Royalty — Sage Publications	$110,000
Sales of review books	952
Royalties and reprint permissions	3,804
Annual meeting revenue	2,868
Miscellaneous	4,000
Total Income	121,624

Operating Expenses
Salaries	76,764
Payroll taxes	7,848
Pension expense	14,340
Employee benefits	4,284
Annual meeting expense	18,768
Depreciation	4,153
Insurance	7,812
Postage	3,012
Repairs and maintenance	9,216

Supplies	2,496
Telephone	2,580
Utilities	8,904
Total Operating Expenses	160,177
Loss from Operations	(38,553)
Other Income (Expenses)	
Investment income (net)	28,356
Gains (loss) on sale of investments	(40,000)
Grant administration overhead	2,000
Total Other Income (Expense)	(9,644)
Net Income (Loss)	(48,197)
Retained Earnings – January 1	249,112
Retained Earnings – December 31	$390,924

Report of the Board of Directors

During 1988, the six volumes of THE ANNALS dealt with the following subjects:

January — *Telescience: Scientific Communication in the Information Age,* edited by Murray Aborn, Senior Scientist, National Science Foundation, Washington, D.C.

March — *State Constitutions in a Federal System,* edited by John Kincaid, Director of Research, U.S. Advisory Commission on Intergovernmental Relations, Washington, D.C.

May — *Anti-Americanism: Origins and Context,* edited by Thomas Perry Thornton, Adjunct Professor, School of Advanced International Studies, Johns Hopkins University, Washington, D.C.

July — *The Private Security Industry: Issues and Trends,* edited by Ira A. Lipman, Chairman and President, Guardsmark, Inc.

September — *Congress and the Presidency: Invitation to Struggle,* edited by Roger H. Davidson, Professor, University of Maryland, College Park

November — *Whither the American Empire: Expansion or Contraction?* edited by Marvin E. Wolfgang, President, American Academy of Political and Social Science, and Professor of Sociology and Law, University of Pennsylvania, Philadelphia.

The publication program for 1989 includes the following volumes:

January — *The Ghetto Underclass: Social Science Perspectives,* edited by William Julius Wilson, Professor, University of Chicago, Illinois

March — *Universities and the Military,* edited by David A. Wilson, Professor, University of California, Los Angeles

May — *The Quality of Aging: Strategies for Interventions,* edited by Matilda White Riley, Associate Director, National Institute on Aging, Bethesda, Maryland, and John W. Riley, Jr., Consulting Sociologist, Chevy Chase, Maryland

July — *Peace Studies: Past and Future,* edited by George A. Lopez, Faculty Fellow, Institute for International Peace Studies, University of Notre Dame, Indiana

September — *The Pacific Rim: Challenges to Policy and Theory,* edited by Peter A. Gourevitch, Dean, Graduate School of International Relations and Pacific Studies, University of California, San Diego

November — *Human Rights around the World,* edited by Marvin E. Wolfgang, President, American Academy of Political and Social Science, Director, Center for Studies in Criminology and Criminal Law, University of Pennsylvania, Philadelphia.

During 1988, the Book Department published over 270 reviews. The majority of these were written by professors, but reviewers also included university presidents, members of private and university-sponsored organizations, government and public officials, and business professionals. Over 900 books were listed in the Other Books section.

Sixty-two requests were granted to reprint material from THE ANNALS. These went to professors and other authors for use in books in preparation and to nonprofit organizations for educational purposes.

MEETINGS

The ninetieth annual meeting, which was held 29-30 April 1988, had as its subject *Whither the American Empire: Expansion or Contraction?* and continued the tradition of our gatherings with respect to the diversity of organizations represented by delegates, the size of the audiences, and the interest displayed. Delegates were sent by American and foreign universities and colleges and international, civic, scientific, and commercial organizations. States, cities, agencies of the federal government, and United Nations missions and embassies were also represented.

The theme of the ninety-first annual meeting, held 28-29 April 1989 at the Barclay Hotel, Philadelphia, was *Human Rights around the World.* The November 1989 volume of THE ANNALS contains the papers presented at the meeting.

OFFICERS AND STAFF

The Board reelected the following officers: Marvin E. Wolfgang, President; Richard D. Lambert, Vice-President; Randall M. Whaley, Secretary; Elmer B. Staats, Treasurer; Henry W. Sawyer, III, Counsel. Reappointed were: Richard D. Lambert, Editor, and Alan W. Heston, Associate Editor.

Respectfully submitted,
THE BOARD OF DIRECTORS

Elmer B. Staats
Marvin E. Wolfgang
Lee Benson
Richard D. Lambert
Thomas L. Hughes
Randall M. Whaley
Lloyd N. Cutler
Henry W. Sawyer, III
William T. Coleman, Jr.
Anthony J. Scirica
Frederick Heldring

Philadelphia, Pennsylvania
22 November 1988

Book Department

INTERNATIONAL RELATIONS AND POLITICS

MANDELBAUM, MICHAEL. *The Fate of Nations: The Search for National Security in the Nineteenth and Twentieth Centuries.* Pp. xi, 416. New York: Cambridge University Press, 1988. $39.50.

Michael Mandelbaum, of the Council of Foreign Relations, has fashioned a tightly reasoned and informative historical analysis of systemic factors that motivate the formulation and execution of a state's national security policy. Predicated upon the view that "a state's security policy is determined in the first instance by the features of the international system, not of the state itself," his subsequent analysis falls easily within the realpolitik tradition of international-relations theory.

Mandelbaum's argument for an outside-in view of a state's security is developed through his critical analysis of the security policies of six states. These case studies are, in chronological order, nineteenth-century Great Britain, France during the interwar period, the United States in the post-World War II era, China, Israel, and Japan. Mandelbaum's objective is to demonstrate that a state's security policy is primarily dependent upon the security rationale found within its contemporary international environment, and its position of power relative to other actors. Consequently, it is the restraints and limits of the international system and the state's position within it that primarily restrain and limit a state's security policy.

The common thread that runs through Mandelbaum's analysis is traditional balance-of-power theory. His approach, while differing from those traditional explanations of foreign policy formation that stress the dominance of internal factors, does not offer many novel insights. It falls prey to many of the common pitfalls associated with the nihilism of power politics.

Of some interest is Mandelbaum's discussion of the differences between security and economic affairs. While the terminology is familiar—that is, the zero-sum nature of security affairs versus the positive-sum nature of economic affairs—the suggestion that the current international economic order is approaching a zero-sum state is interestingly argued and worthy of serious discussion. Little consideration is given, however, to the alternative view that security policy is undergoing a reassessment, transforming from preoccupation with a paranoid sense of insecurity to sharing in a common

165

understanding of the mutually dependent nature of security in the modern era.

In the final analysis, *The Fate of Nations* offers better than average historical analysis, even if it fails to greatly enlighten the theoretical debate. It contributes to our understanding of the evolution of the national security policies of nation-states and of the too often neglected role of the international system in setting the common parameters within which nations, irrespective of their ideological persuasion, seek to further their security interests.

LOUIS FURMANSKI

Fort Hays State University
Kansas

RICE, EDWARD E. *Wars of the Third Kind: Conflict in Underdeveloped Countries*. Pp. 186. Berkeley: University of California Press, 1988. No price.

This is a book by a veteran U.S. foreign service officer about conflict usually labeled "guerrilla war." Edward Rice proposes "wars of the third kind" as the more suitable label for conflicts in the Third World that are "neither nuclear nor conventional" and in which a major power may become "almost inadvertently involved."

Rice, who began his long career in the 1930s, organized the book around six sets of generalizations that he derived about wars of the third kind, supporting them with historical examples and using his vast experience to good advantage. The first generalization is that if problems that gave rise to such wars are fundamental, causes that have been defeated or suppressed are likely to reemerge and become radicalized. The second is that it is in the rural areas of the Third World that wars of the third kind take place, drawing support directly from the people of the country in which the two sides fight. Third, decentralized organization and a unifying cause like nationalism are necessities. Fourth, guerrillas must rely upon a strategy of protracted war and convert themselves into a regular army ultimately capable of conventional

warfare. Fifth, there are a number of approaches to counterinsurgency—siege, blockade, and so forth—none of which will be successful unless political goals and military capabilities are harmonized. Finally, guerrilla wars pose serious dangers to the major powers that become involved in them by risking military disaster and undermining the polity of the state.

Vietnam and Nicaragua are never far from Rice's concern. Specifically, he worries that the United States either has not learned from past Third World involvements or, worse, has learned the wrong lessons. He cites two recent American generals, Gorman and Nutting, who seem not to have felt free to voice their policy preference for minimal U.S. military involvement until they were on the verge of retirement. Rice considers it seriously deficient to believe that the usual explanations are correct: inadequate public and congressional support, unreadiness to commit enough troops, and responsible officials' lack of a clear intention to win.

Though it does not contribute much to the theory of conflict, this is an interesting book that benefits from Rice's insights and long years of experience, coupled with concerns about how the United States might react to the next perceived threat from the Third World. A sequel focusing specifically on mechanisms of conflict resolution would be welcome.

RANDAL L. CRUIKSHANKS

California Polytechnic
State University
San Luis Obispo

AFRICA, ASIA, AND LATIN AMERICA

BETTS, ROBERT D. *The Druze*. Pp. xiv, 161. New Haven, CT: Yale University Press, 1988. $22.50.

MOOSA, MATTI. *Extremist Shiites: The Ghulat Sects*. Pp. xxiii, 580. Syracuse, NY: Syracuse University Press, 1988. $37.50.

These two well-written volumes appear to be intended for college audiences. They summarize in an attractive manner the legends and lore of the Druze and the various Shiite sects. They contain some interesting firsthand accounts of the past decade from the authors' direct research. They also contain summarizations from largely French studies of the Nusayris in Syria, the Ahl-i Haqq, and other groups one could term Alid-Loyalist, meaning following the Imam Ali. Moosa's study also summarizes the main outlines of Shia doctrine. Betts's study of the Druze follows the same approach as Moosa's, commenting on the Druze in modern times in Lebanon, Syria, and Israel.

In general, academic studies of both Islam and Christianity have been undergoing a major change in approach in the past generation. Where in the 1960s the basic model for religious studies was the true church and the sects, the rise of the television evangelists on one hand and the Khomeini revolution of 1979 on the other has led to the perception of religion in terms of cross-cutting modalities such as liberal or fundamentalist. The effect of this reorientation of the field in Islamic studies has been one of downplaying the differences between the creedal positions of Shiites and Sunnis and emphasizing more the social and behavioral positions adopted by individuals across the various communities. The new trend is becoming well known to the readers of the Islamic studies journals. The Koranic commentary of Mahmoud Ayyoub at Temple University is an example. Matti Moosa's source, Professor Mustafa Kamil Shaybi, is another writer of the new trend. His major study on the linkage between Sufism and Shiism across history is now widely read. This trend feeds into and resonates with modernist interpretation in the social history and political economy of Islamic society. For all these writers, the center of gravity is the present day and its dynamics, not the past.

The older trend, led by well-known orientalists such as Bernard Lewis, to which these two books are conceptually in debt, maintains that the key to understanding modern upheavals in Iran and Lebanon can be traced back to medieval extremist sects, collectively called the Ghulat, of which the Order of the Assassins is the best known. Orientalists find evidence for this in the continuity over a thousand years of language and, within language, political vocabulary.

The obvious weak points in orientalism are very much in the public domain, and the two works under review could be criticized on this account. Middle Eastern cultural history is far more than the history of religions. What exists there today in the way of culture is actually modern and/or affirms its own modernity. Surely the great Druze leader Kamil Junbalat, who led the unity movement of the 1970s in Lebanon, was a socialist. It is with difficulty that one can tag his career onto the end of a book on ritual. It would be easier to reconstruct his career from its secular milieu and from secular — and non-Druze — publications such as *Al-Hurriya* and *Al-Safir*. One can well be born into a religious group, experience its education, and become something quite different in a cosmopolitan setting. Husayn Muruwwah, the editor of *Al-Tariq*, the major leftist magazine of Lebanon, and the author of a 2000-page history of Islamic philosophy, was a Communist educated in Shiism in Najaf, the Shiite holy city. The Shiite ayatollah in Iraq, Muhammad Baqir Al-Sadr (d. 1980), wrote a major work criticizing Stalinism but defending collectivism. (Recently Dr. Shams Inati of Villanova University translated this book into English as *Our Philosophy*.) Not all radicals are Shiite by family origin. Individuals of Sunni background dominate the Egyptian Communist Party, for example.

No doubt the writing of communal history tends to be more difficult in a terrain in which a superficial modernism has triumphed over, without fully assimilating, orientalism. Thus, when the authors of these two texts tack a recent chronology onto the end of a frozen weblike account of their community, they do what nearly all other writers do. Still one would expect the typical critic of orientalism to seize on this to show how communal history is decontextualized and largely idealist. For the future, the more subtle point will be not one of attacking authors for studying ritual and custom but one of explaining in a more historical way what the same ritual practice means in different periods. Do people follow rituals because some leader tells them to generation after generation? Of course not! In cases where this has happened, what are the incentives for the masses to do it? Such questions have been bypassed until now by the modernist synthesis of society and religion in Lebanon or Syria. One approach within modernism is to view ethnic experience as pre-capitalist; another and much better one is to look at ethnicities in the Middle East as defeated capitalist efflorescences, as Samir Amin did in *Arab Nation*. A larger synthesis of the culture of the older Middle Eastern merchant capital and the modern capitalist culture of today is still needed. One day, I predict, orientalist studies of arcane practices — for example, the secrecy of the Shia and the codes of the Druze — will be understood in political economy as analogous to the secrets of the Masons in this country, as a part of the culture of merchants.

PETER GRAN

Temple University
Philadelphia
Pennsylvania

LIEBERTHAL, KENNETH and MICHEL OKSENBERG. *Policy Making in China: Leaders, Structures, and Processes.* Pp. xvi, 445. Princeton, NJ: Princeton University Press, 1988. $39.95.

This is a uniquely valuable book that deserves a very wide audience. China specialists will surely flock to it, but many others will find it richly rewarding. Rarely does one book address so incisively a range of issues as broad as this one does, and even more rarely does so broadly conceived a book hold so firmly to its focus and to its roots in detailed case studies. Time and again Lieberthal and Oksenberg suggest, often quite provocatively, the wider implications of their work, only to resist the temptation to overreach themselves. To our great benefit, they do reach far and occasionally even speculate, but when they do so, they tell us what they are about and they know when to stop. Their evidence is massive — they refer to an immense wealth of scholarly literature and doc-

umentation and also draw on personal experience in bureaucracies and on deep familiarity with politics in China; part of the latter is based on extensive interviewing. Indeed, in this last respect, the book is testimony to how far we have come very fast in Chinese studies, especially since we gained the opportunity a decade ago to do extended research in China. A host of excellent publications have appeared in recent years; this one takes us to a new level altogether. Only a few years ago such a book would have been unimaginable.

The major questions addressed in the book concern the relationships between political structures and processes. In particular, Lieberthal and Oksenberg wish to correct a relative lack of attention by China scholars to bureaucratic structures. This they have done in spades — they frankly plead guilty to giving us "numbing detail" on numerous organizations — and serious students of politics will find the details fascinating and edifying. As Lieberthal and Oksenberg intend, the detail makes a crucial point: "it is precisely this complexity of bureaucratic structure that produces such a strong effect on policy process" in the sphere under analysis in this book. That sphere — energy — is a vitally important one whose fortunes may well determine whether China succeeds or fails. The case studies that lie at the heart of this book are three large-scale energy projects. Lieberthal and Oksenberg take great care to point out ways in which these bureaucracies are and are not representative of others in China and elsewhere, and they remind us of how small a sector of a vast, complex, and varied system they are treating and how necessary it is to do further intensive research. Still, I suspect that others will hear, as I did, a solid ring of truth in these pages.

In brief, this book manages to achieve the highest level of rigorous and sophisticated social science while graphically portraying the down-to-earth texture of day-to-day political workings. Lieberthal and Oksenberg weave into their subtle analysis of structures and processes a generous dose of human dealings and elements of political culture. To the extent that they stress a major theme, it is how a "bargaining system" emerges and operates in the massive

Chinese bureaucracy, and they show the system to be made up of real human beings engaged in high-stakes political activity, impossible to capture on an organization chart.

Comparative references dot the book, and it concludes with a powerful chapter on Soviet-style systems that is typically both cautious and stimulating, rigorously addressing basic social science issues and also commenting perceptively and wisely on current problems of reform visible from Prague to Vladivostok. Two leading scholars have produced a major work that no serious student of politics should miss.

MICHAEL GASSTER

Rutgers University
New Brunswick
New Jersey

MORLEY, MORRIS H. *Imperial State and Revolution: The United States and Cuba, 1952-1986.* Pp. ix, 571. New York: Cambridge University Press, 1988. No price.

Morris Morley has written here the most comprehensive and detailed account of contemporary U.S. policy toward Cuba. To do so, he relied on the best secondary sources, on extensive archival material, and on declassified documents obtained through the Freedom of Information Act.

The book provides a compelling account of the way in which the United States supported the Batista dictatorship after the 1952 coup and how the Eisenhower, Kennedy, and Johnson administrations relentlessly attempted to destroy the Cuban revolution after 1959, first by direct intervention and later by economic strangulation and international isolation. While the hope of overthrowing the Cuban government may have waned after 1968, the policy of hostility continued through the Reagan administration, with some diminution during the Ford and Carter years. Through confrontation, each succeeding president hoped to pressure Cuba to alter its foreign policy.

Though it has many strengths, perhaps the book's most important contribution is its detail on the economic embargo against Cuba. An embargo is an act of extreme hostility, and indeed this embargo was initially instituted under provisions of the Trading with the Enemy Act, which dates from World War I. Today it may be largely symbolic, as Cuba trades with most of the world and has replaced much of its U.S.-based infrastructure with goods from other countries. In the 1960s and early 1970s, however, the embargo did stifle and distort Cuban development, which makes the Cuban achievements in health, education, and housing all the more remarkable.

Morley had two exceedingly ambitious goals in this study: first, to describe U.S. policy toward Cuba, and then to explain it by viewing it as an empirical verification of the theoretical framework he has been developing about the imperial state. To say that he succeeded admirably only in his first goal does not diminish his achievement. Indeed, his discussion of the imperial state is, at the least, provocative.

The framework, however, requires and deserves a full treatment rather than the introductory chapter it receives here. Several theoretical problems remain unresolved. Consider one, that of methodology. Morley's notion of the imperial state is that it is an objective phenomenon, much as Marx's notion of class *an sich* is objective, regardless of whether the class — or the state actors — recognize their class interest. Yet his explanation for U.S. policy is rooted in subjective data, in the perceptions and motives of the U.S. policymakers. Ironically, this leads Morley to accept their characterization of Cuba as a threat to U.S. imperial interests, though this proposition is both dubious and largely unexamined in the book. Morley recognizes that state actors may misperceive U.S. interests and may act on mistaken assumptions and that this might even explain conflicts between different actors, but he is not clear on whether he even believes they were mistaken in this case.

Nonetheless, the book deserves a wide readership. As the United States begins to make halting moves now toward a new relationship with Cuba, Morley's study certainly should be a required reference for policymakers. The United States tends to forget its past transgres-

sions against other countries and to enter negotiations as if a new relationship were to be based
on a tabula rasa. Only by appreciating what
Cuba suffered can the United States hope to develop a modus vivendi with this close neighbor.

PHILIP BRENNER

American University
Washington, D.C.

SAHLIYEH, EMILE. *In Search of Leadership:
West Bank Politics since 1967.* Pp. xii, 201.
Washington, DC: Brookings Institution,
1988. $28.95. Paperbound, $10.95.

Since 1967 there have been hundreds of
books written about the Middle East. Because
of the fluidity of events, many of these books
were dated by the time they were published.
Others, quickly researched and published, have
added little to our understanding of events in
this part of the world. Emile Sahliyeh has
avoided both of these traps. His volume deals
with the Middle East conflict from the perspective of Palestinians living on the West Bank and
in Gaza. It is a welcome addition to the literature
on the contemporary history of the Middle East.
Sahliyeh has experienced many of the events
about which he writes. A teacher at Bir Zeit
University between 1978 and 1984, he is currently associate professor of international relations and Middle East politics at the University
of North Texas.

Using a study of elite politics as his vehicle,
Sahliyeh traces the shifting sands of Palestinian
politics from the post-1967 pro-Jordanian leaders through the aggressive new leaders behind
the *intifada,* the uprising in the occupied areas.
The first chapter paints a clear picture of the
issues that characterize the politics on the West
Bank and in Gaza. The middle chapters deal
with the leadership struggles that have characterized Palestinian politics since June 1967. Included are chapters on the traditional elites, the
urban elites who support the Palestine Libera-

tion Organization, the Communists, the students, and the Islamic leadership. In these chapters, Sahliyeh has avoided references in Arabic
and the use of confusing political acronyms
common to books of this type. His writing style
is clear and to the point. If there is confusion in
these chapters, it is because of the constantly
changing positions of the parties involved,
which, of course, is beyond Sahliyeh's control.

The chapter "Islam as an Alternative" is
particularly interesting. Sahliyeh not only
clearly articulates the various positions of the
Islamic elites; he also identifies these Islamic
forces as major players in the current uprising.
In his concluding chapter, Sahliyeh points out
that power in the occupied territories is shifting
from the more traditional elites of earlier years
to a younger, more militant leadership dedicated
both to forcing withdrawal of the Israeli authorities and to the creation of a Palestinian state on
the West Bank and in Gaza. Encouraged by their
ability to continue the *intifada,* the new leaders
have made the point that the Palestinian residents of the territories are a force that can no
longer be ignored by those powers seeking a
settlement to the dispute between the Arabs and
the Israelis.

This book will be of interest to both the
specialist and the general reader interested in
exploring one of the lesser-known aspects of the
Middle East conflict.

JOSEPH N. WEATHERBY

California Polytechnic
State University
San Luis Obispo

EUROPE

BATT, JUDY. *Economic Reform and Political
Change in Eastern Europe.* Pp. x, 353. New
York: St. Martin's Press, 1988. $49.95.

The British scholar presents a lucid, comprehensive, and well-documented picture of Czech

and Hungarian reforms and astutely concludes that all reforms seeking introduction of the market into planned economies are an "unfinished business."

If the analysis contains any shortcomings, they are chiefly attributable to the ingrate nature of the task. The time lag between publication date and the timing of actions rendered the relevance of some of the activities obsolete. The collation of Czech data ended in 1968, the Hungarian, in 1978, with sporadic glimpses into the 1980s. On the eve of the third Hungarian reform wave — 1988 — we are given some fascinating insights into how political limitations have shipwrecked the second Hungarian reform.

In part 1, the arguments in favor of the use of markets in socialism are recapitulated, together with a discussion on the role of political freedom in the various socialist economic models and the realization of the concept of social interest. Part 2 addresses itself to the practical political problems of introducing market-type reform into communist systems.

The precondition of the economic reform during the Kádár regime in Hungary was political change. But by the 1970s, it became obvious that the reform had veered off course and that the system that developed was neither plan nor market. Meanwhile, pressures mounted for recentralization.

The Hungarian case raises fundamental questions about the impact of the political system on economic processes. Although the ruling powers adopted the reform, the political system itself nevertheless remained ultimately unchanged. Bureaucratic centralized institutions remained in place, and, with them, powerful vested interests retained an organizational base, from which to reassert themselves in ways that undermined the actual functioning of the reform.

Solutions to the problem of how far to proceed with the reform were dominated by covert groups within the elite and the state economic organizations. Politics did not develop into the open play of interest groups but remained a "subterranean bargaining process" within the elite. These groups, through concessions, managed to paralyze the blueprint designed by central bodies, without taking responsibility for the impact of their demands on the "social interest."

By the end of the first decade of the reform, the regime faced escalating political crisis joined by domestic and external political difficulties. With the realization of the impossibility of sustaining the structure by the 1980s, once again the issue of a newer economic reform was put forth. The latest version approached the problem through the combination of plan and market, through the dual acknowledgment of individual and group interest, while sustaining the commitment to a concept of the "social interest."

The ideological problem posed by economic reform for the communist one-party state today is that, on one hand, it recognizes the necessity of rule by a large measure of consent, and yet it is haunted by the fear that in abstaining from centralized coercive methods, uncontrolled political liberalization might result in which, as in 1956, the regime would be swept away. Opening up the prospect of democracy as an option undermines the legal basis for the party's absolute claim to the necessity of its "leading role" provided by the totalitarian concept of a "social interest."

PETER S. ELEK

Villanova University
Pennsylvania

FUNIGIELLO, PHILIP J. *American-Soviet Trade in the Cold War.* Pp. xii, 289. Chapel Hill: University of North Carolina Press, 1988. $32.50.

Philip J. Funigiello's *American-Soviet Trade in the Cold War* is an interesting analysis of how cold-war battles were fought on the field of international trade. While its title suggests a broad perspective, it is primarily a chronicle of presidential initiative and congressional response. Over the course of 225 pages and 70 years, Funigiello reconstructs, in meticulous detail, the balance of forces that made U.S.-Soviet trade a political football. From this he derives an important lesson: namely, that it is very difficult to substitute an economic initiative for a diplomatic one.

This book will appeal to historians, political scientists, and Sovietologists. For more general readers, however, it is overly long. They will find the excitement of getting into the minds of the key players overshadowed by the details of legislation. All told, it is an admirable book, but I am troubled by its lack of balance. There is virtually no analysis, firsthand or otherwise, of the Soviet side and the forces lining up behind its positions. Nor is there any serious attempt to reconstruct the European Coordinating Committee (COCOM) perspective from their records and archives. The former lapse is understandable given the availability of Soviet materials, but the latter is not hampered in this respect. Thus an important piece of the puzzle is missing.

MARC RUBIN

Loyola College
Baltimore
Maryland

WHITE, STEPHEN. *The Bolshevik Poster.* Pp. vii, 152. New Haven, CT: Yale University Press, 1989. $39.95.

Stephen White's lavishly illustrated, folio-sized book is actually a history of political posters created for the Bolshevik cause during the Civil War years. During this period — roughly 1918-21 — nearly 4000 different posters were produced, in millions of copies, by 453 institutions. White seeks to "explain the emergence, flowering, and subsequent decline of the Soviet civil war poster," and in this aim he is largely successful. This book will appeal to historians of Russia, of art, and of communications and to the general reader as well as to the scholar.

White finds ancestors and influences of the Bolshevik posters in *lubki,* illustrated woodcut texts dating from the seventeenth century; in religious icons; in late nineteenth-century and early twentieth-century newspaper, magazine, and journal graphics and satirical cartoons; and in advertising. Graphic art, however, took on critical importance for a new regime fighting for its life and needing to win the support of a largely illiterate society. The task of the poster artists, thus, was to "'seize public attention, to compel a crowd of pedestrians, whether they want to or not, by whatever means, to stop in front of the slogans of which we want them to stop,'" according to Vladimir Maiakovskii, poet and unofficial director of the group of 100 artists who created the famed Rosta windows, propaganda displays based on the latest news from the Russian Telegraph Agency (Rosta). Posters were commissioned by organs of the new Soviet government at the highest levels. The themes of the posters were largely political and military, as opposed to economic and cultural, especially during the most intense war years, 1919 and 1920.

White contends that the political poster flourished during the Civil War because it was a time of "transcendent national need," when "the Bolshevik poster artists had at their disposal themes such as social justice, education and female emancipation, and above all the theme of the motherland in danger." Lacking the imperative of national survival, the artists lost their sense of creative urgency during the next two decades, only to regain it, briefly, when the Soviet Union was threatened in World War II. White's biographical sketches of the artists tend to support this thesis, as nearly all of the most important artists, including even Maiakovskii and Dmitrii Moor, had also offered their services to the czarist government in World War I. Defense of the historic Russian state, which the Bolsheviks controlled, ultimately determined the outcome of the Civil War; it also produced an artistic "level of achievement which has scarcely been improved upon in any other country or at any other time." In the absence of any kind of survey of the population, White can offer only anecdotal evidence that the millions who saw the posters during the Civil War were equally inspired. The over 170 posters, mostly in color, reproduced in this book speak for themselves.

LESLEY A. RIMMEL

University of Pennsylvania
Philadelphia

WILLIAMS, WALTER. *Washington, Westminster and Whitehall.* Pp. xii, 233. New York: Cambridge University Press, 1988. No price.

Washington, Westminster and Whitehall is an analysis of the British government system by an American. Walter Williams is a professor in the School of Public Affairs at the University of Washington. He has spent some time in England looking at the Central Policy Review Staff; he has also spent time in federal agencies in Washington.

Overall, he is quite critical of the British system and the divisions between the politicians — Westminster — and the civil servants — Whitehall. He agrees with the assessment that Britain is dying and says that "the British disease lives on."

Williams makes many suggestions, mostly in regard to structural reforms. For example, he thinks there is much need for policy analysis and proposes a policy analysis unit in the prime minister's office. Underlying his recommendations in this area is the separation of the political and administrative sides of government. He is critical of the neutral civil service that allegedly exists in England. For example, he would abolish the single permanent secretary found in the departments and would replace these persons with a layer of top departmental executives through which all subordinates report.

To help him arrive at this point, Williams analyzes various prime ministers and presidents of the United States; in fact, at one point he brings in the French system and particularly Charles de Gaulle. He gives high marks, for example, to President Dwight Eisenhower. On this score, he is part of the revisionist movement that has been moving Eisenhower up on the scales of the presidents. In this process of comparing presidents and prime ministers, he is quite critical of Prime Minister Margaret Thatcher. He says that she has a decision-making approach that can be labeled as "ideological/intuitive."

Some options that Williams spells out for the House of Commons give some idea of his approach. He feels that the Commons should eliminate question time, increase the number of policy analysts, and strengthen the committees as a primary vehicle. Concerning the prime minister and the cabinet, he would have the prime minister responsible for overall strategy. He would create a policy unit in the prime minister's office and new analytic and strategic units in cabinet offices. In the Whitehall departments he would have the ministers control senior appointments, and he would have ministers who are not in the cabinet have full access to the House of Commons. He would create a new civil service promotion structure. He questions the elite training college for the civil service. He feels there is a need for a strong freedom-of-information act. Overall, he wants more checks and balances and wants more citizen input. There are other suggestions as well. Overall, he would bring several American-type concepts into the British government.

Washington, Westminster and Whitehall is an interesting book with many ideas that might be of interest to the British people. But underlying the arguments is a high level of support for American institutions; not all, such as the Congress, should be used as models.

This book would be a good place for an American student or scholar going to England to start his comparative analysis.

SAMUEL K. GOVE

University of Illinois
Urbana

UNITED STATES

BENZE, JAMES G., Jr. *Presidential Power and Management Techniques: The Carter and Reagan Administrations in Historical Perspective.* Pp. xii, 157. Westport, CT: Greenwood Press, 1987. $32.75.

COHEN, JEFFREY E. *The Politics of the United States Cabinet: Representation in the Executive Branch 1789-1984.* Pp. xiv, 204. Pittsburgh, PA: University of Pittsburgh Press, 1988. $34.95.

Scholars wrote these two books for scholars who are versed in data collection and analysis. The same scholars should also be versed in concepts of political theory.

I found Benze's first two chapters difficult to read because the relationships he establishes are new and a bit strange to me. Cohen's collection and analysis of data will be difficult for readers who have not had at least the "elements of statistics." In fact, some of his analysis is quite difficult to understand—yet his conclusions are made clear to the reader.

Cohen places references to his facts and data at the end of each sentence, rather than using the customary numbers and footnotes. For me, this format was disconcerting.

Cohen describes the cabinet as a body of people formed by the different department heads of the U.S. government. The usual assumption of citizens is that the executive division of the U.S. government, headed by the president, will execute the laws. Cohen claims that the executive department does execute the laws but that it also, through the cabinet, represents different interests and constituents.

He uses empirical data to establish relationships between the cabinet heads and different interests; for example, the secretary of the Department of Agriculture represents the interest of farmers. Such relationships could counteract the programs and desires of the president. The tensions created could bring the president and the department head into conflict.

Conflict between the president and department heads arises in the development and implementation of policy. When taking office, presidents resolve to use their cabinets to establish and implement policy. For unexplained reasons, this intention does not continue for the president's tenure in office. Creating policy becomes the sole possession of the Executive Office of the President, and implementing policy, the responsibility of the department heads. It is then that department heads become representatives of the constituency that is served by their department. Having been left out of the policymaking process, department heads feel no urgency or great sense of responsibility to implement the president's policy.

Cohen uses as a data bank cabinets from Washington's administration to Reagan's first administration. To make his data useful, he divides the years from 1789 to 1984 into five time periods, and for each time period he discusses the variation in cabinet members' social standing by statistical analysis of age, education, experience, party relationship, and regional relationship. From this he goes on to discuss the tenure of secretaries and the secretaries' relationships to parties.

Cohen questions why the cabinet has not become an institution as the cabinet in Great Britain has. We have to note the differences in constitutional growth between the two governments—one parliamentary system recruits its cabinet from its legislative members, while our separation of government functions by means of three different branches: executive, legislative, and judicial. Our independent executive branch forms its cabinet from people outside the government. The cabinet therefore is an extension of the president's programs, desires, and style of executing the laws. Thus department heads who do not like the president's operation usually resign and are replaced by people more sympathetic to the president's political wishes. This is one reason for the noninstitutionalization of the cabinet. Cohen discusses this in relation to institutional theory and democratic theory.

In his introduction, Benze says, "Modern presidents have expressed dissatisfaction with their inability to control policy implementation by the federal bureaucracy." His book is a study of presidential management based on investigation of a variety of administrative techniques. "The research is primarily concerned with the relationship between presidential power and presidential management."

Benze discusses how Carter used standard techniques of public administration such as budgeting, reorganization, and personnel management to have his policies implemented by department heads. President Reagan used political leadership and personnel management to obtain policy implementation and was more successful than Carter.

In his conclusion, Benze states, "The central problem is whether it is possible to institutionalize presidential management." The objective is to bring policy implementation more directly under presidential control. The suggestion is that the president's institutional authority for administration be strengthened by either constitutional amendment or congressional action. This will give "all presidents a stronger administrative hand to play and perhaps diminish the importance of presidential leadership."

Unfortunately, both occurrences seem unlikely in the near future. Therefore, the prognosis for successful presidential management is not positive. Most presidents will continue to muddle through. The very few that combine leadership skills with innovative management programs will be successful.

The two books do complement each other, and each reinforces the information contained in the other. In both cases, I believe only political scientists with a strong scholarly bent will find the books interesting. Others may find them difficult to read.

ARTHUR GALLANT

Montgomery College
Germantown
Maryland

EWEN, STUART. *All Consuming Images: The Politics of Style in Contemporary Culture.* Pp. xi, 306. New York: Basic Books, 1988. $19.95.

At the close of 1988, the New York Times News Service reported a survey of architects, designers, artists, cartoonists, and other social observers. The question put to them was, "What is emblematic of today's culture?"—that is, for what will the 1980s be remembered? Answers included the Pee-Wee Herman doll, the Concorde, plastic commuter coffee mugs, the personal computer, the Swatch watch, and the Tizio lamp. A museum curator spoke of a "decade of dematerialization" in which everything from stereo speakers to airplanes "disappeared into thin lines" (*Dallas Morning News,* 20 Dec. 1988).

This terse news story captures the key theme of Stuart Ewen's longer, cogent, and informative *All Consuming Images.* The work's title is not merely a double entendre but a triple entendre, if such is possible. First, what we consume in contemporary culture is not material goods but images of them, style not substance. Second, we all consume images; there are no exceptions. Third, the images are all consuming; they drive our social, economic, and political lives.

Ewen, professor and chair of the Department of Communications at Hunter College, makes it clear that the trend toward all-consuming images began long ago. So, too, did commentaries on the trend. He returns often to Oliver Wendell Holmes's 1859 essay, "The Stereoscope and the Stereograph," describing the impact photography would have on the world. Using phrases with the ring of the 1980s, Holmes described how "form" would be "divorced from matter," "images would become more important than the object itself," making "the object disposable," and progress would be measured by success at "skinning" material goods of their visible images, then marketing the visible images inexpensively. Although never specifically defining "style," the words resounding through this volume make clear what guides contemporary culture—facades, ephemerals, surfaces, skins, invisibles, mystifications, appearances, representations, abstractions, vapors, envelopes, evanescence, indeed "the production and peddling of thin air." Ewen finds thin air everywhere. The person who reads this well-researched effort will never look at another product advertisement, building, automobile, coffee pot, tube of toothpaste, or any other marketed object or person—even one's best friend—without pondering whether the object itself or the person, like beauty, is only skin deep.

It is refreshing to read a scholarly work acknowledging no debts to massive foundation largess, either government or corporate, for research funding. Instead, Ewen thanks staffs of libraries, museums, and art centers for friendship and advice. He also recognizes his students, who, in response to a writing assignment on "what style means to me," provided the insight that style is the legal tender of society. Thus, perhaps, does Ewen hint that form need not always follow profit.

DAN NIMMO

University of Oklahoma
Norman

HOUSE, ERNEST R. *Jesse Jackson and the Politics of Charisma: The Rise and Fall of the PUSH/Excel Program.* Pp. xi, 196. Boulder, CO: Westview Press, 1988. $23.95.

Ernest House, a policy evaluation specialist in the School of Education at the University of Colorado at Boulder, begins by describing the emergence of the Reverend Jesse Jackson as the head of Operation PUSH. He then addresses the politics of the federal evaluation, in which he was involved, of PUSH for Excellence (PUSH/Excel), an education program sponsored by Operation PUSH from 1979 to 1982. House analyzes several factors as responsible for the failure of the program but then settles on Jackson's charismatic leadership style as the subject of the book and attempts to stretch this analysis to cover a brief survey of the Jackson presidential campaign in 1984 and part of 1988. I would have preferred him to have resisted the temptation to give us an evaluation of an evaluation or to address presidential elections and, instead, as he is an education expert, to have used the PUSH/Excel case study to enhance our understanding of the national problem of generalized race conflict over the methods and goals of the education of black youths in America.

House suggests that the failure of the PUSH/Excel program is to be found in four pillars of conflict that he identifies as Jesse Jackson's charismatic style of leadership; the resistance of the public school bureaucracy and

the state and local governments to PUSH/Excel; cultural differences between the PUSH/Excel idea and the programmatic expectations of the federal government bureaucracy and its program evaluators; and interethnic conflict between blacks and Jews. Except for chapter 12, "The Politics of Race and Social Class," his one-dimensional pursuit of Jackson is unsatisfying as either cause or effect, especially since he does not justify the ubiquitous impact of Jackson on the failure of the program to an extent that would warrant a single-minded treatment of his leadership style. In fact, by the end of chapter 9, House concludes:

The truth, in my view, is that American education is entwined inextricably in racial and ethnic politics, in the vying of different social groups for social mobility. Race, ethnic, and class conflict figure prominently in the battle over what the schools should teach, where they should be located, who should go to them, and who should pay for them. And in this general social conflict, PUSH/Excel was no exception (p. 112).

Why was this not a fitting framework for this book?

The central question at the heart of the conflict between the government bureaucracy and the education establishment and PUSH/Excel that House fails to explicate adequately is the differential conceptions of the degree and extent of change envisioned by the program. In fact, PUSH/Excel was not conceived narrowly as a program only to raise test scores but as a vehicle intended by Jackson to mobilize black communities to enhance their empowerment within the school environment.

Perhaps this book should have ended with chapter 12. House's efforts in chapters 13 and 14 to apply insights into Jackson's leadership style to black leadership in general and to the Jackson campaigns of 1984 and 1988 falter. One reason they falter is that, disturbingly, they rely upon only a few sources. For example, relying upon Bob Faw and Nancy Skelton's *Thunder in America,* House suggests that Jackson's 1984 Democratic Convention speech brought "his supporters to anger"; this suggestion is erroneous. Their anger was directed at the absence of returns from the total process of political bargaining rather than just at Jackson's speech. In addition, House's singular reliance upon Adolph Reed's analysis in *The Jesse Jackson Phenomenon* led to the oversimplification that black charismatic leaders eschew processes of consultation. This is, again, a conclusion that is patently erroneous as it applies to both Martin Luther King, Jr. and Jesse Jackson.

This work should be read for the information it provides on the factors that led to the downfall of PUSH/Excel. Although House does not directly answer the question of whether the program failed or was stopped by its detractors, the implication here is that Jesse Jackson's leadership style was the key factor in either case. A more expansive analysis of the political environment of the program might have proven otherwise.

RONALD W. WALTERS

Howard University
Washington, D.C.

LINK, ARTHUR S. et al., eds. *The Papers of Woodrow Wilson*. Vol. 57, *1919*. Pp. xxiv, 659. Princeton, NJ: Princeton University Press, 1987. $52.50.

LINK, ARTHUR S. et al., eds. *The Papers of Woodrow Wilson*. Vol. 58, *1919*. Pp. xxii, 663. Princeton, NJ: Princeton University Press, 1988. $52.50.

The imperial *Wilson Papers* continues its steady march, striving for definitiveness and undeterred by the formidable masses of documents that must be given individual attention to place Wilson's role in perspective. This involves in the present group of volumes the Treaty of Paris conference. Since it is common knowledge that the great powers failed to achieve a treaty that to any degree justified the appalling human sacrifices suffered in the concluded war, and that the League of Nations the powers created is a monument to its futility, questions are raised regarding the best use of these papers. The present volumes add up to some 1277 pages of text, covering the period from 5 April to 9 May 1919. What do they offer historians and political scientists?

For one thing, they give as intimate a record of the postwar efforts of the Allies and other belligerents as can be asked. They chart the push and pull of national ambitions, and the style and substance of the high participants. For example, too often all but forgotten in the vivid presence of Lloyd George, Clemenceau, and Wilson, Orlando of Italy stands out as he gestures and roundly asserts in battling for Italy's right to Fiume on the Dalmatian coast. Today Fiume is long missing under its own name, but in 1919 it loomed large and critical at the conference. Wilson all but left it in his determination that promises to the Serbs must be kept.

In fact, Wilson's very health is a factor in the conference's proceedings, so much so that it requires a special appendix by medical experts, "Wilson's Neurological Illness at Paris." Such are the conference's problems that Wilson loses precious sleep in laboring to adjust his thinking on Fiume with that on the allocation of former German territory in China to Japan. Justice and expedience are all but at odds in numerous massive problems. Should the kaiser be tried as a criminal? — here is a question that reaches into the present. Ought American arms be sold to friendly — that is, presently friendly — nations? General Tasker Howard Bliss is dismayed that this "would make a mockery of the bloody work already done in the name of lasting peace." Ought food to be distributed to starving Russia, considering that it would be in the hands of Bolsheviks with their own evident agenda? Herbert Hoover says no, a judgment held by Colonel E. M. House — Wilson's other self — to be "foolish." House, placed in the forefront of American statesmen by Wilson's fiat and, indeed, sitting in Wilson's chair at the conference when illness keeps him abed, continues to be momentous in any consideration of America's role in the war and its aftermath.

Yet the peace conference must go on. Germans must be found who will accept its harsh reparations demands and loss of territory. The alternative is to keep Germany under military rule, a plan Clemenceau is willing to consider, since he deems Germans a "servile race." But there are desperate people throughout Europe. Communists in Hungary, Bavaria, and greater Germany threaten breakthroughs that might transform the problems of the peacemakers. Moreover, the self-interest of the Allied leaders, notably that of France, which hungers for the Saar coalfields, bewilders Wilson and makes more complicated his will toward an equitable treaty.

The basic problem receives too little notice at the conference of supreme leaders, and that is the deep emotional feelings of the publics involved. All the Allies have lost appalling numbers of people in the war, and their leaders must take into account the feelings of their people back home. Germans have also bled, but they have lost. The victors feel free to put burdens on them that will prove a blight on future hopes of peace. One of the German delegation, Count von Brockdorff-Rantzau, delivers an impassioned defense of German policy that will echo into the 1920s and 1930s.

Still, the peace conference must go on. One of its main uses is that it underscores the power individual leaders may have to wield for good or ill. It also suggests alternative solutions that might be available to them or later leaders. Wilson had, in his War Message, said that we had no quarrel with the German people; yet it was they who would be asked to pay the reparations demanded. Such facts lie under the often brilliant rhetoric and emotional appeals of the participants.

LOUIS FILLER

The Belfry
Ovid
Michigan

PATTERSON, BRADLEY H., Jr. *The Ring of Power: The White House Staff and Its Expanding Role in Government.* Pp. xi, 382. New York: Basic Books, 1988. $19.95.

Books about the presidency tend to fall into set categories: textbooks, memoirs, biographies, or case studies. Bradley Patterson's vol-

ume fits none of those classifications. It is analytic without being hypothetical; that is to say, it does not offer a theory of the presidency. It does have a theme: the necessity of a White House staff and one that exerts a central thrust in contemporary presidential administrations.

That theme is manifested in the structure of the book. Part 1, consisting of 6 chapters—70 pages—demonstrates why cabinet government, not the parliamentary form but that which each president fashions upon entering office, is insufficient to the challenges before our national government. Part 2, running through 17 chapters—220 pages—sets out in detail the various agencies within the presidency, including those of the first lady and the vice-president, that collectively serve the modern president.

While the obvious audience for this book consists of specialists on the presidency, other students of public affairs will benefit from reading it. There is grist for the mills of media experts, those in public policy, as well as those in organizational and legislative behavior. This is a source to which one will turn whenever a controversy emerges around the presidency: to ascertain which office or offices should be principally responsible behind the scenes. Or reference may be made on a more mundane plane: to confirm who—which agency—answered one's telephone inquiry, who replied to one's letter, or how many persons staff the White House garage.

Fresh perspectives are found throughout this volume. Patterson's list of presidential roles may compel a revision of those offered years ago by Clinton Rossiter in *The American Presidency.* Presidential successes and slips are recounted without favoritism. Despite a seemingly unnecessary effort to prevent premature disclosure of the new flag design when the last two states were admitted to the Union, Dwight Eisenhower's administration appears to rate the highest marks in management skills. That, of course, is in accord with several recent assessments of the Eisenhower presidency.

One quibble: the index is not as comprehensive as one would wish. Neither "contra" nor "Nicaragua" is indexed, and although "Iran-contra affair" is, the pages listed for that topic do not include all references for "contra" in the text.

There is a storehouse of insight and anecdotal information in the book that any student of the presidency will find rewarding. Chapter 1 reminds us of the vast scope and great minutiae that come under the purview of our chief executive. Laced throughout the volume are quotations and illustrative incidents, many of which are likely to slip into the public addresses and classroom lectures of the book's readers. Overall, this is an impressive weaving together of information from personal interviews, material from presidential libraries and other archives, memoirs, official documents, and Patterson's firsthand experience in several years at the White House. It is also a tribute, if only a muted one, to the numerous unsung, anonymous, but vital participants in our national executive: the White House staff.

T. PHILLIP WOLF

Indiana University Southeast
New Albany

POMPER, GERALD M. *Voters, Elections, and Parties.* Pp. xviii, 400. New Brunswick, NJ: Transaction Books, 1988. $29.95.

In this volume, Gerald Pomper has collected twenty of his scholarly articles written over the past two decades. His overall goal is to show the connection between democratic theory and performance in voting behavior, elections, and political parties. He demonstrates a commitment to contemporary democracy by arguing that "voters are capable, elections are meaningful and political parties are responsive."

The seven articles on voters emphasize a critique of *The American Voter,* a landmark study of voting behavior in the 1950s. Pomper challenges the findings of that study by arguing that voters are more responsive to issues and ideology than to party labels. He demonstrates this by discussing gender differences on war and the differences between partisan and nonpartisan local elections. Declining voter participa-

tion is not addressed in this section. Perhaps presidential candidates are dealing with trivial issues or nonissues such as in the 1988 campaign. If so, then Pomper's emphasis on responsive voting would result in nonparticipation. Only a bare majority of the eligible voters cast votes in 1988.

The essays on electoral contests focus on party platforms, voter realignment, and the 1972 and 1984 presidential contests. Pomper finds that platform promises are meaningful, in contrast to conventional wisdom. His reassessment of the 1964 election admits that Johnson's landslide victory did not usher in a new era of Democratic Party dominance. Instead, the reverse occurred. Republican presidential candidates won five of the next six elections. Pomper accurately predicted Republican resurgence in the South. Reagan's 1984 reelection landslide is interpreted as a retrospective endorsement of his first term. This was probably repeated in 1988 with Bush's victory largely based on voter approval of the Reagan years and "peace and prosperity."

The concluding section on political parties demonstrates Pomper's concern about the long-term decline of political parties as an effective force in organizing the voters and providing them with a coherent view of the candidates. Instead, party labels have become virtually meaningless, particularly for the presidency. Pomper correctly identifies the problem in the way that presidential nominations take place. Presidential contests have become too lengthy, boring, and expensive. The media, pundits, and pollsters define the candidates while the parties play virtually no role. It is not surprising that most voters were dissatisfied with the candidates in 1988 and found the campaign issueless and negative. Pomper is accurate in calling for party renewal to correct these problems. He offers 10 useful reforms in the concluding essay.

The wide scope and diversity of these essays demonstrate Pomper's basic optimism about the democratic process. At the same time, he argues that party renewal and revival are essential. This concern is shared by many political scientists and ordinary citizens. If the 1988 presidential contest becomes the model for the future, we can expect our future presidents to be the choice of fewer and fewer voters as television spectators watch with dismay. Surely, this will require a reassessment of democratic theory as the plebiscitary presidency becomes the choice of enthusiastic minorities rather than an involved, activist citizenry.

ALAN SHANK

State University of New York
Geneseo

SCHWARTZ, BERNARD. *Behind Bakke: Affirmative Action and the Supreme Court*. Pp. x, 266. New York: New York University Press, 1988. $35.00.

Bernard Schwartz has written a clear-headed insider's account of policymaking within the Supreme Court. The author of *Super Chief* and *Swann's Way,* Schwartz here turns his attention to the decade-old case of *Regents of the University of California* v. *Bakke.* Having gained access to the files of at least one justice — apparently Brennan; to the reminiscences of some justices' law clerks — most obviously, Brennan's; and to the unusual number of memoranda circulated among members of the Court when *Bakke* was decided, Schwartz lets us listen in on conferences and personal conversations within the Marble Palace. Apart from some concerns about the principle of access to court materials and a serious lapse in professional conduct on Schwartz's part, this is a solid addition to a small corpus — including, for example, Walter Murphy's *Elements of Judicial Strategy* — of credible insights into the operations of the Court.

After a few opening chapters recounting what others have already chronicled about the events leading up to the Supreme Court's grant of certiorari in *Bakke,* Schwartz presents fresh materials. We learn about the initial misjudgment of the likely votes for and against the University of California, Davis, Medical School's preferential admissions program — Burger was once thought to be a pro-Davis vote;

Brennan's adroit maneuvering to bring Powell into the grudging acceptance of the principle of race as not per se unconstitutional; and Blackmun's surgery, slow recovery, and occasional outbursts of irrationality — irrational to the point that Brennan feared that Blackmun might be incapable of a well-tempered judgment on the issue. All these offer insights into the personalities and peculiarities of a court that typically resists such disclosure.

Most important, Schwartz reprints in full five key memoranda and recounts in detail several other memoranda, personal letters, conversations, and conference discussions between the justices. Schwartz's entrée to the inner workings of the Court will foster envy and frustration in those of us obliged to rely upon the finished opinion to track the development of judicial doctrine. In addition, except for a few occasions, Schwartz resists the sensational disclosures that made *The Brethren* a number-one best-seller and a less than credible source.

I have two complaints about the book: one small, the other serious. The small complaint concerns Schwartz's refusal to address the "so what" questions posed by his enterprise. How do these particulars cast light on more general and important matters? There are too many missed opportunities for Schwartz to teach us about why the Court acts as it does. Schwartz points to the role of interoffice memoranda, and he emphasizes how law clerks act not only as authors of these memos but conduct negotiations between the justices. Even something as mundane as the installation of a photocopying machine promises to be important, for it removes the need for face-to-face politicking between the justices.

No doubt Schwartz gained access to Brennan's files precisely because he shuns the hard questions. If this is so, it poses disturbing questions about the appropriate rules of access to intra-court materials. The Court's members are usually reluctant to disclose how the published opinions are forged, fearing that disclosure would destroy the mystique of the Court as a finder rather than a maker of law. But given the willingness of justices such as Stevens,

Brennan, Marshall, and Blackmun to make public their continuing differences of opinion over the direction of the Court, perhaps this reticence is no longer proper because it is no longer consistently followed. Moreover, this mystique is myth; the American public can survive the revelation of what actually goes into the making of a decision. The emperor has no clothes if the Court is understood to be swathed in the cover of a neutral finder of law. The danger of failing to delve deeply in the dynamics of judicial deliberations is that, unintentionally, Schwartz provides support to the "court is a mere sum of the individual personalities on it" reductionism. Brennan and Marshall were predictably for affirmative action; Burger and Rehnquist were just as predictably opposed. Other members were not so predictable but could be consistently placed along the spectrum between the sure yeses and nos. This deceptively simple approach returns us to sociological jurisprudence and legal positivism. Do we want to return?

My most serious complaint about the book is directed at Schwartz's lapse of professional judgment and care. In the opening two chapters, he uses direct phrases and sentences from a 1977 *New York Times Magazine* article and a 1985 book without the proper use of quotation marks or the acknowledgment of sources. That so solid a book should be marred by so much carelessness about other authors' words and ideas is tragic.

TIMOTHY J. O'NEILL

Southwestern University
Georgetown
Texas

SOCIOLOGY

BUSH, MALCOLM. *Families in Distress: Public, Private and Civic Responses.* Pp. xv, 350. Berkeley: University of California Press, 1988. $35.00.

This is a comprehensive text on the history, philosophy, rationale, and problems facing the public welfare field. The early chapters begin with a historical review of the charity organizations from colonial days to the mid-1850s and continue to explore the impact of the Great Depression in the 1930s. The major change occurred when the New Deal legislation was instituted. A second important modification followed the 1962 amendments to the Social Security Act. Consequently, the role and function of the public and private social welfare agencies experienced unique changes. Such accepted concepts as responsiveness to need, equity of the client, dealing with difficult children, and the quality of service offered by the professional staff are challenged by Malcolm Bush.

The question raised is whether social services offered by the public welfare agencies result in greater dependency of the client rather than helping impoverished people to become self-sufficient and independent. Bush recommends a number of changes in the practice of social work in social welfare agencies.

In analyzing the text, I find that Bush raises two major issues. First, what professional personnel should staff a social service agency? Second, how should the welfare system function in helping families in distress to resolve their problems and convert them into self-sufficient and independent citizens?

Regarding professionally trained staff, Bush believes that "the link between social welfare legislation, social welfare bureaucracies and clients is the social work profession." He takes issue with the psychological and Freudian orientation of the professional case worker. The functioning professional becomes paternalistic and denies the autonomy of the client. The tools of case records are considered prejudiced and distorted, resulting in diminished citizenship roles and responsibilities of the client.

Concerning the second issue, the Social Security Act aimed for the role and function of the social welfare system to be that of a powerful change agent that would reverse the impoverished and problem-ridden families into economically healthy and independent citizens. Poverty with all of its ills and problems would be eradicated. Unfortunately, the developed dependency on the social welfare system revealed a new phenomenon, the built-in and immovable culture of poverty.

Malcolm Bush makes many insightful recommendations for the improvement of public welfare. Among such changes are clearly defined citizen roles for welfare parents and children; a developed sense of independence, as, for example, by subsidizing natural parents to maintain their family rather than giving the same money to surrogate parents; utilizing volunteers rather than employing social workers exclusively; and, last, opening case records to the clients, instituting public review boards, and treating welfare clients as human beings who are entitled to their rights, privileges, and responsibilities.

One small criticism is that there are some omissions: homelessness, the aggravating housing shortage, and the new projective legislative change in public welfare with its built-in work factor as promulgated by Senator Moynihan.

In conclusion, this is a relatively modest text that packs a big punch. My guess is that the challenge to social work will not go unheeded. Malcolm Bush has produced a commendable, well-documented, competently written book that poses some challenges to the public welfare profession.

MARTIN E. DANZIG

City University of New York

FINGARETTE, HERBERT. *Heavy Drinking: The Myth of Alcoholism as a Disease.* Pp. x, 166. Berkeley: University of California Press, 1988. $16.95.

WOOD, BARBARA L. *Children of Alcoholism: The Struggle for Self and Intimacy in Adult Life.* Pp. xv, 166. New York: New York University Press, 1987. $35.00.

Addictions are the disease of the 1980s. The drug epidemic has increasingly been portrayed as the cause of most serious social problems in cities, and so the new social programs created by government have been heavily oriented toward attacking drug use. Meanwhile, self-help groups modeled on Alcoholics Anonymous are springing up to deal with an array of social problems portrayed as addictions—one thinks of groups like Overeaters Anonymous. Some have portrayed ours as an addictive society with nearly everyone addicted to something.

The two books I am reviewing take nearly opposite points of view on the nature and importance of addictions as social problems. Both of the books deal with alcohol rather than drugs in general. One, Fingarette's book, is a powerful, authoritative attack on the disease model of alcoholism that challenges the accuracy and the legitimacy of the whole addictions movement. The other, Wood's book, is rooted in psychotherapeutic, clinical experience and explores personality problems common among adult children of alcoholics. It accepts the view that alcoholism is a syndrome that affects the family system in a distinctive way.

Fingarette's discussion evaluates the accuracy of the hypothesis that alcoholism exists as a disease. He argues that if we use the term "disease," we should determine whether the phenomenon fits what medical people mean by this concept. It should have definite causes, a distinctive course of development, and identifiable prognoses. Alcoholism fails to meet the definition of a disease on all of these counts. There is no clear cause or set of steps that lead to heavy drinking. There may be some weak association between one's genetic susceptibility to alcohol and heavy drinking, but at best it accounts for a small fraction of the variation in alcoholic behavior. Researchers have not been able to show that any specific intervention limits alcoholism any better than does no treatment at all. Contrary to the argument of disease proponents, research suggests that most alcoholics—and most drug abusers, by the way—eventually taper down their rate of drinking. Alcoholism seems to be a self-limiting condition for most people. Heavy drinking is strongly influenced by social and cultural contexts, and it also is one way people have of coping with stress. They self-medicate.

Wood's book roots a description of common emotional problems among adult children of alcoholics in the British object relations theory of psychoanalysis. In contrast to Freudian psychoanalysis, which interprets psychological problems as being products of repression associated with psychosocial development, object relations theorists argue that psychopathology arises when subjects have learned that frank expression of emotions and feelings is likely to be attacked by significant others.

According to Wood, children of alcoholics (COAs) often grow up in families where the drinking adults will not allow their children to express their feelings or needs openly. Children often must play the responsible role of adult in alcoholic families, and this teaches them to repress and hide their true feelings. This lays the foundation for a pattern of psychological problems among adult COAs, and it poses characteristic strategic difficulties to therapists seeking to treat them. Wood does a compelling job of describing this psychopathology and discusses her treatment strategies by drawing on case examples from her clinical practice.

While on the surface these two books seem based in opposite views of the world, their differences mostly have to do with the level of action they are concerned with. Wood's presentation is useful as a sensitizing framework for people who themselves come from families with heavy drinkers and for people who must work with COAs. To say that alcoholism is a disease from this viewpoint is primarily to make a metaphorical statement that can help people organize their world and find a framework for taking personal action.

Fingarette's attack is more directed at the reification of the disease concept in public policy. The disease model suggests that there are single best treatments and that if someone is not treated, he or she will always be an alcoholic. That simply is not true. But if social policy is based on that model, it legitimates treating alcoholics and other addicts as tainted people and directs attention away from social practices that encourage abuse, like allowing bars to be built

on highways far from public transportation. Fingarette's book is an important one because it forces us to reconsider the way we think about substance abuse. It convinces me that we will make headway in attacking substance abuse only when more realistic theories inform policymaking on alcoholism and drugs.

CARL MILOFSKY

Bucknell University
Lewisburg
Pennsylvania

MAYO, JAMES M. *War Memorials as Political Landscape: The American Experience and Beyond.* Pp. xvi, 306. Westport, CT: Praeger, 1988. $42.95.

With its high cost in human life, war is one of a nation's most drastic acts and the most likely to be memorialized in public monuments. War monuments commemorate both a nation's political ideals and its historical actions, but that commemoration is selective, reflecting as much what society wants to remember as what actually occurred. This study approaches war memorials as a visual effort to orchestrate society's collective memory of particular wars, and it analyzes how different types of memorials parallel a hierarchy of social purpose: humanitarianism, honor, service, and identity. James Mayo, a professor of architecture and urban design at the University of Kansas, argues that war memorials reflect not only the political history of the nation but the efforts of subsequent generations to symbolize and justify that history.

Mayo classifies monuments into four general categories: "monuments to victory as justice," "monuments to victory as manifest destiny," "monuments to defeat," and "memories of horror." Monuments built to commemorate the Revolutionary War and the two world wars fall into the first category. Mayo argues that a broad national consensus exists that these "righteous wars" embodied the nation's most basic values and that the monuments built to them were designed to project an image of a nation that was not only strong but just. The wars of "manifest destiny" — identified as the War of 1812, the Mexican wars, the American Indian wars, and the Spanish-American War — provoked more ambivalent national feelings. Memorials to these wars are relatively few, given the immense territorial gains that resulted from them. Mayo contends that while most of those that were built were intended to legitimize American actions, these monuments today send out contradictory messages. They memorialize important advances in the nation's development, but the victories they celebrate are tainted by the knowledge that greed and racism were as much factors in these wars as were America's traditional moral values.

Monuments of the Civil War, along with those of the Korean and Vietnam wars, are discussed in the chapter on "monuments to defeat." Mayo maintains that whatever the outcome of the Civil War, the nation as a whole had lost because the political process had failed to resolve the issues separating North and South. He argues that many Civil War memorials, particularly those on battlefield sites, convey a sense of communal guilt over the nation's failure to resolve its differences in accord with its own democratic principles and processes. Monuments to the Korean and Vietnam wars are far fewer in number and have a very different focus. Whereas Civil War monuments commemorate specific battles, leaders, or regiments, the commemoration of the later wars is much more general. What these "monuments to defeat" do share in common, according to Mayo, is a tendency to treat war as past history, a product of political forces from which contemporary society has successfully distanced itself.

Monuments commemorating American Indian massacres, Japanese American internment camps, Civil War prison camps, atomic bomb victims, and Nazi war crimes are all cited as examples of "memories of horror." Mayo's book is generally limited to monuments on the American landscape, but in this section, his primary focus is on European memorials to the Holocaust. The question of how a nation can

deal in a constructive way with the knowledge that it has been guilty of unspeakable horrors is one of the most profound raised in this book, but the relatively short discussion treats it only superficially.

War Memorials as Political Landscape provides a useful framework for analyzing the social and political functions of these frequently seen but rarely analyzed landmarks. Guilty at times of belaboring the obvious, Mayo does offer some interesting insights that will enhance appreciation of war memorials as agents of political socialization. Mayo's discussion reveals that war monuments often reflect much more than an effort to orchestrate the political meaning of a particular conflict. He notes, for example, that there was a close tie between the City Beautiful movement and memorials to both the Spanish-American and the first world wars. City planners in cities like Indianapolis and Kansas City used the patriotic fervor following these wars to mobilize public support for their City Beautiful plans by featuring war memorials as the centerpieces of these plans. Monument building during this period was also influenced by the rapid growth of cities, new technologies, and the availability of wealth. That these other kinds of forces were often at work in shaping the type and level of monument-building activity taking place makes clear that monuments serve many functions and that their major significance may not always be political, at least in the sense in which Mayo uses the term. There is some tendency in this book toward overgeneralization about society's motives and goals in erecting monuments and about their contemporary meanings, but most of the analysis is balanced. This is an interesting work that can be appreciated by both the academic specialist and the general reader.

JAMES D. FAIRBANKS

University of Houston — Downtown
Texas

PAYER, LYNN. *Medicine and Culture: Varieties of Treatment in the United States, England,*

West Germany, and France. Pp. 204. New York: Henry Holt, 1988. $18.95.

DUTTON, DIANA B. with THOMAS A. PRESTON and NANCY E. PFUND. *Worse Than the Disease: Pitfalls of Medical Progress.* Pp. xvi, 528. New York: Cambridge University Press, 1988. No price.

Perspectives on biomedicine tend to cluster near two extremes. Some — let us call them realist — identify medical phenomena as objectively real. Others — let us call them relativist — claim that medical phenomena are contingent on what medical systems recognize as real. Physicians typically favor the former perspective and anthropologists the latter, though some, like the physician-anthropologist Arthur Kleinman, occupy an interesting middle ground.

Payer and Dutton start from relativist, not realist, assumptions and therefore agree that biomedicine's scope is contingent on something other than preexisting objective states. They differ radically, however, on the sources of this contingency. Payer, the author of *Medicine and Culture,* argues that seemingly autonomous structures, like biomedicine, reflect variable cultural assumptions about the way the world works. In France, for example, the importance of *terrain* — a totalistic concept similar to "constitution" — underwrites French doctors' preference for improving bodies and not treating diseases. Dutton, the author — with Preston and Pfund — of *Worse Than the Disease,* argues that medical phenomena reflect structures that support existing political and economic relationships of capitalist America. New techniques, like artificial heart implantation, and new technologies, like genetic engineering, advance despite questionable benefits because developing them is good for business.

Payer and Dutton differ as Emile Durkheim and Karl Marx, or Clifford Geertz and Milton Friedman, differ on similar issues: How are societies constituted? What role does individual judgment play? How do systems change? Where the hermeneutical approach of one recognizes cultural systems of shared meaning, the political-economic approach of the other recognizes economic systems of differential access to power. The first is good at explaining shared values but less effective in describing how values are manipulated. The second is good at explaining people's manipulations but less effective in articulating their values, which usually end up being ignored as irrelevant or assumed as universal. These contrasts will be clearer if we focus on just one issue — the development of the artificial heart.

Dutton's book examines four medical developments — including swine flu inoculation, genetic engineering, and diethylstibestrol (DES) — whose benefits were either questionable from the beginning or outweighed ultimately by their side effects, ethical implications, or costs. The artificial heart is one of these. In the 1960s, Congress enthusiastically supported efforts to improve health care. Congress funded the National Institutes of Health (NIH) and NIH funded artificial-heart programs. Competition for research funds — always intense — increased after the cutbacks of the early 1970s, causing some researchers to adopt market-based tactics. Utah-based specialist Dr. Kolff and his associate Jarvik started a company to make artificial hearts. To attract investments, they needed publicity, and so they attempted the first permanent implantation. Barney Clark, the recipient, attracted worldwide media attention, and this resulted in huge corporate investments in the company. Meanwhile, the surgeon who performed the operation was lured away to a private hospital corporation, ensuring that both the device and the methods used for its implantation would be governed by market forces.

The artificial-heart program reveals many flaws. First, researchers who depended on public funds for most of their work were able to circumvent public accountability. By forming a private company, to which, technically, no public funds were committed, the developers avoided NIH reviews. Second, decisions as to how to develop and when to implant the artificial heart were made largely on business, not health-related, grounds. Publicity was clearly a factor, and successful advertising an important determinant of the program's direction and outcome. Third, the artificial heart itself proved to be an expensive boondoggle, in failing to meet the least optimistic predictions of its proponents. But even if it had worked, it would have created a dilemma common to all expensive technologies: who would receive it and who would pay for it? Finally, by devoting vast resources to its development, were not other, less glamorous programs — preventive medicine, for instance — necessarily shortchanged, with disastrous consequences for the nation's health?

Dutton's book asks us to consider why things like this happen. It identifies several culprits — profit-hungry big business, prestige-conscious research scientists, and dilatory, self-compromising big government. Dutton advocates greater public participation through a "substantial redistribution of decision-making power." The public could then decide what it wants, what it is willing to pay, and what risks it is willing to accept. Surely the same point has been made before with reference to housing, education, and environmental policy. Short of revolution, however, it is difficult to see how this redistribution can happen, since, as Dutton points out, "the most formidable obstacle . . . is the present structure of economic and political power."

The exclusionary process Dutton criticizes, and the greater participatory democracy she advocates, repeat an argument represented in its classical form in the debate between Adam Smith and Karl Marx over the issue of capitalist competition. Dutton's point — that competition between scientists, entrepreneurs, and industries is no way to ensure the public's good — is based on the well-argued contention that competition restricts information, limits participation, and defines success by what sells in the short run and not by what works in the long run. Further, competition degrades humanitarian values by making them subservient to the profit motive. Marx said the same thing. The reverse contention — Smith's "invisible hand" argument that competition creates innovation and enhances the common good by making each competitor accountable to the market — suggests that an unencumbered capitalism is the best way to ensure the good life for the greatest number of people.

Dutton argues forcefully from a Marxian perspective. But the fact that she does not acknowledge that perspective or speak in terms of the historically long-standing debate that her argument joins is symptomatic of a certain myopia. The mechanisms of capitalist competition are simply insufficient as explanations of the artificial heart's social importance. For this, a more sensitive cultural approach is needed, which Payer supplies in a study of cross-cultural differences in medical beliefs and decision making. Payer notes that in America the heart is viewed as a pump. Hearts, like pumps, get clogged up, and so we replace their pipes through coronary bypass. Hearts, like pumps, wear out, and so we replace them with real or artificial substitutes. It all makes sense because of the way Americans think about the heart. But in West Germany, it does not, since Germans do not see the heart as a pump. Payer believes that it is not coincidental that fewer bypass and replacement operations are performed in West Germany than in America.

These are valuable and worthwhile books that should attract broad interest. Dutton presents evidence that argues for a reappraisal of the American medical establishment. Her studies show that there is a lot happening behind the scenes in an area increasingly dominated by competitive business interests. But her work badly neglects the rootedness of the problem in a distinctively American cultural worldview. Moreover, her solution — the reordering of American political economy — mistakenly attributes to formal social structures a primary role in determining how people think and act. This, of course, is understandable if we adopt Payer's perspective: Dutton's faith in political solutions reflects her culture's strongly held belief that society, like a machine, can be fixed by tinkering with its parts.

CHARLES W. NUCKOLLS
University of Kentucky
Lexington

PHILLIPS, RODERICK. *Putting Asunder: A History of Divorce in Western Society.* Pp. xx,

672. New York: Cambridge University Press, 1988. No price.

This ambitious, impressive, and absorbing book seeks to chronicle the history of divorce in Western society from the Middle Ages to the present. It begins by describing the ideological positions on divorce of the Catholic Church and of the Protestant reformers. From this description grows the book's first theme, the story of the development of divorce legislation. Phillips examines the insistence of Catholic states on marital indissolubility, traces the acceptance in Protestant states of divorce — primarily for adultery — and reviews the strikingly liberal law of revolutionary France. After noting that divorce law was procedurally and substantively secularized in the seventeenth and eighteenth centuries, Phillips details the liberalization of divorce law in the early nineteenth century and the conservative reaction in the later nineteenth century. The liberalization of divorce law resumed after World War I, a process that culminated in the explosion of no-fault divorce from the 1960s through the 1980s. Intertwined with this history of divorce statutes is the book's second theme, the study of the incidence of divorce. Rates were trivially low for centuries, increased in the nineteenth century, and culminated in the rise of mass divorce in the twentieth century.

Phillips's third theme is the related but separate question of the extent of marriage breakdown. He argues that for many centuries marriages were stable because spouses had no economic and social alternative to marriage and because spouses accommodated themselves to these realities with low expectations of marital happiness. As economic and social circumstances changed, those expectations rose, and with them rose the incidence of marriage breakdowns.

Phillips has undertaken to study an important social phenomenon over a major part of the globe over a millennium of history. Considering the difficulties, he does admirably. But the difficulties are formidable. Phillips is rightly anxious to show that divorce legislation, divorce rates, and marriage breakdowns must be seen in their fullest context, but showing them in this context is dauntingly complex. He is unable to deal with some crucial aspects of divorce: questions of child custody, marital property, and alimony are hardly considered; the intellectual history of divorce with which he opens gets lost in the shuffle. Moreover, except for his discussion of legislation, he is dealing not only with an area in which research must be difficult to conduct but with one in which research has hardly begun. It is thus understandable that Phillips gives more fully studied countries like France, whose divorce history Phillips himself has examined before, England, and the United States perhaps disproportionate prominence.

In a sense, then, this imposing book is premature. In a better sense, however, *Putting Asunder* is very much what we need now to draw our attention to a neglected area of family history, to analyze what we know, and to chart a course that others can profitably follow.

CARL E. SCHNEIDER

University of Michigan
Ann Arbor

TITON, JEFF TODD. *Powerhouse for God: Speech, Chant, and Song in an Appalachian Baptist Church.* Pp. xviii, 523. Austin: University of Texas Press, 1988. $35.00.

While most books on religion focus on narrow topics limited to subjects like ethics, prayer, and belief, this book presents, just as the author states it, a holistic approach. While Titon considers it "a key to the world of ordinary people," the term "ordinary" would be acceptable to refer to any person or to any group. Principally, Titon stresses the term "folklike"; however, any human activity can be listed under the term "folklike." Titon is a specialist in folklore and ethnomusicology. His book is very thorough in its analysis, both in detail and in depth. It describes the life and the activities of the people in an Appalachian Baptist church.

In his first chapter, Titon feels that the approach to reach the Almighty is not a distant search but rather a homecoming. In the second chapter, he describes thoroughly the activity of farming, since the constituents of the church are mostly farmers. Farming is not just a technical activity but rather a total involvement of its people. In the third chapter, he tries to describe folk religion in comparison to "official religion." Again, religion is an involvement of people and not just technical words and pronouncements. While the term "old-fashioned" seems to be rather derogatory in modern language, Titon indicates how relevant and appropriate the term really becomes in this church's activities. In the fourth chapter, he describes the value of language in prayer and communication. In the fifth chapter, ideas about music are discussed. Titon indicates that good music actually makes people reflective. The sixth chapter brings us a description of the nature and effect of prayer, which is not simply a technical expression of words but a depth of feeling and self-understanding. In the seventh chapter, Titon talks about teaching and preaching, indicating that preaching is not simply a professional performance in a technical sense but rather "a cast of mind" coming from "a call to preach."

In almost all cases Titon gives many examples and samples. He has a number of appendixes, giving many facts and figures and listing interviews as well as types of recordings. A full bibliography is listed with a very definitive index.

Generally speaking, the work would be most interesting in giving us what Titon considers to be a depth of meaning for the activities of the church he has studied. Some of those meanings might easily be helpful in the organization and process of many kinds of religious institutions.

SAMUEL J. FOX

Lynn
Massachusetts

WOLFGANG, MARVIN E., TERENCE P. THORNBERRY, and ROBERT M. FIGLIO. *From Boy to Man, from Delinquency to Crime.* Pp. xiv, 221. Chicago: University of Chicago Press, 1988. $29.95.

In 1972, Marvin Wolfgang, Robert Figlio, and Thorsten Sellin published their important book *Delinquency in a Birth Cohort,* which examined the delinquent careers of 9945 boys who were born in 1945 and lived in Philadelphia from their tenth to eighteenth birthdays. *From Boy to Man, from Delinquency to Crime* is the long-awaited follow-up to that book, tracing a 10 percent sample of the original cohort through adulthood to age 30. As any movie enthusiast will attest, sequels to blockbuster hits are usually disappointing. In this case, however, the follow-up is every bit as insightful as the original study and should garner just as much attention from criminological audiences.

In chapters 3-6, Wolfgang, Thornberry, and Figlio "examine the extent to which the patterns observed in the original study were observed during the adult years as well." Generally, the findings for the adult years are consistent with those presented in the original study for the juvenile years. For example, a finding in the original study, one that ran counter to the conventional wisdom of the time, was that offenders did not become specialists in particular types of offenses as their delinquent careers unfolded. Consistent with that finding, the authors discover little evidence of offense specialization when the analysis is extended to adulthood.

Chapters 7-14 were written by the authors' graduate students. Representing shorter versions of their doctoral dissertations, some of these chapters complement the earlier ones, focusing on such issues as the time intervals between arrests and the factors affecting the dispositions of adult arrests. Many of these chapters break new ground, however. While the earlier chapters used only official — arrest — data as measures of law-violating behavior, the later chapters incorporate interview data collected from a subset — 567 men — of the 10 percent sample, including firsthand accounts from respondents about their offending and victimization experiences. The interview data allow for examination of a wide range of issues such as race and class differences in delinquency, the degree of planning involved in committing crimes, desistance from crime, and the relation between individuals' experiences as victims and offenders.

This book merits the careful attention not only of students of crime and delinquency but also of policymakers and practitioners. It is not without flaws, however. A minor irritant is that the book contains many production errors. For example, on the same page — page 83 — readers are told both that "the arrests of the whites were more likely to occur during the juvenile years" and that "arrests of the whites were more likely to occur in the adult years." A more serious flaw is that many of the chapters, especially many of chapters 7-14, seem to be first cuts of the data. The findings are often based on preliminary analyses, which are certainly suggestive of general patterns but must be regarded cautiously.

MARK C. STAFFORD

Washington State University
Pullman

ECONOMICS

GOLDFIELD, MICHAEL. *The Decline of Organized Labor in the United States.* Pp. xv, 294. Chicago: University of Chicago Press, 1987. No price.

A high percentage of doctoral candidates rather wishfully expect to see their theses published. Few actually do and fewer still achieve great popular acclaim. Here we have the exception, a well-written, well-documented book that thoroughly reviews, assesses, and analyzes the very provocative question, What are the reasons behind the dramatic losses in union membership, particularly in the private sector? The question has intrigued and continues to puzzle any number of scholars, philosophers, and practitioners of all sorts. The search for answers has resulted in a spate of literature attempting to diagnose and to explain the phenomenon.

The core argument of the book is that organized labor in the United States has been declining steadily over the last three decades. Contrary to some conventional wisdom, there is little evidence that the decline is due primarily to events that have occurred in the 1970s or the 1980s. This book — as well as, presumably, the

projected second volume — analyzes the decline not only in structural and economic terms but also in "more traditional Marxist forms of class analysis."

There are four parts and 11 rather brief chapters organized in very logical order. Part 1 reviews organized labor in the United States, its general weakness and recent decline; part 2 treats the significance and meaning of union decline; part 3 explores the reasons behind the trade union decline; and part 4 is the conclusion. Additionally, as befits a good doctoral thesis, there are useful appendixes and an exhaustive bibliography.

Goldfield's statistical and factual analysis of the long-run decline in U.S. organized labor is both conservative and sound, using, as he does, available data sources such as the National Labor Relations Board's certification results, membership of U.S. international unions — discounting for the obvious softness in this particular source — and union membership as a percentage of the total labor force. With these and other measures he makes his case and places himself in league with the majority of today's scholars who see the decline as being driven by multiple forces over decades of time. He asserts that John Dunlop, one of the country's senior industrial relations gurus, is simply wrong in his conclusion that U.S. labor unions are strong even in light of the economic and political developments of the 1970s and 1980s. When compared to unions in other capitalist countries, U.S. unions, again contrary to Dunlop, are weak rather than strong. Unfortunately, when making this assertion, Goldfield does not display the same diligence with the relevant comparative data as he does when referring to U.S. data. He relies primarily on the fact that social welfare programs in Canada and in Western Europe, for example, are more highly developed than they are in the United States and, by implication but without explicit evidence, that organized labor in these countries played a significant role in such developments.

Does it make any difference that union membership in the United States is on the decline? To critics on the right the answer may be good riddance, while those on the left may argue that

U.S. unions are really irrelevant. Goldfield suggests, however, that the decline be viewed from a deeper theoretical context. From a Marxist perspective he sees that the decline is not only the natural result of economic and social trends but also the product of ongoing class struggles, which in turn will determine some of the future shape and dimensions of our society. To his credit, his explanation is made less in terms of dogmatic — scientific — assertions and more in terms of a logical conclusion that weak unions unable even to defend their own interests will certainly not be able to establish the socialist society.

In explaining the decline of American unions, Goldfield does not rely solely on ideology but instead covers all possible explanations fairly and exhaustively. Three main categories of explanations are delineated, none of them mutually exclusive: sociological, cyclical, and political.

Each of the potential explanations is analyzed using statistical, historical, and econometric approaches. Goldfield concludes that the sociological explanations cannot be viewed as the primary reasons for union decline. Similarly, after constructing and analyzing several econometric models, he finds that the cyclical type of explanation also fails definitively to explain the bulk of the decline. With regard to his third category of hypothesis, he finds: workers today are not averse to unionism, they can organize; public policy in the United States poses greater difficulties for unions in the private sector than those in other economically developed countries; the antiunion employer offensive has been effective; and the unions themselves have not applied sufficient energy and resources to counter the antiunion offensive. Of all these forces and factors, he favors several class forces as most explanatory for union decline, namely, the growing aggressiveness of U.S. capitalists; the changes made in public policy that favor employers; and the inability and/or the unwillingness of U.S. unions to combat their decline.

As mentioned earlier, this is an impressive book. Nevertheless, there are a few things over which to quibble. Concerning language,

Goldfield's use of the term "capitalist" rather than "employer" becomes awkward when, as he does from time to time, he refers to union growth in the public sector. At one point he singles out the American Federation of State, County and Municipal Employees (AFSCME) as one of the few unions that is aggressive and growing stronger rather than declining. While AFSCME negotiates with governors, mayors, county executives, and the like, most of these would probably not refer to themselves as capitalists. In addition, when referring to categories of workers he uses the term "proletarianized."

More important caveats relate to errors per se or in interpretations. Goldfield writes that unorganized U.S. workers have few legal rights and can be fired summarily. This overlooks the burgeoning legal movement in this country: more than one-half of the states have passed employment-at-will legislation curtailing summary dismissals and providing for the concepts of just cause and due process. His reference to the Professional Air Traffic Controllers Organization (PATCO) strike and ultimate demise is a bit misleading because many observers of those events argue that it was PATCO's poor strategy and leadership that led to its defeat. Another error is in his reference to highly unionized industries like construction, mining, and trucking, where industry-wide bargaining has been destroyed. It never existed in the construction industry. Finally, his uncritical acceptance of statements from unionists like R. Georgine and J. Turner when referring to the antiunion offensive is less than objective. But these are minor matters in the total scheme of things.

FELICIAN F. FOLTMAN

Cornell University
Ithaca
New York

HUNNICUTT, BENJAMIN KLINE. *Work without End: Abandoning Shorter Hours for the Right to Work.* Pp. x, 404. Philadelphia: Temple University Press, 1988. $34.95.

From the early 1800s through the 1930s, American labor was preoccupied with reducing the length of the workweek. Major strikes and political campaigns were conducted to win a shorter workweek in the 1830s, the 1860s, and again in 1886 and 1890. This pressure began to show results in the 1890s. The manufacturing workweek, for example, fell from about 60 hours in 1890 to 50 by 1914 and to under 40 hours in the 1930s. Since then, however, less attention has been paid to the length of the workweek; instead, organized labor has devoted its energies to campaigning for full employment and high wages. Perhaps as a result, there has been little change in the average number of hours worked. Indeed, with the increasing labor force involvement of married women, the average adult is employed for more hours now than in the 1930s.

Benjamin Hunnicutt's work is a careful study of the changing political and intellectual struggle over reducing the workweek in the early part of the New Deal. This was a crucial period when liberal social reformers abandoned attempts to promote employment and leisure as an alternative to work and consumption. Instead, under the leadership of the Roosevelt administration, reformers developed what Hunnicutt labels a new "gospel of consumption" in which social welfare and full employment are maintained by increasing demand for commodities and "superfluous consumption." In excruciating detail, Hunnicutt chronicles the New Deal debate over mandated shorter hours from 1933 through the National Recovery Administration's codes until the Fair Labor Standards Act of 1938 marked the final defeat of attempts to mandate a standard workweek of fewer than 40 hours. At each turn of the debate, he shows how Roosevelt sidetracked pressure for shorter hours, substituting instead a program to increase employment by increasing production.

Hunnicutt's detailed recounting of political debates and intellectual fashions might be of interest to political historians of the New Deal era. It adds little, however, to our understanding of the relationship between changes in the workweek and unemployment. Hunnicutt never explains unemployment; he never examines the casual assumption that reducing the supply of labor by shortening the workweek will by itself reduce unemployment. Lacking a supply-side model of unemployment, however, Hunnicutt can scarcely present shorter hours as an alternative to effective demand as a means for reducing unemployment.

Hunnicutt's focus on politics and intellectual fashion also leads him to neglect the impact of worker preferences and their unions' activities on the length of the workweek. Most of the reduction in the workweek came before the passage of federal hours legislation in the 1930s. Employers before 1930 responded to worker preferences and the efforts of labor unions by reducing the workweek. Given these successes without government action, were the legislative battles and intellectual disputes of the 1930s really crucial for achieving further reductions in the workweek? Hunnicutt clearly wishes that workers valued leisure more highly, but lacking direct evidence of dissatisfaction, should one assume that most workers wanted government-mandated shorter hours? Or did the shorter-hours campaign end in the 1930s because workers were satisfied that a workweek in the range of 35-40 hours suited their preferences for work and nonwork?

Hunnicutt's work will contribute to a growing debate over the role of work, employment, and leisure in modern America. This is an important debate, but it needs a more solid foundation. By focusing almost exclusively on national politics, Hunnicutt never examines the meaning of employment for workers. He never distinguishes between productive, self-directed labor, which may be essential for the fulfillment of human potential, and a job, alienating employment under the direction and supervision of a capitalist boss. Lacking this distinction, Hunnicutt contrasts all work, including frustrating jobs and productive, fulfilling labor, with nonwork, including both constructive leisure and barren idleness. Given that choice, most

Americans choose jobs; the real issue is to give them the opportunity to choose productive labor.

GERALD FRIEDMAN

University of Massachusetts
Amherst

McGAW, JUDITH A. *Most Wonderful Machine: Mechanization and Social Change in Berkshire Paper Making 1801-1885*. Pp. xv, 439. Princeton, NJ: Princeton University Press, 1987. $40.00.

Most Wonderful Machine is really a most wonderful book. In fact, it can confidently be said that the study belongs on a list with the mere handful that have offered deep insights into the American industrial revolution and especially into the social relations of mechanization. This may seem a great deal to claim for a book devoted to a single industry that no one has termed central to the industrial revolution, located in a single county in a corner of the United States that has recently passed out of fashion as the cradle of industrialization. Nevertheless, the claim is made seriously and I think can be justified partly in terms of that very selectivity.

By concentrating on a small space, McGaw is able to look at practically everything that happened in Berkshire County, Massachusetts, between 1801, when the first paper mill commenced operation, and 1885, when the growing use of wood pulp instead of rags was already forcing some of the county's mills to close and had deprived it of its leadership. Under such conditions the processes of technological change can more readily be seen and the relationship to social change more easily analyzed. Then, too, McGaw is doubtless correct in pointing out that the paper worker better typified the situation of most American workers than the more frequently studied Lowell system textile workers, shoemakers, or metalworkers. The textile, shoe, and metal industries all featured large congregations of workers, sharp differen-

tiation of management from labor, and marked changes in skill and job control. McGaw consequently portrays a very different worker—a member of a small work force who knew his employer as a fellow man, experienced some mobility, and through all the technological changes retained considerable skill.

In fact, her picture of the typical skilled worker during that time is sharply different from most others, for she argues that the adoption of papermaking machinery brought increased well-being and increased supervisory responsibilities to the mills' principal male employees and that the machines did not replace workers, reduce their level of skill, or subdivide their tasks. Mechanization, rather, functioned primarily as intended, by multiplying the output of the always limited number of skilled workers available. The result is that instead of the alienation and protest emphasized by most other students, McGaw finds that under these more typical conditions, mechanization reinforced most of the preindustrial craftsman's sense of common interest with his employer. In fact, such contemporary buzz words as "deskilling," "alienation," and "anomie" are refreshingly missing from the index.

On the other hand, however, this book should not be written off as a celebration of mechanization, either. Although McGaw appears to believe that, on balance, workers and society in general prospered from mechanization, she knows it was not without its problems. For one thing, the conditions of work became more hectic and the work pace became less flexible; in the short term, there were longer workdays, periodic unemployment, and more dangerous and unpleasant surroundings. The effect on women workers in the mills was especially demeaning, but McGaw is certainly correct in pointing out that this was not something forced by machines—in fact, their work was almost entirely in the unmechanized part of the process involving counting, sorting, quality checking, and other traditional women's jobs—and that it was simply a working out of widely held notions of a separate sphere. Here, as elsewhere, McGaw finds little support for either conspiracy theories or for "paralyzing technological determinism prevalent in contemporary and nineteenth century American rhetoric."

I have emphasized McGaw's conclusions about the impact on workers simply because on these points she is probably at her most controversial, but that does not exhaust either the richness or the freshness of the work. It contains material on cooperation between mill owners that will suggest serious revisions of many fac-

ile conclusions about the supposed dog-eat-dog world of nineteenth-century industrialism, and it contains a wealth of insightful material on the process of technological change itself. There is also an excellent account of how social control actually worked. All in all, this book is an extraordinary achievement that will be of value to scholars in a variety of fields.

GEORGE H. DANIELS
University of South Alabama
Mobile

OTHER BOOKS

ALESANDER, LARRY and PAUL HORTON. *Whom Does the Constitution Command? A Conceptual Analysis with Practical Implications.* Pp. xii, 169. Westport, CT: Greenwood Press, 1988. $37.95.

ALLEN, WILLIAM B., comp. and ed. *George Washington: A Collection.* Pp. xxviii, 714. Indianapolis, IN: Liberty Classics, 1988. $26.00. Paperbound, $9.50.

ANDERSON, ANNELISE and DENNIS L. BARK, eds. *Thinking about America: The United States in the 1990s.* Pp. xlvii, 590. Stanford, CA: Hoover Institution Press, 1988. Distributed by National Book Network, Lanham, MD. $24.95.

ANDRIANOPOULOS, ARGYRIS G. *Western Europe in Kissinger's Global Strategy.* Pp. xiii, 262. New York: St. Martin's Press, 1988. $47.50.

ARENDELL, TERRY. *Mothers and Divorce: Legal, Economic, and Social Dilemmas.* Pp. xiv, 221. Berkeley: University of California Press, 1986. Paperbound, no price.

ARNOLD, LIND. *Bureaucracy and Bureaucrats in Mexico City, 1742-1835.* Pp. xii, 202. Tucson: University of Arizona Press, 1988. No price.

BABCOCK, BARBARA A. and NANCY J. PAREZO. *Daughters of the Desert: Women Anthropologists and the Native American Southwest, 1880-1980.* Pp. xii, 241. Albuquerque: University of New Mexico Press, 1988. No price.

BERLIN, GILLES V. and SALLY WYATT. *Multinationals and Industrial Property: The Control of the World's Technology.* Pp. xxi, 177. Atlantic Highlands, NJ: Humanities Press International, 1988. No price.

BHAGWATI, JAGDISH. *Protectionism.* Pp. xiii, 147. Cambridge: MIT Press, 1988. $16.95.

BOULDING, KENNETH E. *Conflict and Defense: A General Theory.* Pp. xvii, 349. Lanham, MD: University Press of America, 1988. Paperbound, $16.75.

BRAMS, STEVEN J. and D. MARC KILGOUR. *Game Theory and National Security.* Pp. xiii, 199. New York: Basil Blackwell, 1988. $49.95.

BROADBENT, SIR EWEN. *The Military and Government: From Macmillan to Heseltine.* Pp. xiii, 238. New York: St. Martin's Press, 1988. $45.00.

BROWN, ANTHONY E. *The Politics of Airline Deregulation.* Pp. xiii, 224. Knoxville: University of Tennessee Press, 1987. $22.95.

CARGILL, THOMAS F. and SHOICHI ROYAMA. *The Transition of Finance in Japan and the United States: A Comparative Perspective.* Pp. ix, 246. Stanford, CA: Hoover Institution Press, 1988. Paperbound, $18.95.

CHRISTY, CAROL A. *Sex Differences in Political Participation: Processes of Change in Fourteen Nations.* Pp. xii, 195. New York: Praeger, 1987. $37.95.

CHUBB, JOHN E. and PAUL E. PETERSON, eds. *Can the Government Govern.* Pp. x, 339. Washington, DC: Brookings Institution, 1989. $29.95.

COHEN, BENJAMIN J. *In Whose Interest? International Banking and American Foreign Policy.* Pp. xi, 347. New Haven, CT: Yale University Press, 1988. No price.

COHLER, ANNE M. *Montesquieu's Comparative Politics and the Spirit of American Constitutionalism.* Pp. x, 210. Lawrence: University Press of Kansas, 1988. $22.50.

COOPER, RICHARD N. *The International Monetary System: Essays in World Economics.* Pp. xvii, 286. Cambridge: MIT Press, 1988. Paperbound, $9.95.

DEWEY, CLIVE, ed. *The State and the Market: Studies in the Economic and Social History of the Third World.* Pp. xx, 355. Riverdale, MD: Riverdale, 1988. $34.00.

EPSTEIN, JOSHUA M. *Strategy and Force Planning: The Case of the Persian Gulf.* Pp. xiii, 169. Washington, DC: Brookings Institution, 1986. $28.95. Paperbound, $10.95.

ESTES, RICHARD J. *Trends in World Social Development: The Social Progress of Na-*

tions, 1970-1987. Pp. xx, 218. New York: Praeger, 1988. $39.95.

FELKAY, ANDREW. *Hungary and the USSR, 1956-1988: Kadar's Political Leadership.* Pp. x, 334. Westport, CT: Greenwood Press, 1989. No price.

FERGUSON, SHERRY D. and STEWART FERGUSON, eds. *Organizational Communication.* 2d ed. Pp. xxii, 734. New Brunswick, NJ: Transaction Books, 1988. $39.95.

FEUCHTWANG, S. et al., eds. *Transforming China's Economy in the Eighties.* Vol. 1, *The Rural Sector, Welfare and Employment.* Pp. xii, 259. Boulder, CO: Westview Press, 1988. $40.00.

FEUCHTWANG, S. et al., eds. *Transforming China's Economy in the Eighties.* Vol. 2, *Management, Industry, and the Urban Economy.* Pp. xii, 168. Boulder, CO: Westview Press, 1988. $38.50.

FIELDHOUSE, ROBERT, ed. *The Political Education of Servants of the State.* Pp. vii, 208. New York: St. Martin's Press, 1988. $45.00.

FIRESTONE, BERNARD J. and ROBERT C. VOGT, eds. *Lyndon Baines Johnson and the Uses of Power.* Pp. xvii, 418. Westport, CT: Greenwood Press, 1988. No price.

FISHMAN, MARK. *Manufacturing the News.* Pp. 180. Austin: University of Texas Press, 1988. Paperbound, $8.95.

FRIEDMAN, DAVID. *The Misunderstood Miracle: Industrial Development and Political Change in Japan.* Pp. viii, 252. Cambridge, MA: Harvard University Press, 1987. $25.00.

GALLAGHER, TOM. *Glasgow: The Uneasy Peace.* Pp. ix, 382. Wolfeboro, NH: Manchester University Press, 1987. No price.

GAYLORD, MARK S. and JOHN F. GALLIGHER. *The Criminology of Edwin Sutherland.* Pp. xiv, 183. New Brunswick, NJ: Transaction Books, 1988. $24.95.

GEIGER, THEODORE. *The Future of the International System: The United States and the World Political Economy.* Pp. xiv, 190. Winchester, MA: Unwin Hyman, 1988. $34.95. Paperbound, $12.95.

GLEICK, JAMES. *Chaos: Making a New Science.* Pp. xi, 352. New York: Penguin Books, 1988. Paperbound, $8.95.

GOEHLERT, ROBERT and HUGH REYNOLDS, comp. *The Executive Branch of the U.S. Government: A Bibliography.* Pp. ix, 380. Westport, CT: Greenwood Press, 1988. $49.95.

GOEL, M. LAL. *Political Science Research: A Methods Workbook.* Pp. vii, 194. Ames: Iowa State University Press, 1988. No price.

GOLDMAN, NATHAN C. *American Space Law: International and Domestic.* Pp. xii, 374. Ames: Iowa State University Press, 1988. $34.95.

GOLDSTEIN, THOMAS. *Dawn of Modern Science.* Pp. xvii, 296. New York: Houghton Mifflin, 1988. Paperbound, $9.95.

GUTOWSKI, ARMIN and MANFRED HOLTHUS, eds. *Limits to International Indebtedness.* Pp. 344. New Brunswick, NJ: Transaction Books, 1988. Paperbound, $18.95.

HAAS, KENNETH C. and JAMES A. INCIARDI. *Challenging Capital Punishment: Legal and Social Science Approaches.* Pp. 302. Newbury Park, CA: Sage, 1988. No price.

HARRIS, MARVIN and ERIC B. ROSS. *Death, Sex, and Fertility: Population Regulation in Preindustrial and Developing Societies.* Pp. 227. New York: Columbia University Press, 1987. $25.00.

HENSLIN, JAMES M., ed. *Deviance in American Life.* Pp. xii, 406. New Brunswick, NJ: Transaction Books, 1988. Paperbound, $16.95.

HERTZ, ROSANNA. *More Equal Than Others: Women and Men in Dual-Career Marriages.* Pp. xvi, 245. Berkeley: University of California Press, 1986. Paperbound, no price.

HOLST, JOHAN JØRGEN, ed. *Norwegian Foreign Policy in the 1980s.* Pp. 176. Oslo: Norwegian University Press, 1988. Distributed by Oxford University Press, New York. $29.95.

JALLAND, PAT. *Women, Marriage and Politics, 1860-1914.* Pp. xii, 366. New York: Oxford University Press, 1987. $37.00.

JAY, MARTIN. *Fin de Siècle Socialism and Other Essays.* Pp. 216. New York: Routledge, Chapman & Hall, 1989. $35.00. Paperbound, $13.95.

JOHNSON, ALLEN W. and TIMOTHY EARLE. *The Evolution of Human Societies: From Foraging Group to Agrarian State.* Pp. xii, 360. Stanford, CA: Stanford University Press, 1987. $39.50.

KAPLAN, ROBERT D. *Surrender or Starve: The Wars behind the Famine.* Pp. x, 188. Boulder, CO: Westview Press, 1988. $24.95.

KEOHANE, ROBERT O. and JOSEPH S. NYE. *Power and Interdependence.* 2d ed. Pp. xix, 315. Glenview, IL: Scott, Foresman/Little, Brown, 1988. Paperbound, $12.50.

KOHLI, ATUL. *The State and Poverty in India: The Politics of Reform.* Pp. x, 262. New York: Cambridge University Press, 1987. No price.

KOVEN, STEVEN G. *Ideological Budgeting: The Influence of Political Philosophy on Public Policy.* Pp. viii, 193. New York: Praeger, 1988. $35.95.

LAWTON, HENRY. *The Psychohistorian's Handbook.* Pp. 241. New York: Psychohistory Press, 1988. $25.95.

LEWIS, DAN A. et al. *Social Construction of Reform: Crime Prevention and Community Organizations.* Pp. vii, 152. New Brunswick, NJ: Transaction Books, 1987. $26.95.

LIPPMAN, MATTHEW et al. *Islamic Criminal Law and Procedure, an Introduction.* Pp. xv, 168. New York: Praeger, 1988. $35.95.

LITAN, ROBERT E. et al., eds. *American Living Standards: Threats and Challenges.* Pp. xvi, 250. Washington, DC: Brookings Institution, 1988. $29.95.

LOEWENBERG, GERHARD and SAMUEL C. PATTERSON. *Comparing Legislatures.* Pp. xv, 344. Lanham, MD: University Press of America, 1988. No price.

LUARD, EVAN. *Conflict and Peace in the Modern International System: A Study of the Principles of International Order.* Pp. xii, 318. Albany: SUNY, 1988. $44.50.

LYMAN, STANFORD M. and ARTHUR J. VIDICH. *Social Order and the Public Philosophy: An Analysis and Interpretation of the Work of Herbert Blumer.* Pp. xx, 378. Fayetteville: University of Arkansas Press, 1988. No price.

MARMOR, THEODORE R. and MASHAW, JERRY L., eds. *Social Security: Beyond the Rhetoric of Crisis.* Pp. xvi, 249. Princeton, NJ: Princeton University Press, 1988. $35.00.

McKELVEY, JEAN T., ed. *Cleared for Takeoff: Airline Labor Relations since Deregulation.* Pp. xii, 391. Ithaca, NY: Cornell University Press, 1988. $38.00.

NAFZIGER, E. WAYNE. *Inequality in Africa: Political Elites, Proletariat, Peasants and the Poor.* Pp. xiii, 204. New York: Cambridge University Press, 1988. No price.

NAGEL, STUART S. *Policy Studies: Integration and Evaluation.* Pp. xvi, 303. Westport, CT: Greenwood Press, 1988. No price.

PLANT, RAYMOND et al., eds. *Information Technology: The Public Issues.* Pp. vi, 197. New York: Manchester University Press, 1988. Distributed by St. Martin's Press, New York. No price.

PLISCHKE, ELMER. *Foreign Relations: Analysis of Its Anatomy.* Pp. xii, 315. Westport, CT: Greenwood Press, 1988. $39.95.

PROCTER, IAN. *Service Sector Workers in a Manufacturing City.* Pp. xi, 178. Brockfield, VT: Gower, 1988. $38.95.

PROVIZER, NORMAN W. and WILLIAM D. PEDERSON, eds. *Grassroots Constitutionalism: Shreveport, the South, and the Supreme Law of the Land.* Pp. xiii, 192. Lanham, MD: University Press of America, 1989. $26.50.

QUALE, G. ROBINA. *A History of Marriage Systems.* Pp. xii, 399. Westport, CT: Greenwood Press, 1988. $45.00.

QUANDY, WILLIAM B., ed. *The Middle East: Ten Years after Camp David.* Pp. xiii, 517. Washington, DC: Brookings Institution, 1988. $35.95.

RISSE-KAPPEN, THOMAS. *The Zero Option: INF, West Germany, and Arms Control.* Pp. x, 202. Boulder, CO: Westview Press, 1988. $24.95.

RODMAN, KENNETH A. *Sanctity vs. Sovereignty: The United States and the National-*

ization of Natural Resource Investments. Pp. xvii, 403. New York: Columbia University Press, 1988. $45.00.

SADIKOV, O. N., ed. *Soviet Civil Law.* Pp. xv, 542. Armonk, NY: M. E. Sharpe, 1988. $90.00.

SANTOLI, AL. *New Americans: An Oral History.* Pp. xviii, 392. New York: Viking, 1988. $19.95.

SARKESIAN, SAM C. with ROBERT A. VITAS. *U.S. National Security Policy and Strategy: Documents and Policy Proposals.* Pp. xix, 440. Westport, CT: Greenwood Press, 1988. No price.

SCHUMAN, HOWARD et al. *Racial Attitudes in America: Trends and Interpretations.* Pp. xiv, 260. Cambridge, MA: Harvard University Press, 1985. $25.00. Paperbound, $10.95.

SCHWARTZ, MICHAEL. *Radical Protest and Social Structure: The Southern Farmers' Alliance and Cotton Tenancy, 1880-1890.* Pp. xi, 302. Chicago: University of Chicago Press, 1988. Paperbound, $12.95.

SHERRY, MICHAEL S. *The Rise of American Air Power: The Creation of Armageddon.* Pp. xiii, 435. New Haven, CT: Yale University Press, 1989. Paperbound, $14.95.

SHOREY, KENNETH et al., eds. *Collected Letters of John Randolph of Roanoke to Dr. John Brockenbrough, 1812-1833.* Pp. xxiv, 157. New Brunswick, NJ: Transaction Books, 1988. No price.

SICKER, MARTIN. *The Strategy of Soviet Imperialism: Expansion in Eurasia.* Pp. 172. New York: Praeger, 1988. $37.95.

SIGEL, ROBERTA S., ed. *Political Learning in Adulthood: A Sourcebook of Theory and Research.* Pp. xvi, 483. Chicago: University of Chicago Press, 1989. $65.00.

SMITH, JESSIE CARNEY. *Images of Blacks in American Culture: A Reference Guide to Information Sources.* Pp. xvii, 390. Westport, CT: Greenwood Press, 1988. $49.95.

SMITH, JOAN et al., eds. *Racism, Sexism, and the World-System.* Pp. xii, 221. Westport, CT: Greenwood Press, 1988. No price.

STEINBERG, DAVID I. *The Republic of Korea: Economic Transformation and So-* *cial Change.* Pp. xiv, 218. Boulder, CO: Westview Press, 1989. $34.50.

STEINITZ, VICTORIA A. and ELLEN R. SOLOMON. *Starting Out: Class and Community in the Lives of Working-Class Youth.* Pp. xvi, 273. Philadelphia: Temple University Press, 1987. $29.95.

STELLER, GEORG W. *Journal of a Voyage with Bering, 1741-1742.* Translated by Margritt A. Engel and O. W. Frost. Pp. vi, 252. Stanford, CA: Stanford University Press, 1988. $35.00.

STEWART, ROBERT. *Party and Politics, 1830-1852.* Pp. v, 131. New York: St. Martin's Press, 1989. $39.95.

SUTTON, JOHN R. *Stubborn Children: Controlling Delinquency in the United States, 1640-1981.* Pp. xii, 299. Berkeley: University of California Press, 1988. No price.

SYLVIA, RONALD D. *Critical Issues in Public Personnel Policy.* Pp. xii, 192. Pacific Grove, CA: Brooks/Cole, 1989. Paperbound, $16.25.

SZENT-MIKLOSY, ISTVAN. *With the Hungarian Independence Movement, 1943-1947: An Eyewitness Account.* Pp. xxxiv, 242. New York: Praeger, 1988. $42.95.

TEUNE, HENRY. *Growth.* Pp. 139. Newbury Park, CA: Sage, 1988. $35.00.

TOBIN, JAMES and MURRAY WEDENBAUM, eds. *Two Revolutions in Economic Policy: The First Economic Reports of Presidents Kennedy and Reagan.* Pp. ix, 533. Cambridge: MIT Press, 1988. $30.00.

URBAN, GEORGE R., ed. *Social and Economic Rights in the Soviet Bloc: A Documentary Review Seventy Years after the Bolshevik Revolution.* Pp. xii, 249. New Brunswick, NJ: Transaction Books, 1988. No price.

WALKER, SAMUEL. *Sense and Nonsense about Crime: A Policy Guide.* 2d ed. Pp. xvi, 276. Pacific Grove, CA: Brooks/Cole, 1989. Paperbound, $17.00.

WALLENSTEEN, PETER. *Peace Research: Achievements and Challenges.* Pp. ix, 275. Boulder, CO: Westview Press, 1988. $24.50.

WEISNER, LOUIS A. *Victims and Survivors: Displaced Persons and Other War Victims in*

Viet-Nam, 1954-1975. Pp. xxx, 448. Westport, CT: Greenwood Press, 1988. No price.

WEISS, MARC A. *The Rise of the Community Builders: The American Real Estate Industry and Urban Land Planning.* Pp. xii, 228. New York: Columbia University Press, 1987. $30.00.

WHICKER, MARCIA L. and RAYMOND A. MOORE. *Making America Competitive: Policies for a Global Future.* Pp. ix, 216. New York: Praeger, 1988. $39.95.

YAVETZ, ZVI. *Slaves and Slavery in Ancient Rome.* Pp. viii, 182. New Brunswick, NJ: Transaction Books, 1988. No price.

YIM, YONG-SOON. *Politics of Korean Unification: A Comparative Study of Systemic Outputs.* Pp. ix, 232. Seoul: Research Center for Peace and Unification of Korea, 1988. $10.50.

YUNDT, KEITH W. *Latin American States and Political Refugees.* Pp. xi, 236. New York: Praeger, 1988. No price.

INDEX

199

CHINA REPORT

A Journal of East Asian Studies

Editor: C.R.M. RAO
Centre for the Study of Developing Societies, Delhi

Launched in 1964 with the specific aim of disseminating reliable information about contemporary China, **China Report** has over the years widened its interests and aims and transformed itself into a scholarly journal. It encourages the free expression and discussion of different ideas, approaches and viewpoints which assist a better understanding of China and its East Asian neighbours.

China Report looks beyond China to the whole of Asia; it attempts to provide a new approach — one which goes beyond the strictly utilitarian area studies without becoming antiquarian, one which leads to scholarly understanding without being scholastic and one that is at the same time policy relevant.

Since its inception, **China Report** has received the support of scholars, journalists, specialists in the field of chinese studies and, above all, the Centre for the Study of Developing Societies who took over the journal in 1972 and continue to have the journal's editorial responsibilities.

China Report is published quarterly in February, May, August and November.

SPECIAL ISSUES

- **India-China Relations**
- **Bangladesh and Sino-Indian Relations**
- **25 Years of People's China**
- **Lu Xun — Literature, Society and Revolution**
- **The New Course in China**

SAGE PUBLICATIONS
New Delhi • Newbury Park • London
The Publishers of Professional Social Science

NEW from Sage

SUPERPOWER DETENTE: A REAPPRAISAL
by MIKE BOWKER, *Queens University, Belfast*
& PHIL WILLIAMS, *University of Southampton*
Published for the Royal Institute of International Affairs

As the superpowers move once again toward a more open and cooperative relationship, supporters as well as skeptics of detente question its efficacy and durability. Have the superpowers learned from the failure of detente in the 1970s? Is detente possible in the nuclear age?

The early 1970s had seen the most far-reaching moves toward detente since the inception of the Cold War. But, Bowker and Williams suggest that the coincidence of interests between the superpowers hid divergent conceptions of what detente was and what kind of behavior it required. **Superpower Detente: A Reappraisal** first examines the superpowers' differing interpretations of detente and the history of their interests in detente. After considering the impact of events in the Middle East, the volume goes on to discuss the competition in Angola and the Horn of Africa and concludes that it was not the competition but Soviet success in the competition which helped to sour detente. Bowker and Williams analyze the Soviet and American domestic debates over detente and conclude that the major shift in attitude occurred in Washington rather than Moscow. Finally, the authors suggest that the detente experience of the 1970s has some lessons for the future success of the new detente of the 1980s.

Royal Institute of International Affairs
1988 (Autumn) / 288 pages / $48.00 (c) / $18.95 (p)

SAGE PUBLICATIONS, INC.
2111 W. Hillcrest Dr.
Newbury Park, CA 91320

SAGE PUBLICATIONS LTD
28 Banner Street
London EC1Y 8QE, England

SAGE PUBLICATIONS INDIA PVT LTD
M-32 Market, Greater Kailash I
New Delhi 110 048 India

CALL FOR MANUSCRIPTS

Violence, Cooperation, Peace

Editors: Francis A. Beer & Ted Robert Gurr,
University of Colorado, Boulder

Violence, Cooperation, Peace focuses on violent conflict and the dynamics of peaceful change within and among political communities. Studies in the series may include the perspectives and evidence of any of the social sciences or humanities, as well as applied fields such as conflict management.

Among the topics of particular interest to the series editors are: 1) the origins, processes, and outcomes of war; 2) mediation and avoidance of global and regional conflicts; 3) processes of political protest, violence, and accommodation in civil society; 4) the uses and abuses of state power, including arms races and arms control, state terrorism and genocide, and means for checking massive violations of human rights; 5) socio-psychological inquiries into the causes and patterns of political cooperation; and 6) structures and dynamics of stable peaceful systems.

Manuscript Submission

The editors prefer to receive proposals and sample chapters for book projects preliminary to reviewing complete manuscripts.

During 1988-89 authors may correspond individually with either editor at the addresses shown below, or preferably, send duplicate sets of materials to both.

Prof. Francis A. Beer
Department of Political Science
Campus Box 333
University of Colorado
Boulder, CO 80309

Prof. Ted Robert Gurr, Fellow
U.S. Institute of Peace
Suite 700
1550 M. Street, N.W.
Washington, D.C. 20005-1708

SAGE PUBLICATIONS, INC.
2111 W. Hillcrest Dr.
Newbury Park, CA 91320

SAGE PUBLICATIONS LTD
28 Banner Street
London EC1Y 8QE, England

SAGE PUBLICATIONS INDIA PVT LTD
M-32 Market, Greater Kailash I
New Delhi 110 048 India